Wiley Study Guide for 2016 Level II CFA Exam

Volume 1: Ethics & Quantitative Methods

Thousands of candidates from more than 100 countries have relied on these Study Guides to pass the CFA® Exam. Covering every Learning Outcome Statement (LOS) on the exam, these review materials are an invaluable tool for anyone who wants a deep-dive review of all the concepts, formulas, and topics required to pass.

Originally published by Élan Guides, this study material was produced by CFA® charterholders, CFA® Institute members, and investment professionals. In 2014 John Wiley & Sons, Inc. purchased the rights to Élan Guides content, and now this material is part of the Wiley Efficient Learning suite of exam review products. For more information, contact us at info@efficientlearning.com.

Wiley Study Guide for 2016 Level II CFA Exam

Volume 1: Ethics & Quantitative Methods

WILEY

Published by John Wiley & Sons, Inc., Hoboken, New Jersey.

Prior to 2014, the material was published by Élan Guides.

Published simultaneously in Canada.

For general information on our other products and services or for technical support, please contact our Customer Care Department within the United States at (800) 762-2974, outside the United States at (317) 572-3993 or fax (317) 572-4002.

Wiley publishes in a variety of print and electronic formats and by print-on-demand. Some material included with standard print versions of this book may not be included in e-books or in print-on-demand. If this book refers to media such as a CD or DVD that is not included in the version you purchased, you may download this material at http://booksupport.wiley.com. For more information about Wiley products, visit www.wiley.com.

ISBN 978-1-119-18272-6

Contents

ABOUT THE AUTHORS

Wiley's Study Guides are written by a team of highly qualified CFA charterholders and leading CFA instructors from around the globe. Our team of CFA experts work collaboratively to produce the best study materials for CFA candidates available today.

Wiley's expert team of contributing authors and instructors is led by Content Director Basit Shajani, CFA. Basit founded online education start-up Élan Guides in 2009 to help address CFA candidates' need for better study materials. As lead writer, lecturer, and curriculum developer, Basit's unique ability to break down complex topics helped the company grow organically to be a leading global provider of CFA Exam prep materials. In January 2014, Élan Guides was acquired by John Wiley & Sons, Inc., where Basit continues to serve as director of CFA content. Basit graduated magna cum laude from the Wharton School of Business at the University of Pennsylvania with majors in finance and legal studies. He went on to obtain his CFA charter in 2006, passing all three levels on the first attempt. Prior to Élan Guides, Basit ran his own private wealth management business. He is a past president of the Pakistani CFA Society.

Study Session 1: Ethical and Professional Standards

Reading 1: Code of Ethics and Standards of Professional Conduct

LESSON 1: CODE OF ETHICS AND STANDARDS OF PROFESSIONAL CONDUCT

LOS 1a: Describe the six components of the Code of Ethics and the seven Standards of Professional Conduct. Vol 1, pp 9–10

CFA Institute Professional Conduct Program

All CFA Institute members and candidates enrolled in the CFA Program are required to comply with the Code and Standards. The CFA Institute Board of Governors maintains oversight and responsibility for the Professional Conduct Program (PCP), which, in conjunction with the Disciplinary Review Committee (DRC), is responsible for enforcement of the Code and Standards. The DRC is a volunteer committee of CFA charterholders who serve on panels to review conduct and partner with Professional Conduct staff to establish and review professional conduct policies. The CFA Institute Bylaws and Rules of Procedure for Professional Conduct (Rules of Procedure) form the basic structure for enforcing the Code and Standards. The Professional Conduct division is also responsible for enforcing testing policies of other CFA Institute education programs as well as the professional conduct of Certificate in Investment Performance Measurement (CIPM) certificates.

Professional Conduct inquiries come from a number of sources.

- Members and candidates must self-disclose on the annual Professional Conduct Statement all matters that question their professional conduct, such as involvement in civil litigation or a criminal investigation or being the subject of a written complaint.
- Written complaints received by Professional Conduct staff can bring about an investigation.
- CFA Institute staff may become aware of questionable conduct by a member or candidate through the media, regulatory notices, or another public source.
- Candidate conduct is monitored by proctors who complete reports on candidates suspected to have violated testing rules on exam day.
- CFA Institute may also conduct analyses of scores and exam materials after the exam, as well as monitor online and social media to detect disclosure of confidential exam information.

When an inquiry is initiated, the Professional Conduct staff conducts an investigation that may include:

- Requesting a written explanation from the member or candidate.
- Interviewing the member or candidate, complaining parties, and third parties.
- Collecting documents and records relevant to the investigation.

Upon reviewing the material obtained during the investigation, the Professional Conduct staff may:

- Take no disciplinary sanction.
- Issue a cautionary letter.
- Continue proceedings to discipline the member or candidate.

If the Professional Conduct staff believes a violation of the Code and Standards or testing policies has occurred, the member or candidate has the opportunity to reject or accept any charges and the proposed sanctions. If the member or candidate does not accept the charges and proposed sanction, the matter is referred to a panel composed of DRC members. Panels review materials and presentations from Professional Conduct staff and from the member or candidate. The panel's task is to determine whether a violation of the Code and Standards or testing policies occurred and, if so, what sanction should be imposed.

Sanctions imposed by CFA Institute may have significant consequences; they include public censure, suspension of membership and use of the CFA designation, and revocation of the CFA charter. Candidates enrolled in the CFA Program who have violated the Code and Standards or testing policies may be suspended or prohibited from further participation in the CFA Program.

Adoption of the Code and Standards

The Code and Standards apply to individual members of CFA Institute and candidates in the CFA Program. CFA Institute does encourage firms to adopt the Code and Standards, however, as part of their code of ethics. Those who claim compliance should fully understand the requirements of each of the principles of the Code and Standards.

Once a party—nonmember or firm—ensures its code of ethics meets the principles of the Code and Standards, that party should make the following statement whenever claiming compliance:

"[Insert name of party] claims compliance with the CFA Institute Code of Ethics and Standards of Professional Conduct. This claim has not been verified by CFA Institute."

CFA Institute welcomes public acknowledgment, when appropriate, that firms are complying with the CFA Institute Code of Ethics and Standards of Professional Conduct and encourages firms to notify it of the adoption plans.

CFA Institute has also published the Asset Manager Code of Professional Conduct, which is designed, in part, to help asset managers comply with the regulations mandating codes of ethics for investment advisers. Whereas the Code and Standards are aimed at individual investment professionals who are members of CFA Institute or candidates in the CFA Program, the Asset Manager Code was drafted specifically for firms. The Asset Manager Code provides specific, practical guidelines for asset managers in the following areas:

- Loyalty to clients.
- The investment process.
- Trading.
- Compliance.
- Performance evaluation
- Disclosure.

Why Ethics Matters

Ethics can be defined as a set of moral principles or rules of conduct that provide guidance for our behavior when it affects others. Widely acknowledged fundamental ethical principles include honesty, fairness, diligence, and care and respect for others. Ethical conduct follows those principles and balances self-interest with both the direct and the indirect consequences of that behavior for other people.

Not only does unethical behavior by individuals have serious personal consequences—ranging from job loss and reputational damage to fines and even jail—but unethical conduct from market participants, investment professionals, and those who service investors can damage investor trust and thereby impair the sustainability of the global capital markets as a whole. Unfortunately, there seems to be an unending parade of stories bringing to light accounting frauds and manipulations, Ponzi schemes, insider-trading scandals, and other misdeeds. Not surprisingly, this has led to erosion in public confidence in investment professionals. Empirical evidence from numerous surveys documents the low standing in the eyes of the investing public of banks and financial services firms—the very institutions that are entrusted with the economic well-being and retirement security of society.

Governments and regulators have historically tried to combat misconduct in the industry through regulatory reform, with various levels of success. Global capital markets are highly regulated to protect investors and other market participants. However, compliance with regulation alone is insufficient to fully earn investor trust. Individuals and firms must develop a "culture of integrity" that permeates all levels of operations and promotes the ethical principles of stewardship of investor assets and working in the best interests of clients, above and beyond strict compliance with the law. A strong ethical culture that helps honest, ethical people engage in ethical behavior will foster the trust of investors, lead to robust global capital markets, and ultimately benefit society.

LOS 1b: Explain the ethical responsibilities required of CFA Institute members and candidates in the CFA Program by the Code and Standards. **Vol 1, pp 15–19**

CFA INSTITUTE CODE OF ETHICS AND STANDARDS OF PROFESSIONAL CONDUCT

Preamble

The CFA Institute Code of Ethics and Standards of Professional Conduct are fundamental to the values of CFA Institute and essential to achieving its mission to lead the investment profession globally by promoting the highest standards of ethics, education, and professional excellence for the ultimate benefit of society. High ethical standards are critical to maintaining the public's trust in financial markets and in the investment profession. Since their creation in the 1960s, the Code and Standards have promoted the integrity of CFA Institute members and served as a model for measuring the ethics of investment professionals globally, regardless of job function, cultural differences, or local laws and regulations. All CFA Institute members (including holders of the Chartered Financial Analyst [CFA] designation) and CFA candidates have the personal responsibility to embrace and uphold the provisions of the Code and Standards and are encouraged to notify their employer of this responsibility. Violations may result in disciplinary sanctions by CFA Institute. Sanctions can include revocation of membership, revocation of candidacy in the CFA Program, and revocation of the right to use the CFA designation.

The Code of Ethics

Members of CFA Institute (including CFA charterholders) and candidates for the CFA designation ("Members and Candidates") must:

- Act with integrity, competence, diligence, and respect and in an ethical manner with the public, clients, prospective clients, employers, employees, colleagues in the investment profession, and other participants in the global capital markets.
- Place the integrity of the investment profession and the interests of clients above their own personal interests.
- Use reasonable care and exercise independent professional judgment when conducting investment analysis, making investment recommendations, taking investment actions, and engaging in other professional activities.
- Practice and encourage others to practice in a professional and ethical manner that will reflect credit on themselves and the profession.
- Promote the integrity and viability of the global capital markets for the ultimate benefit of society.
- Maintain and improve their professional competence and strive to maintain and improve the competence of other investment professionals.

Standards of Professional Conduct

I. Professionalism

A. Knowledge of the Law
B. Independence and Objectivity
C. Misrepresentation
D. Misconduct

II. Integrity of Capital Markets

A. Material Nonpublic Information
B. Market Manipulation

III. Duties to Clients

A. Loyalty, Prudence and Care
B. Fair Dealing
C. Suitability
D. Performance Presentation
E. Preservation of Confidentiality

IV. Duties to Employers

A. Loyalty
B. Additional Compensation Arrangements
C. Responsibilities of Supervisors

V. Investment Analysis, Recommendations and Actions

A. Diligence and Reasonable Basis
B. Communication with Clients and Prospective Clients
C. Record Retention

VI. Conflicts of Interest

A. Disclosure of Conflicts
B. Priority of Transactions
C. Referral Fees

VII. Responsibilities as a CFA Institute Member or CFA Candidate

A. Conduct as members and candidates in the CFA program

B. Reference to CFA Institute, the CFA Designation, and the CFA Program

We discuss the next four LOS together to make for easier reading and understanding. They are covered in Volume 1, pages 22–176 of the Level I curriculum. The Code of Ethics and the Standards of Practice apply to *all* candidates in the CFA program and members of CFA Institute. All examples and other extracts from the Standards of Practice Handbook that are included in this Reading are reprinted with permission of CFA Institute.

Reading 2: Guidance for Standards I-VII

LESSON 1: STANDARD I: PROFESSIONALISM

A. Knowledge of the Law
B. Independence and Objectivity
C. Misrepresentation
D. Misconduct

LOS 2a: Demonstrate a thorough knowledge of the Code of Ethics and Standards of Professional Conduct by applying the Code and Standards to specific situations. Vol 1, pp 21–176

LOS 2b: Recommend practices and procedures designed to prevent violations of the Code of Ethics and Standards of Professional Conduct. Vol 1, pp 21–176

Standard I(A): Knowledge of the Law

The Standard

Members and candidates must understand and comply with all applicable laws, rules, and regulations (including the CFA Institute Code of Ethics and Standards of Professional Conduct) of any government, regulatory organization, licensing agency, or professional association governing their professional activities. In the event of conflict, members and candidates must comply with the more strict law, rule, or regulation. Members and Candidates must not knowingly participate or assist in and must dissociate from any violation of such laws, rules, or regulations.

Guidance

- Members and candidates must understand the applicable laws and regulations of the countries and jurisdictions where they engage in professional activities.
- On the basis of their reasonable and good faith understanding, members and candidates must comply with the laws and regulations that directly govern their professional activities and resulting outcomes and that protect the interests of the clients.
- When questions arise, members and candidates should know their firm's policies and procedures for accessing compliance guidance.
- During times of changing regulations, members and candidates must remain vigilant in maintaining their knowledge of the requirements for their professional activities.

Relationship between the Code and Standards and Applicable Law

- When applicable law and the Code and Standards require different conduct, members and candidates must follow the stricter of the applicable law or the Code and Standards.
    - "Applicable law" is the law that governs the member's or candidate's conduct. Which law applies will depend on the particular facts and circumstances of each case.
    - The "more strict" law or regulation is the law or regulation that imposes greater restrictions on the action of the member or candidate, or calls for the member or candidate to exert a greater degree of action that protects the interests of investors.

Global Application of the Code and Standards

Members and candidates who practice in multiple jurisdictions may be subject to varied securities laws and regulations. The following chart provides illustrations involving a member who may be subject to the securities laws and regulations of three different types of countries:

NS: country with no securities laws or regulations

LS: country with *less* strict securities laws and regulations than the Code and Standards

MS: country with *more* strict securities laws and regulations than the Code and Standards

Applicable Law	Duties	Explanation
Member resides in NS country, does business in LS country; LS law applies.	Member must adhere to the Code and Standards.	Because applicable law is less strict than the Code and Standards, the member must adhere to the Code and Standards.
Member resides in NS country, does business in MS country; MS law applies.	Member must adhere to the law of MS country.	Because applicable law is stricter than the Code and Standards, member must adhere to the more strict applicable law.
Member resides in LS country, does business in NS country; LS law applies.	Member must adhere to the Code and Standards.	Because applicable law is less strict than the Code and Standards, member must adhere to the Code and Standards.
Member resides in LS country, does business in MS country; MS law applies.	Member must adhere to the law of MS country.	Because applicable law is stricter than the Code and Standards, member must adhere to the more strict applicable law.
Member resides in LS country, does business in NS country; LS law applies, but it states that law of locality where business is conducted governs.	Member must adhere to the Code and Standards.	Because applicable law states that the law of the locality where the business is conducted governs and there is no local law, the member must adhere to the Code and Standards.
Member resides in LS country, does business in MS country; LS law applies, but it states that law of locality where business is conducted governs.	Member must adhere to the law of MS country.	Because applicable law of the locality where the business is conducted governs and local law is stricter than the Code and Standards, member must adhere to the more strict applicable law.
Member resides in MS country, does business in LS country; MS law applies.	Member must adhere to the law of MS country.	Because applicable law is stricter than the Code and Standards, member must adhere to the more strict applicable law.
Member resides in MS country, does business in LS country; MS law applies, but it states that law of locality where business is conducted governs.	Member must adhere to the Code and Standards.	Because applicable law states that the law of the locality where the business is conducted governs and local law is less strict than the Code and Standards, member must adhere to the Code and Standards.

Applicable Law	Duties	Explanation
Member resides in MS country, does business in LS country with a client who is a citizen of LS country; MS law applies, but it states that the law of the client's home country governs.	Member must adhere to the Code and Standards.	Because applicable law states that the law of the client's home country governs (which is less strict than the Code and Standards), member must adhere to the Code and Standards.
Member resides in MS country, does business in LS country with a client who is a citizen of MS country; MS law applies, but it states that the law of the client's home country governs.	Member must adhere to the law of MS country.	Because applicable law states that the law of the client's home country governs and the law of the client's home country is stricter than the Code and Standards, the member must adhere to the more strict applicable law.

Participation in or Association with Violations by Others

- Members and candidates are responsible for violations in which they *knowingly* participate or assist. Standard I(A) applies when members and candidates know or should know that their conduct may contribute to a violation of applicable laws, rules, or regulations or the Code and Standards.
- If a member or candidate has reasonable grounds to believe that imminent or ongoing client or employer activities are illegal or unethical, the member or candidate must dissociate, or separate, from the activity.
- In extreme cases, dissociation may require a member or candidate to leave his or her employment.
- Members and candidates may take the following intermediate steps to dissociate from ethical violations of others when direct discussions with the person or persons committing the violation are unsuccessful.
  - Attempt to stop the behavior by bringing it to the attention of the employer through a supervisor or the firm's compliance department.
  - If this attempt is unsuccessful, then members and candidates have a responsibility to step away and dissociate from the activity. Inaction combined with continuing association with those involved in illegal or unethical conduct may be construed as participation or assistance in the illegal or unethical conduct.
- CFA Institute strongly encourages members and candidates to report potential violations of the Code and Standards committed by fellow members and candidates, although a failure to report is less likely to be construed as a violation than a failure to dissociate from unethical conduct.

Investment Products and Applicable Laws

- Members and candidates involved in creating or maintaining investment services or investment products or packages of securities and/or derivatives should be mindful of where these products or packages will be sold as well as their places of origination.
- They should understand the applicable laws and regulations of the countries or regions of origination and expected sale, and should make reasonable efforts to review whether associated firms that are distributing products or services developed by their employing firms also abide by the laws and regulations of the countries and regions of distribution.

- Finally, they should undertake the necessary due diligence when transacting cross-border business to understand the multiple applicable laws and regulations in order to protect the reputation of their firms and themselves.

Recommended Procedures for Compliance

Members and Candidates
Suggested methods by which members and candidates can acquire and maintain understanding of applicable laws, rules, and regulations include the following:

- Stay informed: Members and candidates should establish or encourage their employers to establish a procedure by which employees are regularly informed about changes in applicable laws, rules, regulations, and case law.
- Review procedures: Members and candidates should review, or encourage their employers to review, the firm's written compliance procedures on a regular basis to ensure that the procedures reflect current law and provide adequate guidance to employees about what is permissible conduct under the law and/or the Code and Standards.
- Maintain current files: Members and candidates should maintain or encourage their employers to maintain readily accessible current reference copies of applicable statutes, rules, regulations, and important cases.

Distribution Area Laws
- Members and candidates should make reasonable efforts to understand the applicable laws—both country and regional—for the countries and regions where their investment products are developed and are most likely to be distributed to clients.

Legal Counsel
- When in doubt about the appropriate action to undertake, it is recommended that a member or candidate seek the advice of compliance personnel or legal counsel concerning legal requirements.
- If a potential violation is being committed by a fellow employee, it may also be prudent for the member or candidate to seek the advice of the firm's compliance department or legal counsel.

Dissociation
- When dissociating from an activity that violates the Code and Standards, members and candidates should document the violation and urge their firms to attempt to persuade the perpetrator(s) to cease such conduct. Note that in order to dissociate from the conduct, a member or candidate may have to resign his or her employment.

Firms
Members and candidates should encourage their firms to consider the following policies and procedures to support the principles of Standard I(A):

- Develop and/or adopt a code of ethics.
- Provide information on applicable laws.
- Establish procedures for reporting violations.

Application of the Standard

Example 1 (Notification of Known Violations)

Michael Allen works for a brokerage firm and is responsible for an underwriting of securities. A company official gives Allen information indicating that the financial statements Allen filed with the regulator overstate the issuer's earnings. Allen seeks the advice of the brokerage firm's general counsel, who states that it would be difficult for the regulator to prove that Allen has been involved in any wrongdoing.

Comment: Although it is recommended that members and candidates seek the advice of legal counsel, the reliance on such advice does not absolve a member or candidate from the requirement to comply with the law or regulation. Allen should report this situation to his supervisor, seek an independent legal opinion, and determine whether the regulator should be notified of the error.

Example 2 (Dissociating from a Violation)

Lawrence Brown's employer, an investment banking firm, is the principal underwriter for an issue of convertible debentures by the Courtney Company. Brown discovers that the Courtney Company has concealed severe third-quarter losses in its foreign operations. The preliminary prospectus has already been distributed.

Comment: Knowing that the preliminary prospectus is misleading, Brown should report his findings to the appropriate supervisory persons in his firm. If the matter is not remedied and Brown's employer does not dissociate from the underwriting, Brown should sever all his connections with the underwriting. Brown should also seek legal advice to determine whether additional reporting or other action should be taken.

Example 3 (Following the Highest Requirements)

Laura Jameson works for a multinational investment adviser based in the United States. Jameson lives and works as a registered investment adviser in the tiny, but wealthy, island nation of Karramba. Karramba's securities laws state that no investment adviser registered and working in that country can participate in initial public offerings (IPOs) for the adviser's personal account. Jameson, believing that, as a U.S. citizen working for a U.S.–based company, she should comply only with U.S. law, has ignored this Karrambian law. In addition, Jameson believes that as a charterholder, as long as she adheres to the Code and Standards requirement that she disclose her participation in any IPO to her employer and clients when such ownership creates a conflict of interest, she is meeting the highest ethical requirements.

Comment: Jameson is in violation of Standard I(A). As a registered investment adviser in Karramba, Jameson is prevented by Karrambian securities law from participating in IPOs regardless of the law of her home country. In addition, because the law of the country where she is working is stricter than the Code and Standards, she must follow the stricter requirements of the local law rather than the requirements of the Code and Standards.

Example 4 (Reporting Potential Unethical Actions)

Krista Blume is a junior portfolio manager for high-net-worth portfolios at a large global investment manager. She observes a number of new portfolios and relationships coming from a country in Europe where the firm did not have previous business and is told that a broker in that country is responsible for this new business. At a meeting on allocation of research resources to third-party research firms, Blume notes that this broker has been added to the list and is allocated payments for research. However, she knows the portfolios do not invest in securities in the broker's country, and she has not seen any research come from this broker. Blume asks her supervisor about the name being on the list and is told that someone in marketing is receiving the research and that the name being on the list is OK. She believes that what may be going on is that the broker is being paid for new business through the inappropriate research payments, and she wishes to dissociate from the misconduct.

Comment: Blume should follow the firm's policies and procedures for reporting potential unethical activity, which may include discussions with her supervisor or someone in a designated compliance department. She should communicate her concerns appropriately while advocating for disclosure between the new broker relationship and the research payments.

Example 5 (Failure to Maintain Knowledge of the Law)

Colleen White is excited to use new technology to communicate with clients and potential clients. She recently began posting investment information, including performance reports and investment opinions and recommendations, to her Facebook page. In addition, she sends out brief announcements, opinions, and thoughts via her Twitter account (for example, "Prospects for future growth of XYZ company look good! #makingmoney4U"). Prior to White's use of these social media platforms, the local regulator had issued new requirements and guidance governing online electronic communication. White's communications appear to conflict with the recent regulatory announcements.

Comment: White is in violation of Standard I(A) because her communications do not comply with the existing guidance and regulation governing use of social media. White must be aware of the evolving legal requirements pertaining to new and dynamic areas of the financial services industry that are applicable to her. She should seek guidance from appropriate, knowledgeable, and reliable sources, such as her firm's compliance department, external service providers, or outside counsel, unless she diligently follows legal and regulatory trends affecting her professional responsibilities.

Standard I(B) Independence and Objectivity

The Standard

Members and candidates must use reasonable care and judgment to achieve and maintain independence and objectivity in their professional activities. Members and candidates must not offer, solicit, or accept any gift, benefit, compensation, or consideration that reasonably could be expected to compromise their own or another's independence and objectivity.

Guidance

- Members and candidates should endeavor to avoid situations that could cause or be perceived to cause a loss of independence or objectivity in recommending investments or taking investment action.

- Modest gifts and entertainment are acceptable, but special care must be taken by members and candidates to resist subtle and not-so-subtle pressures to act in conflict with the interests of their clients. Best practice dictates that members and candidates reject any offer of gift or entertainment that could be expected to threaten their independence and objectivity.
- Receiving a gift, benefit, or consideration from a *client* can be distinguished from gifts given by entities seeking to influence a member or candidate to the detriment of other clients.
- When possible, prior to accepting "bonuses" or gifts from clients, members and candidates should disclose to their employers such benefits offered by clients. If notification is not possible prior to acceptance, members and candidates must disclose to their employer benefits previously accepted from clients.
- Members and candidates are personally responsible for maintaining independence and objectivity when preparing research reports, making investment recommendations, and taking investment action on behalf of clients. Recommendations must convey the member's or candidate's true opinions, free of bias from internal or external pressures, and be stated in clear and unambiguous language.
- When seeking corporate financial support for conventions, seminars, or even weekly society luncheons, the members or candidates responsible for the activities should evaluate both the actual effect of such solicitations on their independence and whether their objectivity might be perceived to be compromised in the eyes of their clients.

Investment-Banking Relationships

- Some sell-side firms may exert pressure on their analysts to issue favorable research reports on current or prospective investment banking clients. Members and candidates must not succumb to such pressures.
- Allowing analysts to work with investment bankers is appropriate only when the conflicts are adequately and effectively managed and disclosed. Firm managers have a responsibility to provide an environment in which analysts are neither coerced nor enticed into issuing research that does not reflect their true opinions. Firms should require public disclosure of actual conflicts of interest to investors.
- Any "firewalls" between the investment banking and research functions must be managed to minimize conflicts of interest. Key elements of enhanced firewalls include:
    - Separate reporting structures for personnel on the research side and personnel on the investment banking side.
    - Compensation arrangements that minimize pressures on research analysts and reward objectivity and accuracy.

Public Companies

- Analysts may be pressured to issue favorable reports and recommendations by the companies they follow. In making an investment recommendation, the analyst is responsible for anticipating, interpreting, and assessing a company's prospects and stock price performance in a factual manner.
- Due diligence in financial research and analysis involves gathering information from a wide variety of sources, including public disclosure documents (such as proxy statements, annual reports, and other regulatory filings) and also company management and investor-relations personnel, suppliers, customers, competitors, and other relevant sources. Research analysts may justifiably fear that companies will limit their ability to conduct thorough research by denying analysts who have "negative" views direct access to company managers and/or barring them from conference calls and other communication venues. This concern may make it difficult for them to conduct the comprehensive research needed to make objective recommendations.

Buy-Side Clients

- Portfolio managers may have significant positions in the security of a company under review. A rating downgrade may adversely affect the portfolio's performance, particularly in the short term, because the sensitivity of stock prices to ratings changes has increased in recent years. A downgrade may also affect the manager's compensation, which is usually tied to portfolio performance. Moreover, portfolio performance is subject to media and public scrutiny, which may affect the manager's professional reputation. Consequently, some portfolio managers implicitly or explicitly support sell-side ratings inflation.
- Portfolio managers have a responsibility to respect and foster the intellectual honesty of sell-side research. Therefore, it is improper for portfolio managers to threaten or engage in retaliatory practices, such as reporting sell-side analysts to the covered company in order to instigate negative corporate reactions.

Fund Manager and Custodial Relationships

- Research analysts are not the only people who must be concerned with maintaining their independence. Members and candidates who are responsible for hiring and retaining outside managers and third-party custodians should not accepts gifts, entertainment, or travel funding that may be perceived as impairing their decisions.

Credit Rating Agency Opinions

- Members and candidates employed at rating agencies should ensure that procedures and processes at the agencies prevent undue influences from a sponsoring company during the analysis. Members and candidates should abide by their agencies' and the industry's standards of conduct regarding the analytical process and the distribution of their reports.
- When using information provided by credit rating agencies, members and candidates should be mindful of the potential conflicts of interest. And because of the potential conflicts, members and candidates may need to independently validate the rating granted.

Issuer-Paid Research

- Some companies hire analysts to produce research reports in case of lack of coverage from sell-side research, or to increase the company's visibility in financial markets.
- Analysts must engage in thorough, independent, and unbiased analysis and must fully disclose potential conflicts, including the nature of their compensation. It should also be clearly mentioned in the report that the research has been paid for by the subject company. At a minimum, research should include a thorough analysis of the company's financial statements based on publicly disclosed information, benchmarking within a peer group, and industry analysis.
- Analysts must try to limit the type of compensation they accept for conducting research. This compensation can be direct, such as payment based on the conclusions of the report or more indirect, such as stock warrants or other equity instruments that could increase in value based on positive coverage in the report. In those instances, analysts would have an incentive to avoid negative information or conclusions that would diminish their potential compensation.
- Best practice is for analysts to accept only a flat fee for their work prior to writing the report, without regard to their conclusions or the report's recommendations.

Travel Funding

- The benefits related to accepting paid travel extend beyond the cost savings to the member or candidate and his firm, such as the chance to talk exclusively with the executives of a company or learning more about the investment options provided by an investment organization. Acceptance also comes with potential concerns; for example, members and candidates may be influenced by these discussions when flying on a corporate or chartered jet, or attending sponsored conferences where many expenses, including airfare and lodging, are covered.

- To avoid the appearance of compromising their independence and objectivity, best practice dictates that analysts always use commercial transportation at their expense or at the expense of their firm rather than accept paid travel arrangements from an outside company.
- In case of unavailability of commercial travel, they may accept modestly arranged travel to participate in appropriate information gathering events, such as a property tour.

Performance Measurement and Attribution

- Members and candidates working within a firm's investment performance measurement department may also be presented with situations that challenge their independence and objectivity. As performance analysts, their analyses may reveal instances where managers may appear to have strayed from their mandate. Additionally, the performance analyst may receive requests to alter the construction of composite indices owing to negative results for a selected account or fund. Members or candidates must not allow internal or external influences to affect their independence and objectivity as they faithfully complete their performance calculation and analysis-related responsibilities.

Influence during the Manager Selection/Procurement Process

- When serving in a hiring capacity, members and candidates should not solicit gifts, contributions, or other compensation that may affect their independence and objectivity. Solicitations do not have to benefit members and candidates personally to conflict with Standard I(B). Requesting contributions to a favorite charity or political organization may also be perceived as an attempt to influence the decision-making process. Additionally, members and candidates serving in a hiring capacity should refuse gifts, donations, and other offered compensation that may be perceived to influence their decision-making process.
- When working to earn a new investment allocation, members and candidates should not offer gifts, contributions, or other compensation to influence the decision of the hiring representative. The offering of these items with the intent to impair the independence and objectivity of another person would not comply with Standard I(B). Such prohibited actions may include offering donations to a charitable organization or political candidate referred by the hiring representative.

Recommended Procedures for Compliance

Members and candidates should adhere to the following practices and should encourage their firms to establish procedures to avoid violations of Standard I(B):

- Protect the integrity of opinions: Members, candidates, and their firms should establish policies stating that every research report concerning the securities of a corporate client should reflect the unbiased opinion of the analyst.
- Create a restricted list: If the firm is unwilling to permit dissemination of adverse opinions about a corporate client, members and candidates should encourage the firm to remove the controversial company from the research universe and put it on a restricted list so that the firm disseminates only factual information about the company.
- Restrict special cost arrangements: When attending meetings at an issuer's headquarters, members and candidates should pay for commercial transportation and hotel charges. No corporate issuer should reimburse members or candidates for air transportation. Members and candidates should encourage issuers to limit the use of corporate aircraft to situations in which commercial transportation is not available or in which efficient movement could not otherwise be arranged.

- Limit gifts: Members and candidates must limit the acceptance of gratuities and/or gifts to token items. Standard I(B) does not preclude customary, ordinary business-related entertainment as long as its purpose is not to influence or reward members or candidates. Firms should consider a strict value limit for acceptable gifts that is based on the local or regional customs and should address whether the limit is per gift or an aggregate annual value.
- Restrict investments: Members and candidates should encourage their investment firms to develop formal polices related to employee purchases of equity or equity-related IPOs. Firms should require prior approval for employee participation in IPOs, with prompt disclosure of investment actions taken following the offering. Strict limits should be imposed on investment personnel acquiring securities in private placements.
- Review procedures: Members and candidates should encourage their firms to implement effective supervisory and review procedures to ensure that analysts and portfolio managers comply with policies relating to their personal investment activities.
- Independence policy: Members, candidates, and their firms should establish a formal written policy on the independence and objectivity of research and implement reporting structures and review procedures to ensure that research analysts do not report to and are not supervised or controlled by any department of the firm that could compromise the independence of the analyst.
- Appointed officer: Firms should appoint a senior officer with oversight responsibilities for compliance with the firm's code of ethics and all regulations concerning its business.

Application of the Standard

Example 1 (Research Independence and Intrafirm Pressure)

Walter Fritz is an equity analyst with Hilton Brokerage who covers the mining industry. He has concluded that the stock of Metals & Mining is overpriced at its current level, but he is concerned that a negative research report will hurt the good relationship between Metals & Mining and the investment banking division of his firm. In fact, a senior manager of Hilton Brokerage has just sent him a copy of a proposal his firm has made to Metals & Mining to underwrite a debt offering. Fritz needs to produce a report right away and is concerned about issuing a less-than-favorable rating.

Comment: Fritz's analysis of Metals & Mining must be objective and based solely on consideration of company fundamentals. Any pressure from other divisions of his firm is inappropriate. This conflict could have been eliminated if, in anticipation of the offering, Hilton Brokerage had placed Metals & Mining on a restricted list for its sales force.

Example 2 (Research Independence and Issuer Relationship Pressure)

As in Example 1, Walter Fritz has concluded that Metals & Mining stock is overvalued at its current level, but he is concerned that a negative research report might jeopardize a close rapport that he has nurtured over the years with Metals & Mining's CEO, chief finance officer, and investment relations officer. Fritz is concerned that a negative report might result also in management retaliation—for instance, cutting him off from participating in conference calls when a quarterly earnings release is made, denying him the ability to ask questions on such calls, and/or denying him access to top management for arranging group meetings between Hilton Brokerage clients and top Metals & Mining managers.

Comment: As in Example 1, Fritz's analysis must be objective and based solely on consideration of company fundamentals. Any pressure from Metals & Mining is inappropriate. Fritz should reinforce the integrity of his conclusions by stressing that his investment recommendation is based on relative valuation, which may include qualitative issues with respect to Metals & Mining's management.

Example 3 (Gifts and Entertainment from Related Party)

Edward Grant directs a large amount of his commission business to a New York–based brokerage house. In appreciation for all the business, the brokerage house gives Grant two tickets to the World Cup in South Africa, two nights at a nearby resort, several meals, and transportation via limousine to the game. Grant fails to disclose receiving this package to his supervisor.

Comment: Grant has violated Standard I(B) because accepting these substantial gifts may impede his independence and objectivity. Every member and candidate should endeavor to avoid situations that might cause or be perceived to cause a loss of independence or objectivity in recommending investments or taking investment action. By accepting the trip, Grant has opened himself up to the accusation that he may give the broker favored treatment in return.

Example 4 (Gifts and Entertainment from Client)

Theresa Green manages the portfolio of Ian Knowlden, a client of Tisbury Investments. Green achieves an annual return for Knowlden that is consistently better than that of the benchmark she and the client previously agreed to. As a reward, Knowlden offers Green two tickets to Wimbledon and the use of Knowlden's flat in London for a week. Green discloses this gift to her supervisor at Tisbury.

Comment: Green is in compliance with Standard I(B) because she disclosed the gift from one of her clients in accordance with the firm's policies. Members and candidates may accept bonuses or gifts from clients as long as they disclose them to their employer because gifts in a client relationship are deemed less likely to affect a member's or candidate's objectivity and independence than gifts in other situations. Disclosure is required, however, so that supervisors can monitor such situations to guard against employees favoring a gift-giving client to the detriment of other fee-paying clients (such as by allocating a greater proportion of IPO stock to the gift-giving client's portfolio).

Best practices for monitoring include comparing the transaction costs of the Knowlden account with the costs of other accounts managed by Green and other similar accounts within Tisbury. The supervisor could also compare the performance returns with the returns of other clients with the same mandate. This comparison will assist in determining whether a pattern of favoritism by Green is disadvantaging other Tisbury clients or the possibility that this favoritism could affect her future behavior.

Example 5 (Research Independence and Compensation Arrangements)

Javier Herrero recently left his job as a research analyst for a large investment adviser. While looking for a new position, he was hired by an investor-relations firm to write a research report on one of its clients, a small educational software company. The investor-relations firm hopes to generate investor interest in the technology company. The firm will pay Herrero a flat fee plus a bonus if any new investors buy stock in the company as a result of Herrero's report.

Comment: If Herrero accepts this payment arrangement, he will be in violation of Standard I(B) because the compensation arrangement can reasonably be expected to compromise his independence and objectivity. Herrero will receive a bonus for attracting investors, which provides an incentive to draft a positive report regardless of the facts and to ignore or play down any negative information about the company. Herrero should accept only a flat fee that is not tied to the conclusions or recommendations of the report. Issuer-paid research that is objective and unbiased can be done under the right circumstances as long as the analyst takes steps to maintain his or her objectivity and includes in the report proper disclosures regarding potential conflicts of interest.

Example 6 (Influencing Manager Selection Decisions)

Adrian Mandel, CFA, is a senior portfolio manager for ZZYY Capital Management who oversees a team of investment professionals who manage labor union pension funds. A few years ago, ZZYY sought to win a competitive asset manager search to manage a significant allocation of the pension fund of the United Doughnut and Pretzel Bakers Union (UDPBU). UDPBU's investment board is chaired by a recognized key decision maker and long-time leader of the union, Ernesto Gomez. To improve ZZYY's chances of winning the competition, Mandel made significant monetary contributions to Gomez's union reelection campaign fund. Even after ZZYY was hired as a primary manager of the pension, Mandel believed that his firm's position was not secure. Mandel continued to contribute to Gomez's reelection campaign chest as well as to entertain lavishly the union leader and his family at top restaurants on a regular basis. All of Mandel's outlays were routinely handled as marketing expenses reimbursed by ZZYY's expense accounts and were disclosed to his senior management as being instrumental in maintaining a strong close relationship with an important client.

Comment: Mandel not only offered but actually gave monetary gifts, benefits, and other considerations that reasonably could be expected to compromise Gomez's objectivity. Therefore, Mandel was in violation of Standard I(B).

Example 7 (Influencing Manager Selection Decisions)

Adrian Mandel, CFA, had heard about the manager search competition for the UDPBU Pension Fund through a broker/dealer contact. The contact told him that a well-known retired professional golfer, Bobby "The Bear" Finlay, who had become a licensed broker/dealer serving as a pension consultant, was orchestrating the UDPBU manager search. Finlay had gained celebrity status with several labor union pension fund boards by entertaining their respective board members and regaling them with colorful stories of fellow pro golfers' antics in clubhouses around the world. Mandel decided to improve ZZYY's chances of being invited to participate in the search competition by befriending Finlay to curry his favor. Knowing

Finlay's love of entertainment, Mandel wined and dined Finlay at high-profile bistros where Finlay could glow in the fan recognition lavished on him by all the other patrons. Mandel's endeavors paid off handsomely when Finlay recommended to the UDPBU board that ZZYY be entered as one of three finalist asset management firms in its search.

Comment: Mandel lavished gifts, benefits, and other considerations in the form of expensive entertainment that could reasonably be expected to influence the consultant to recommend the hiring of his firm. Therefore, Mandel was in violation of Standard I(B).

Example 8 (Fund Manager Relationships)

Amie Scott is a performance analyst within her firm with responsibilities for analyzing the performance of external managers. While completing her quarterly analysis, Scott notices a change in one manager's reported composite construction. The change concealed the bad performance of a particularly large account by placing that account into a new residual composite. This change allowed the manager to remain at the top of the list of manager performance. Scott knows her firm has a large allocation to this manager, and the fund's manager is a close personal friend of the CEO. She needs to deliver her final report but is concerned with pointing out the composite change.

Comment: Scott would be in violation of Standard I(B) if she did not disclose the change in her final report. The analysis of managers' performance should not be influenced by personal relationships or the size of the allocation to the outside managers. By not including the change, Scott would not be providing an independent analysis of the performance metrics for her firm.

Example 9 (Intrafirm Pressure)

Jill Stein is head of performance measurement for her firm. During the last quarter, many members of the organization's research department were removed because of the poor quality of their recommendations. The subpar research caused one larger account holder to experience significant underperformance, which resulted in the client withdrawing his money after the end of the quarter. The head of sales requests that Stein remove this account from the firm's performance composite because the performance decline can be attributed to the departed research team and not the client's adviser.

Comment: Pressure from other internal departments can create situations that cause a member or candidate to violate the Code and Standards. Stein must maintain her independence and objectivity and refuse to exclude specific accounts from the firm's performance composites to which they belong. As long as the client invested under a strategy similar to that of the defined composite, it cannot be excluded because of the poor stock selections that led to the underperformance and asset withdrawal.

Example 10 (Travel Expenses)

Steven Taylor, a mining analyst with Bronson Brokers, is invited by Precision Metals to join a group of his peers in a tour of mining facilities in several western U.S. states. The company arranges for chartered group flights from site to site and for accommodations in Spartan Motels, the only chain with accommodations near the mines, for three nights. Taylor allows Precision Metals to pick up his tab, as do the other analysts, with one exception—John Adams, an employee of a large trust company who insists on following his company's policy and paying for his hotel room himself.

Comment: The policy of the company where Adams works complies closely with Standard I(B) by avoiding even the appearance of a conflict of interest, but Taylor and the other analysts were not necessarily violating Standard I(B). In general, when allowing companies to pay for travel and/or accommodations in these circumstances, members and candidates must use their judgment. They must be on guard that such arrangements not impinge on a member's or candidate's independence and objectivity. In this example, the trip was strictly for business and Taylor was not accepting irrelevant or lavish hospitality. The itinerary required chartered flights, for which analysts were not expected to pay. The accommodations were modest. These arrangements are not unusual and did not violate Standard I(B) as long as Taylor's independence and objectivity were not compromised. In the final analysis, members and candidates should consider both whether they can remain objective and whether their integrity might be perceived by their clients to have been compromised.

Example 11 (Travel Expenses from External Manager)

Tom Wayne is the investment manager of the Franklin City Employees Pension Plan. He recently completed a successful search for a firm to manage the foreign equity allocation of the plan's diversified portfolio. He followed the plan's standard procedure of seeking presentations from a number of qualified firms and recommended that his board select Penguin Advisors because of its experience, well-defined investment strategy, and performance record. The firm claims compliance with the Global Investment Performance Standards (GIPS) and has been verified. Following the selection of Penguin, a reporter from the *Franklin City Record* calls to ask if there was any connection between this action and the fact that Penguin was one of the sponsors of an "investment fact-finding trip to Asia" that Wayne made earlier in the year. The trip was one of several conducted by the Pension Investment Academy, which had arranged the itinerary of meetings with economic, government, and corporate officials in major cities in several Asian countries. The Pension Investment Academy obtains support for the cost of these trips from a number of investment managers, including Penguin Advisors; the Academy then pays the travel expenses of the various pension plan managers on the trip and provides all meals and accommodations. The president of Penguin Advisors was also one of the travelers on the trip.

Comment: Although Wayne can probably put to good use the knowledge he gained from the trip in selecting portfolio managers and in other areas of managing the pension plan, his recommendation of Penguin Advisors may be tainted by the possible conflict incurred when he participated in a trip partly paid for by Penguin Advisors and when he was in the daily company of the president of Penguin Advisors. To avoid violating Standard I(B), Wayne's basic expenses for travel and accommodations should have been paid by his employer or the pension plan; contact with the president of Penguin Advisors should have been limited to informational or educational events only; and the trip, the organizer, and the sponsor should have been made a matter of public record. Even if his actions were not in violation of Standard I(B), Wayne should have been sensitive to the public perception of the trip when reported in the newspaper and the extent to which the subjective elements of his decision might have been affected by the familiarity that the daily contact of such a trip would encourage. This advantage would probably not be shared by firms competing with Penguin Advisors.

Example 12 (Recommendation Objectivity)

Bob Thompson has been doing research for the portfolio manager of the fixed-income department. His assignment is to do sensitivity analysis on securitized subprime mortgages. He has discussed with the manager possible scenarios to use to calculate expected returns. A key assumption in such calculations is housing price appreciation (HPA) because it drives "prepays" (prepayments of mortgages) and losses. Thompson is concerned with the significant appreciation experienced over the previous five years as a result of the increased availability of funds from subprime mortgages. Thompson insists that the analysis should include a scenario run with –10% for Year 1, –5% for Year 2, and then (to project a worst-case scenario) 0% for Years 3 through 5. The manager replies that these assumptions are too dire because there has never been a time in their available database when HPA was negative.

Thompson conducts his research to better understand the risks inherent in these securities and evaluates these securities in the worst-case scenario, an unlikely but possible environment. Based on the results of the enhanced scenarios, Thompson does not recommend the purchase of the securitization. Against the general market trends, the manager follows Thompson's recommendation and does not invest. The following year, the housing market collapses. In avoiding the subprime investments, the manager's portfolio outperforms its peer group that year.

Comment: Thompson's actions in running the worst-case scenario against the protests of the portfolio manager are in alignment with the principles of Standard I(B). Thompson did not allow his research to be pressured by the general trends of the market or the manager's desire to limit the research to historical norms.

Example 13 (Research Independence and Prior Coverage)

Jill Jorund is a securities analyst following airline stocks and a rising star at her firm. Her boss has been carrying a "buy" recommendation on International Airlines and asks Jorund to take over coverage of that airline. He tells Jorund that under no circumstances should the prevailing buy recommendation be changed.

Comment: Jorund must be independent and objective in her analysis of International Airlines. If she believes that her boss's instructions have compromised her, she has two options: She can tell her boss that she cannot cover the company under these constraints, or she can take over coverage of the company, reach her own independent conclusions, and if they conflict with her boss's opinion, share the conclusions with her boss or other supervisors in the firm so that they can make appropriate recommendations. Jorund must issue only recommendations that reflect her independent and objective opinion.

Standard I(C) Misrepresentation

The Standard

Members and candidates must not knowingly make any misrepresentations relating to investment analysis, recommendations, actions, or other professional activities.

Guidance

- A misrepresentation is any untrue statement or omission of a fact or any statement that is otherwise false or misleading.

- A member or candidate must not knowingly omit or misrepresent information or give a false impression of a firm, organization, or security in the member's or candidate's oral representations, advertising (whether in the press or through brochures), electronic communications, or written materials (whether publicly disseminated or not).
    - In this context, "knowingly" means that the member or candidate either knows or should have known that the misrepresentation was being made or that omitted information could alter the investment decision-making process.
- Members and candidates who use webpages should regularly monitor materials posted on these sites to ensure that they contain current information. Members and candidates should also ensure that all reasonable precautions have been taken to protect the site's integrity and security and that the site does not misrepresent any information and does provide full disclosure.
- Members and candidates should not guarantee clients any specific return on volatile investments. Most investments contain some element of risk that makes their return inherently unpredictable. For such investments, guaranteeing either a particular rate of return or a guaranteed preservation of investment capital (e.g., "I can guarantee that you will earn 8% on equities this year" or "I can guarantee that you will not lose money on this investment") is misleading to investors.
- Note that Standard I(C) does not prohibit members and candidates from providing clients with information on investment products that have guarantees built into the structure of the products themselves or for which an institution has agreed to cover any losses.

Impact on Investment Practice

- Members and candidates must not misrepresent any aspect of their practice, including (but not limited to) their qualifications or credentials, the qualifications or services provided by their firm, their performance record and the record of their firm, and the characteristics of an investment.
- Members and candidates should exercise care and diligence when incorporating third-party information. Misrepresentations resulting from the use of the credit ratings, research, testimonials, or marketing materials of outside parties become the responsibility of the investment professional when it affects that professional's business practices.
- Members and candidates must disclose their intended use of external managers and must not represent those managers' investment practices as their own.

Performance Reporting

- Members and candidates should not misrepresent the success of their performance record by presenting benchmarks that are not comparable to their strategies. The benchmark's results should be reported on a basis comparable to that of the fund's or client's results.
- Note that Standard I(C) does not require that a benchmark always be provided in order to comply. Some investment strategies may not lend themselves to displaying an appropriate benchmark because of the complexity or diversity of the investments included.
- Members and candidates should discuss with clients on a continuous basis the appropriate benchmark to be used for performance evaluations and related fee calculations.
- Members and candidates should take reasonable steps to provide accurate and reliable security pricing information to clients on a consistent basis. Changing pricing providers should not be based solely on the justification that the new provider reports a higher current value of a security.

Social Media

- When communicating through social media channels, members and candidates should provide only the same information they are allowed to distribute to clients and potential clients through other traditional forms of communication.

- Along with understanding and following existing and newly developing rules and regulations regarding the allowed use of social media, members and candidates should also ensure that all communications in this format adhere to the requirements of the Code and Standards.
- The perceived anonymity granted through these platforms may entice individuals to misrepresent their qualifications or abilities or those of their employer. Actions undertaken through social media that knowingly misrepresent investment recommendations or professional activities are considered a violation of Standard I(C).

Omissions

- Members and candidates should not knowingly omit inputs used in any models and processes they use to scan for new investment opportunities, to develop investment vehicles, and to produce investment recommendations and ratings as resulting outcomes may provide misleading information. Further, members and candidates should not presented outcomes from their models as facts because they only represent expected results.
- Members and candidates should encourage their firms to develop strict policies for composite development to prevent cherry picking—situations in which selected accounts are presented as representative of the firm's abilities. The omission of any accounts appropriate for the defined composite may misrepresent to clients the success of the manager's implementation of its strategy.

Plagiarism

- Plagiarism refers to the practice of copying, or using in substantially the same form, materials prepared by others without acknowledging the source of the material or identifying the author and publisher of the material. Plagiarism includes:
  - Taking a research report or study performed by another firm or person, changing the names, and releasing the material as one's own original analysis.
  - Using excerpts from articles or reports prepared by others either verbatim or with only slight changes in wording without acknowledgment.
  - Citing specific quotations supposedly attributable to "leading analysts" and "investment experts" without specific reference.
  - Presenting statistical estimates of forecasts prepared by others with the source identified but without qualifying statements or caveats that may have been used.
  - Using charts and graphs without stating their sources.
  - Copying proprietary computerized spreadsheets or algorithms without seeking the cooperation or authorization of their creators.
- In the case of distributing third-party, outsourced research, members and candidates can use and distribute these reports as long as they do not represent themselves as the author of the report. They may add value to clients by sifting through research and repackaging it for them, but should disclose that the research being presented to clients comes from an outside source.
- The standard also applies to plagiarism in oral communications, such as through group meetings; visits with associates, clients, and customers; use of audio/video media (which is rapidly increasing); and telecommunications, such as through electronic data transfer and the outright copying of electronic media. One of the most egregious practices in violation of this standard is the preparation of research reports based on multiple sources of information without acknowledging the sources. Such information would include, for example, ideas, statistical compilations, and forecasts combined to give the appearance of original work.

Work Completed for Employer

- Members and candidates may use research conducted by other analysts within their firm. Any research reports prepared by the analysts are the property of the firm and may be issued by it even if the original analysts are no longer with the firm.
- Therefore, members and candidates are allowed to use the research conducted by analysts who were previously employed at their firms. However, they cannot reissue a previously released report solely under their own name.

Recommended Procedures for Compliance

Factual presentations: Firms should provide guidance for employees who make written or oral presentations to clients or potential clients by providing a written list of the firm's available services and a description of the firm's qualifications. Firms can also help prevent misrepresentation by specifically designating which employees are authorized to speak on behalf of the firm.

Qualification summary: In order to ensure accurate presentations to clients, the member or candidate should prepare a summary of her own qualifications and experience, as well as a list of the services she is capable of performing.

Verify outside information: When providing information to clients from third parties, members and candidates should ensure the accuracy of the marketing and distribution materials that pertain to the third party's capabilities, services, and products. This is because inaccurate information can damage their individual and their firm's reputations as well as the integrity of the capital markets.

Maintain webpages: If they publish a webpage, members and candidates should regularly monitor materials posted to the site to ensure the site maintains current information.

Plagiarism policy: To avoid plagiarism in preparing research reports or conclusions of analysis, members and candidates should take the following steps:

- *Maintain copies:* Keep copies of all research reports, articles containing research ideas, material with new statistical methodology, and other materials that were relied on in preparing the research report.
- *Attribute quotations:* Attribute to their sources any direct quotations, including projections, tables, statistics, model/product ideas, and new methodologies prepared by persons other than recognized financial and statistical reporting services or similar sources.
- *Attribute summaries:* Attribute to their sources paraphrases or summaries of material prepared by others.

Application of the Standard

Example 1 (Disclosure of Issuer-Paid Research)

Anthony McGuire is an issuer-paid analyst hired by publicly traded companies to electronically promote their stocks. McGuire creates a website that promotes his research efforts as a seemingly independent analyst. McGuire posts a profile and a strong buy recommendation for each company on the website indicating that the stock is expected to increase in value. He does not disclose the contractual relationships with the companies he covers on his website, in the research reports he issues, or in the statements he makes about the companies in internet chat rooms.

Comment: McGuire has violated Standard I(C) because the website is misleading to potential investors. Even if the recommendations are valid and supported with thorough research, his omissions regarding the true relationship between himself and the companies he covers constitute a misrepresentation. McGuire has also violated Standard VI(A)—Disclosure of Conflicts by not disclosing the existence of an arrangement with the companies through which he receives compensation in exchange for his services.

Example 2 (Correction of Unintentional Errors)

Hijan Yao is responsible for the creation and distribution of the marketing materials for his firm, which claims compliance with the GIPS standards. Yao creates and distributes a presentation of performance by the firm's Asian equity composite that states the composite has ¥350 billion in assets. In fact, the composite has only ¥35 billion in assets, and the higher figure on the presentation is a result of a typographical error. Nevertheless, the erroneous material is distributed to a number of clients before Yao catches the mistake.

Comment: Once the error is discovered, Yao must take steps to cease distribution of the incorrect material and correct the error by informing those who have received the erroneous information. Because Yao did not knowingly make the misrepresentation, however, he did not violate Standard I(C). Because his firm claims compliance with the GIPS standards, it must also comply with the GIPS Guidance Statement on Error Correction in relation to the error.

Example 3 (Noncorrection of Known Errors)

Syed Muhammad is the president of an investment management firm. The promotional material for the firm, created by the firm's marketing department, incorrectly claims that Muhammad has an advanced degree in finance from a prestigious business school in addition to the CFA designation. Although Muhammad attended the school for a short period of time, he did not receive a degree. Over the years, Muhammad and others in the firm have distributed this material to numerous prospective clients and consultants.

Comment: Even though Muhammad may not have been directly responsible for the misrepresentation of his credentials in the firm's promotional material, he used this material numerous times over an extended period and should have known of the misrepresentation. Thus, Muhammad has violated Standard I(C).

Example 4 (Misrepresentation of Information)

When Ricki Marks sells mortgage-backed derivatives called "interest-only strips" (IOs) to public pension plan clients, she describes them as "guaranteed by the U.S. government." Purchasers of the IOs are entitled only to the interest stream generated by the mortgages, however, not the notional principal itself. One particular municipality's investment policies and local law require that securities purchased by its public pension plans be guaranteed by the U.S. government. Although the underlying mortgages are guaranteed, neither the investor's investment nor the interest stream on the IOs is guaranteed. When interest rates decline, causing an increase in prepayment of mortgages, interest payments to the IOs' investors decline, and these investors lose a portion of their investment.

Comment: Marks violated Standard I(C) by misrepresenting the terms and character of the investment.

Example 5 (Potential Information Misrepresentation)

Khalouck Abdrabbo manages the investments of several high-net-worth individuals in the United States who are approaching retirement. Abdrabbo advises these individuals that a portion of their investments be moved from equity to bank-sponsored certificates of deposit and money market accounts so that the principal will be "guaranteed" up to a certain amount. The interest is not guaranteed.

Comment: Although there is risk that the institution offering the certificates of deposits and money market accounts could go bankrupt, in the United States, these accounts are insured by the U.S. government through the Federal Deposit Insurance Corporation. Therefore, using the term "guaranteed" in this context is not inappropriate as long as the amount is within the government-insured limit. Abdrabbo should explain these facts to the clients.

Example 6 (Plagiarism)

Steve Swanson is a senior analyst in the investment research department of Ballard and Company. Apex Corporation has asked Ballard to assist in acquiring the majority ownership of stock in the Campbell Company, a financial consulting firm, and to prepare a report recommending that stockholders of Campbell agree to the acquisition. Another investment firm, Davis and Company, had already prepared a report for Apex analyzing both Apex and Campbell and recommending an exchange ratio. Apex has given the Davis report to Ballard officers, who have passed it on to Swanson. Swanson reviews the Davis report and other available material on Apex and Campbell. From his analysis, he concludes that the common stocks of Campbell and Apex represent good value at their current prices; he believes, however, that the Davis report does not consider all the factors a Campbell stockholder would need to know to make a decision. Swanson reports his conclusions to the partner in charge, who tells him to "use the Davis report, change a few words, sign your name, and get it out."

Comment: If Swanson does as requested, he will violate Standard I(C). He could refer to those portions of the Davis report that he agrees with if he identifies Davis as the source; he could then add his own analysis and conclusions to the report before signing and distributing it.

Example 7 (Plagiarism)

Claude Browning, a quantitative analyst for Double Alpha, Inc., returns from a seminar in great excitement. At that seminar, Jack Jorrely, a well-known quantitative analyst at a national brokerage firm, discussed one of his new models in great detail, and Browning is intrigued by the new concepts. He proceeds to test the model, making some minor mechanical changes but retaining the concepts, until he produces some very positive results. Browning quickly announces to his supervisors at Double Alpha that he has discovered a new model and that clients and prospective clients should be informed of this positive finding as ongoing proof of Double Alpha's continuing innovation and ability to add value.

Comment: Although Browning tested Jorrely's model on his own and even slightly modified it, he must still acknowledge the original source of the idea. Browning can certainly take credit for the final, practical results; he can also support his conclusions with his own test. The credit for the innovative thinking, however, must be awarded to Jorrely.

Example 8 (Plagiarism)

Fernando Zubia would like to include in his firm's marketing materials some "plain-language" descriptions of various concepts, such as the price-to-earnings (P/E) multiple and why standard deviation is used as a measure of risk. The descriptions come from other sources, but Zubia wishes to use them without reference to the original authors. Would this use of material be a violation of Standard I(C)?

Comment: Copying verbatim any material without acknowledgment, including plain-language descriptions of the P/E multiple and standard deviation, violates Standard I(C). Even though these concepts are general, best practice would be for Zubia to describe them in his own words or cite the sources from which the descriptions are quoted. Members and candidates would be violating Standard I(C) if they either were responsible for creating marketing materials without attribution or knowingly use plagiarized materials.

Example 9 (Plagiarism)

Through a mainstream media outlet, Erika Schneider learns about a study that she would like to cite in her research. Should she cite both the mainstream intermediary source as well as the author of the study itself when using that information?

Comment: In all instances, a member or candidate must cite the actual source of the information. Best practice for Schneider would be to obtain the information directly from the author and review it before citing it in a report. In that case, Schneider would not need to report how she found out about the information. For example, suppose Schneider read in the *Financial Times* about a study issued by CFA Institute; best practice for Schneider would be to obtain a copy of the study from CFA Institute, review it, and then cite it in her report. If she does not use any interpretation of the report from the *Financial Times* and the newspaper does not add value to the report itself, the newspaper is merely a conduit of the original information and does not need to be cited. If she does not obtain the report and review the information, Schneider runs the risk of relying on secondhand information that may misstate facts. If, for example, the *Financial Times* erroneously reported some information from the original CFA Institute study and Schneider copied that erroneous information without acknowledging CFA Institute, she could be the object of complaints. Best practice would be either to obtain the complete study from its original author and cite only that author or to use the information provided by the intermediary and cite both sources.

Example 10 (Misrepresentation of Information)

Tom Stafford is part of a team within Appleton Investment Management responsible for managing a pool of assets for Open Air Bank, which distributes structured securities to offshore clients. He becomes aware that Open Air is promoting the structured securities as a much less risky investment than the investment management policy followed by him and the team to manage the original pool of assets. Also, Open Air has procured an independent rating for the pool that significantly overstates the quality of the investments. Stafford communicates his concerns to his supervisor, who responds that Open Air owns the product and is responsible for all marketing and distribution. Stafford's supervisor goes on to say that the product is outside of the U.S. regulatory regime that Appleton follows and that all risks of the product are disclosed at the bottom of page 184 of the prospectus.

Comment: As a member of the investment team, Stafford is qualified to recognize the degree of accuracy of the materials that characterize the portfolio, and he is correct to be worried about Appleton's responsibility for a misrepresentation of the risks. Thus, he should continue to pursue the issue of Open Air's inaccurate promotion of the portfolio according to the firm's policies and procedures. The Code and Standards stress protecting the reputation of the firm and the sustainability and integrity of the capital markets. Misrepresenting the quality and risks associated with the investment pool may lead to negative consequences for others well beyond the direct investors.

Example 11 (Misrepresenting Composite Construction)

Robert Palmer is head of performance for a fund manager. When asked to provide performance numbers to fund rating agencies, he avoids mentioning that the fund manager is quite liberal in composite construction. The reason accounts are included/excluded is not fully explained. The performance values reported to the rating agencies for the composites, although accurate for the accounts shown each period, may not present a true representation of the fund manager's ability.

Comment: "Cherry picking" accounts to include in either published reports or information provided to rating agencies conflicts with Standard I(C). Moving accounts into or out of a composite to influence the overall performance results materially misrepresents the reported values over time. Palmer should work with his firm to strengthen its reporting practices concerning composite construction to avoid misrepresenting the firm's track record or the quality of the information being provided.

Example 12 (Overemphasis of Firm Results)

Bob Anderson is chief compliance officer for Optima Asset Management Company, a firm currently offering eight funds to clients. Seven of the eight had 10-year returns below the median for their respective sectors. Anderson approves a recent advertisement, which includes this statement: "Optima Asset Management is achieving excellent returns for its investors. The Optima Emerging Markets Equity fund, for example, has 10-year returns that exceed the sector median by more than 10%."

Comment: From the information provided it is difficult to determine whether a violation has occurred as long as the sector outperformance is correct. Anderson may be attempting to mislead potential clients by citing the performance of the sole fund that achieved such results. Past performance is often used to demonstrate a firm's skill and abilities in comparison to funds in the same sectors.

However, if all the funds outperformed their respective benchmarks, then Anderson's assertion that the company "is achieving excellent returns" may be factual. Funds may exhibit positive returns for investors, exceed benchmarks, and yet have returns below the median in their sectors.

Members and candidates need to ensure that their marketing efforts do not include statements that misrepresent their skills and abilities to remain compliant with Standard I(C). Unless the returns of a single fund reflect the performance of a firm as a whole, the use of a singular fund for performance comparisons should be avoided.

Standard I(D) Misconduct

The Standard

Members and candidates must not engage in any professional conduct involving dishonesty, fraud, or deceit, or commit any act that reflects adversely on their professional reputation, integrity, or competence.

Guidance

- While Standard I(A) addresses the obligation of members and candidates to comply with applicable law that governs their professional activities, Standard I(D) addresses *all* conduct that reflects poorly on the professional integrity, good reputation, or competence of members and candidates. Any act that involves lying, cheating, stealing, or other dishonest conduct is a violation of this standard if the offense reflects adversely on a member's or candidate's professional activities.
- Conduct that damages trustworthiness or competence may include behavior that, although not illegal, nevertheless negatively affects a member's or candidate's ability to perform his or her responsibilities. For example:
    - Abusing alcohol during business hours might constitute a violation of this standard because it could have a detrimental effect on the member's or candidate's ability to fulfill his or her professional responsibilities.
    - Personal bankruptcy may not reflect on the integrity or trustworthiness of the person declaring bankruptcy, but if the circumstances of the bankruptcy involve fraudulent or deceitful business conduct, the bankruptcy may be a violation of this standard.
- In some cases, the absence of appropriate conduct or the lack of sufficient effort may be a violation of Standard I(D). The integrity of the investment profession is built on trust. A member or candidate—whether an investment banker, rating or research analyst, or portfolio manager—is expected to conduct the necessary due diligence to properly understand the nature and risks of an investment before making an investment recommendation. By not taking these steps and, instead, relying on someone else in the process to perform them, members or candidates may violate the trust their clients have placed in them. This loss of trust may have a significant impact on the reputation of the member or candidate and the operations of the financial market as a whole.
- Note that Standard I(D) or any other standard should not be used to settle personal, political, or other disputes unrelated to professional ethics.

Recommended Procedures for Compliance

Members and candidates should encourage their firms to adopt the following policies and procedures to support the principles of Standard I(D):

- Code of ethics: Develop and/or adopt a code of ethics to which every employee must subscribe, and make clear that any personal behavior that reflects poorly on the individual involved, the institution as a whole, or the investment industry will not be tolerated.
- List of violations: Disseminate to all employees a list of potential violations and associated disciplinary sanctions, up to and including dismissal from the firm.
- Employee references: Check references of potential employees to ensure that they are of good character and not ineligible to work in the investment industry because of past infractions of the law.

Application of the Standard

Example 1 (Professionalism and Competence)

Simon Sasserman is a trust investment officer at a bank in a small affluent town. He enjoys lunching every day with friends at the country club, where his clients have observed him having numerous drinks. Back at work after lunch, he clearly is intoxicated while making investment decisions. His colleagues make a point of handling any business with Sasserman in the morning because they distrust his judgment after lunch.

Comment: Sasserman's excessive drinking at lunch and subsequent intoxication at work constitute a violation of Standard I(D) because this conduct has raised questions about his professionalism and competence. His behavior reflects poorly on him, his employer, and the investment industry.

Example 2 (Fraud and Deceit)

Howard Hoffman, a security analyst at ATZ Brothers, Inc., a large brokerage house, submits reimbursement forms over a two-year period to ATZ's self-funded health insurance program for more than two dozen bills, most of which have been altered to increase the amount due. An investigation by the firm's director of employee benefits uncovers the inappropriate conduct. ATZ subsequently terminates Hoffman's employment and notifies CFA Institute.

Comment: Hoffman violated Standard I(D) because he engaged in intentional conduct involving fraud and deceit in the workplace that adversely reflected on his integrity.

Example 3 (Personal Actions and Integrity)

Carmen Garcia manages a mutual fund dedicated to socially responsible investing. She is also an environmental activist. As the result of her participation in nonviolent protests, Garcia has been arrested on numerous occasions for trespassing on the property of a large petrochemical plant that is accused of damaging the environment.

Comment: Generally, Standard I(D) is not meant to cover legal transgressions resulting from acts of civil disobedience in support of personal beliefs because such conduct does not reflect poorly on the member's or candidate's professional reputation, integrity, or competence.

Example 4 (Professional Misconduct)

Meredith Rasmussen works on a buy-side trading desk of an investment management firm and concentrates on in-house trades for a hedge fund subsidiary managed by a team at the investment management firm. The hedge fund has been very successful and is marketed globally by the firm. From her experience as the trader for much of the activity of the fund, Rasmussen has become quite knowledgeable about the hedge fund's strategy, tactics, and performance. When a distinct break in the market occurs and many of the securities involved in the hedge fund's strategy decline markedly in value, Rasmussen observes that the reported performance of the hedge fund does not reflect this decline. In her experience, the lack of effect is a very unlikely occurrence. She approaches the head of trading about her concern and is told that she should not ask any questions and that the fund is big and successful and is not her concern. She is fairly sure something is not right, so she contacts the compliance officer, who also tells her to stay away from the issue of the hedge fund's reporting.

Comment: Rasmussen has clearly come across an error in policies, procedures, and compliance practices within the firm's operations. According to the firm's procedures for reporting potentially unethical activity, she should pursue the issue by gathering some proof of her reason for doubt. Should all internal communications within the firm not satisfy her concerns, Rasmussen should consider reporting the potential unethical activity to the appropriate regulator.

See also Standard IV(A) for guidance on whistleblowing and Standard IV(C) for the duties of a supervisor.

LESSON 2: STANDARD II: INTEGRITY OF CAPITAL MARKETS

A. Material Nonpublic Information
B. Market Manipulation

Standard II(A) Material Nonpublic Information

The Standard

Members and Candidates who possess material nonpublic information that could affect the value of an investment must not act or cause others to act on the information.

Guidance

- Standard II(A) is related to information that is material and is nonpublic. Such information must not be used for direct buying and selling of individual securities or bonds, nor to influence investment actions related to derivatives, mutual funds, or other alternative investments.

Material Information

Information is "material" if its disclosure would likely have an impact on the price of a security, or if reasonable investors would want to know the information before making an investment decision. Material information may include, but is not limited to, information relating to the following:

- Earnings.
- Mergers, acquisitions, tender offers, or joint ventures.
- Changes in assets.
- Innovative products, processes, or discoveries.
- New licenses, patents, registered trademarks, or regulatory approval/rejection of a product.
- Developments regarding customers or suppliers (e.g., the acquisition or loss of a contract).
- Changes in management.
- Change in auditor notification or the fact that the issuer may no longer rely on an auditor's report or qualified opinion.
- Events regarding the issuer's securities (e.g., defaults on senior securities, calls of securities for redemption, repurchase plans, stock splits, changes in dividends, changes to the rights of security holders, public or private sales of additional securities, and changes in credit ratings).
- Bankruptcies.
- Significant legal disputes.
- Government reports of economic trends (employment, housing starts, currency information, etc.).
- Orders for large trades before they are executed.
- New or changing equity or debt ratings issued by a third party (e.g., sell-side recommendations and credit ratings).
- To determine if information is material, members and candidates should consider the source of information and the information's likely effect on the relevant stock price.
    - The less reliable a source, the less likely the information provided would be considered material.
    - The more ambiguous the effect on price, the less material the information becomes.
    - If it is unclear whether the information will affect the price of a security and to what extent, information may not be considered material.

Nonpublic Information

- Information is "nonpublic" until it has been disseminated or is available to the marketplace in general (as opposed to a select group of investors). "Disseminated" can be defined as "made known."
    - For example, a company report of profits that is posted on the internet and distributed widely through a press release or accompanied by a filing has been effectively disseminated to the marketplace.
- Members and candidates must be particularly aware of information that is selectively disclosed by corporations to a small group of investors, analysts, or other market participants. Information that is made available to analysts remains nonpublic until it is made available to investors in general.
- Analysts should also be alert to the possibility that they are selectively receiving material nonpublic information when a company provides them with guidance or interpretation of such publicly available information as financial statements or regulatory filings.
- A member or candidate may use insider information provided legitimately by the source company for the specific purpose of conducting due diligence according to the business agreement between the parties for such activities as mergers, loan underwriting, credit ratings, and offering engagements. However, the use of insider information provided by the source company for other purposes, especially to trade or entice others to trade the securities of the firm, conflicts with this standard.

Mosaic Theory

- A financial analyst may use significant conclusions derived from the analysis of public information and nonmaterial nonpublic information as the basis for investment recommendations and decisions. Under the "mosaic theory," financial analysts are free to act on this collection, or mosaic, of information without risking violation, even when the conclusion they reach would have been material inside information had the company communicated the same.
- Investment professionals should note, however, that although analysts are free to use mosaic information in their research reports, they should save and document all their research [see Standard V(C)].

Social Media

- Members and candidates participating in online discussion forums/groups with membership limitations should verify that material information obtained from these sources can also be accessed from a source that would be considered available to the public (e.g., company filings, webpages, and press releases).
- Members and candidates may use social media platforms to communicate with clients or investors without conflicting with this standard.
- Members and candidates, as required by Standard I(A), should also complete all appropriate regulatory filings related to information distributed through social media platforms.

Using Industry Experts

- The increased demand for insights for understanding the complexities of some industries has led to an expansion of engagement with outside experts. Members and candidates may provide compensation to individuals for their insights without violating this standard.
- However, members and candidates are ultimately responsible for ensuring that they are not requesting or acting on confidential information received from external experts, which is in violation of security regulations and laws or duties to others.

Investment Research Reports

- It might often be the case that reports prepared by well-known analysts may have an effect on the market and thus may be considered material information. Theoretically, such a report might have to be made public before it was distributed to clients. However, since the analyst is not a company insider, and presumably prepared the report based on publicly available information, the report does not need to be made public just because its conclusions are material. Investors who want to use that report must become clients of the analyst.

Recommended Procedures for Compliance

Achieve public dissemination: If a member or candidate determines that some nonpublic information is material, she should encourage the issuer to make the information public. If public dissemination is not possible, she must communicate the information only to the designated supervisory and compliance personnel in her firm and must not take investment action on the basis of the information.

Adopt compliance procedures: Members and candidates should encourage their firms to adopt compliance procedures to prevent the misuse of material nonpublic information. Particularly important is improving compliance in areas such as review of employee and proprietary trading, documentation of firm procedures, and the supervision of interdepartmental communications in multi-service firms.

Adopt disclosure procedures: Members and candidates should encourage their firms to develop and follow disclosure policies designed to ensure that information is disseminated in the marketplace in an equitable manner. An issuing company should not discriminate among analysts in the provision of information or blackball particular analysts who have given negative reports on the company in the past.

Issue press releases: Companies should consider issuing press releases prior to analyst meetings and conference calls and scripting those meetings and calls to decrease the chance that further information will be disclosed.

Firewall elements: An information barrier commonly referred to as a "firewall" is the most widely used approach to prevent communication of material nonpublic information within firms. The minimum elements of such a system include, but are not limited to, the following:

- Substantial control of relevant interdepartmental communications, preferably through a clearance area within the firm in either the compliance or legal department;
- Review of employee trading through the maintenance of "watch," "restricted," and "rumor" lists;
- Documentation of the procedures designed to limit the flow of information between departments and of the enforcement actions taken pursuant to those procedures;
- Heightened review or restriction of proprietary trading while a firm is in possession of material nonpublic information.

Appropriate interdepartmental communications: Based on the size of the firm, procedures concerning interdepartmental communication, the review of trading activity, and the investigation of possible violations should be compiled and formalized.

Physical separation of departments: As a practical matter, to the extent possible, firms should consider the physical separation of departments and files to prevent the communication of sensitive information.

Prevention of personnel overlap: There should be no overlap of personnel between the investment banking and corporate finance areas of a brokerage firm and the sales and research departments or between a bank's commercial lending department and its trust and research departments. For a firewall to be effective in a multi-service firm, an employee can be allowed to be on only one side of the wall at any given time.

A reporting system: The least a firm should do to protect itself from liability is have an information barrier in place. It should authorize people to review and approve communications between departments. A single supervisor or compliance officer should have the specific authority and responsibility of deciding whether or not information is material and whether it is sufficiently public to be used as the basis for investment decisions.

Personal trading limitations: Firms should also consider restrictions or prohibitions on personal trading by employees and should carefully monitor both proprietary trading and personal trading by employees. Further, they should require employees to make periodic reports (to the extent that such reporting is not already required by securities laws) of their own transactions and transactions made for the benefit of family members.

Securities should be placed on a restricted list when a firm has or may have material nonpublic information. Further, the watch list should be shown to only the few people responsible for compliance to monitor transactions in specified securities. The use of a watch list in combination with a restricted list has become a common means of ensuring an effective procedure.

Record maintenance: Multi-service firms should maintain written records of communications among various departments. Firms should place a high priority on training and should consider instituting comprehensive training programs, to enable employees to make informed decisions.

Proprietary trading procedures: Procedures concerning the restriction or review of a firm's proprietary trading while it possesses material nonpublic information will necessarily depend on the types of proprietary trading in which a firm may engage. For example, when a firm acts as a market maker, a prohibition on proprietary trading may be counterproductive to the goals of maintaining the confidentiality of information and market liquidity. However, in case of risk-arbitrage trading, a firm should suspend arbitrage activity when a security is placed on the watch list.

Communication to all employees: Written compliance policies and guidelines should be circulated to all employees of a firm. Further, they must be given sufficient training to either be able to make an informed decision or to realize that they need to consult a compliance officer before engaging in questionable transactions.

Application of the Standard

Example 1 (Acting on Nonpublic Information)

Frank Barnes, the president and controlling shareholder of the SmartTown clothing chain, decides to accept a tender offer and sell the family business at a price almost double the market price of its shares. He describes this decision to his sister (SmartTown's treasurer), who conveys it to her daughter (who owns no stock in the family company at present), who tells her husband, Staple. Staple, however, tells his stockbroker, Alex Halsey, who immediately buys SmartTown stock for himself.

Comment: The information regarding the pending sale is both material and nonpublic. Staple has violated Standard II(A) by communicating the inside information to his broker. Halsey also has violated the standard by buying the shares on the basis of material nonpublic information.

Example 2 (Controlling Nonpublic Information)

Samuel Peter, an analyst with Scotland and Pierce Incorporated, is assisting his firm with a secondary offering for Bright Ideas Lamp Company. Peter participates, via telephone conference call, in a meeting with Scotland and Pierce investment banking employees and Bright Ideas' CEO. Peter is advised that the company's earnings projections for the next year have significantly dropped. Throughout the telephone conference call, several Scotland and Pierce salespeople and portfolio managers walk in and out of Peter's office, where the telephone call is taking place. As a result, they are aware of the drop in projected earnings for Bright Ideas. Before the conference call is concluded, the salespeople trade the stock of the company on behalf of the firm's clients and other firm personnel trade the stock in a firm proprietary account and in employees' personal accounts.

Comment: Peter has violated Standard II(A) because he failed to prevent the transfer and misuse of material nonpublic information to others in his firm. Peter's firm should have adopted information barriers to prevent the communication of nonpublic information among departments of the firm. The salespeople and portfolio managers who traded on the information have also violated Standard II(A) by trading on inside information.

Example 3 (Selective Disclosure of Material Information)

Elizabeth Levenson is based in Taipei and covers the Taiwanese market for her firm, which is based in Singapore. She is invited, together with the other 10 largest shareholders of a manufacturing company, to meet the finance director of that company. During the meeting, the finance director states that the company expects its workforce to strike next Friday, which will cripple productivity and distribution. Can Levenson use this information as a basis to change her rating on the company from "buy" to "sell"?

Comment: Levenson must first determine whether the material information is public. According to Standard II(A), if the company has not made this information public (a small group forum does not qualify as a method of public dissemination), she cannot use the information.

Example 4 (Determining Materiality)

Leah Fechtman is trying to decide whether to hold or sell shares of an oil-and-gas exploration company that she owns in several of the funds she manages. Although the company has underperformed the index for some time already, the trends in the industry sector signal that companies of this type might become takeover targets. While she is considering her decision, her doctor, who casually follows the markets, mentions that she thinks that the company in question will soon be bought out by a large multinational conglomerate and that it would be a good idea to buy the stock right now. After talking to various investment professionals and checking their opinions on the company as well as checking industry trends, Fechtman decides the next day to accumulate more stock in the oil-and-gas exploration company.

Comment: Although information on an expected takeover bid may be of the type that is generally material and nonpublic, in this case, the source of information is unreliable, so the information cannot be considered material. Therefore, Fechtman is not prohibited from trading the stock on the basis of this information.

Example 5 (Applying the Mosaic Theory)

Jagdish Teja is a buy-side analyst covering the furniture industry. Looking for an attractive company to recommend as a buy, he analyzes several furniture makers by studying their financial reports and visiting their operations. He also talks to some designers and retailers to find out which furniture styles are trendy and popular. Although none of the companies that he analyzes are a clear buy, he discovers that one of them, Swan Furniture Company (SFC), may be in financial trouble. SFC's extravagant new designs have been introduced at substantial cost. Even though these designs initially attracted attention, the public is now buying more conservative furniture from other makers. Based on this information and on a profit-and-loss analysis, Teja believes that SFC's next quarter earnings will drop substantially. He issues a sell recommendation for SFC. Immediately after receiving that recommendation, investment managers start reducing the SFC stock in their portfolios.

Comment: Information on quarterly earnings data is material and nonpublic. Teja arrived at his conclusion about the earnings drop on the basis of public information and on pieces of nonmaterial nonpublic information (such as opinions of designers and retailers). Therefore, trading based on Teja's correct conclusion is not prohibited by Standard II(A).

Example 6 (Mosaic Theory)

John Doll is a research analyst for a hedge fund that also sells its research to a select group of paying client investment firms. Doll's focus is medical technology companies and products, and he has been in the business long enough and has been successful enough to build up a very credible network of friends and experts in the business. Doll has been working on a major research report recommending Boyce Health, a medical device manufacturer. He recently ran into an old acquaintance at a wedding who is a senior executive at Boyce, and Doll asked about the business. Doll was drawn to a statement that the executive, who has responsibilities in the new products area, made about a product: "I would not get too excited about the medium-term prospects; we have a lot of work to do first." Doll incorporated this and other information about the new Boyce product in his long-term recommendation of Boyce.

Comment: Doll's conversation with the senior executive is part of the mosaic of information used in recommending Boyce. When holding discussions with a firm executive, Doll would need to guard against soliciting or obtaining material nonpublic information. Before issuing the report, the executive's statement about the continuing development of the product would need to be weighed against the other known public facts to determine whether it would be considered material.

Example 7 (Materiality Determination)

Larry Nadler, a trader for a mutual fund, gets a text message from another firm's trader, whom he has known for years. The message indicates a software company is going to report strong earnings when the firm publicly announces in two days. Nadler has a buy order from a portfolio manager within his firm to purchase several hundred thousand shares of the stock. Nadler is aggressive in placing the portfolio manager's order and completes the purchases by the following morning, a day ahead of the firm's planned earnings announcement.

Comment: There are often rumors and whisper numbers before a release of any kind. The text message from the other trader would most likely be considered market noise. Unless Nadler knew that the trader had an ongoing business relationship with the public firm, he had no reason to suspect he was receiving material nonpublic information that would prevent him from completing the trading request of the portfolio manager.

Example 8 (Using an Expert Network)

Tom Watson is a research analyst working for a hedge fund. To stay informed, Watson relies on outside experts for information on such industries as technology and pharmaceuticals, where new advancements occur frequently. The meetings with the industry experts often are arranged through networks or placement agents that have specific policies and procedures in place to deter the exchange of material nonpublic information.

Watson arranges a call to discuss future prospects for one of the fund's existing technology company holdings, a company that was testing a new semiconductor product. The scientist leading the tests indicates his disappointment with the performance of the new semiconductor. Following the call, Watson relays the insights he received to others at the fund. The fund sells its current position in the company and writes many put options because the market is anticipating the success of the new semiconductor and the share price reflects the market's optimism.

Comment: Watson has violated Standard II(A) by passing along material nonpublic information concerning the ongoing product tests, which the fund used to trade in the securities and options of the related company. Watson cannot simply rely on the agreements signed by individuals who participate in expert networks that state that he has not received information that would prohibit his trading activity. He must make his own determination whether information he received through these arrangements reaches a materiality threshold that would affect his trading abilities.

Standard II(B) Market Manipulation

The Standard

Members and candidates must not engage in practices that distort prices or artificially inflate trading volume with the intent to mislead market participants.

Guidance

- Members and candidates must uphold market integrity by prohibiting market manipulation. Market manipulation includes practices that distort security prices or trading volume with the intent to deceive people or entities that rely on information in the market.

- Market manipulation includes (1) the dissemination of false or misleading information and (2) transactions that deceive or would be likely to mislead market participants by distorting the price-setting mechanism of financial instruments.

Information-Based Manipulation

- Information-based manipulation includes, but is not limited to, spreading false rumors to induce trading by others.
  - For example, members and candidates must refrain from "pumping up" the price of an investment by issuing misleading positive information or overly optimistic projections of a security's worth only to later "dump" the investment (i.e., sell it) once the price, fueled by the misleading information's effect on other market participants, reaches an artificially high level.

Transaction-Based Manipulation

- Transaction-based manipulation involves instances where a member or candidate knew or should have known that his or her actions could affect the pricing of a security. This type of manipulation includes, but is not limited to, the following:
  - Transactions that artificially affect prices or volume to give the impression of activity or price movement in a financial instrument, which represent a diversion from the expectations of a fair and efficient market.
  - Securing a controlling, dominant position in a financial instrument to exploit and manipulate the price of a related derivative and/or the underlying asset.

Note that Standard II(B) is not intended to preclude transactions undertaken on legitimate trading strategies based on perceived market inefficiencies. The intent of the action is critical to determining whether it is a violation of this standard.

Application of the Standard

Example 1 (Independent Analysis and Company Promotion)

The principal owner of Financial Information Services (FIS) entered into an agreement with two microcap companies to promote the companies' stock in exchange for stock and cash compensation. The principal owner caused FIS to disseminate e-mails, design and maintain several websites, and distribute an online investment newsletter—all of which recommended investment in the two companies. The systematic publication of purportedly independent analyses and recommendations containing inaccurate and highly promotional and speculative statements increased public investment in the companies and led to dramatically higher stock prices.

Comment: The principal owner of FIS violated Standard II(B) by using inaccurate reporting and misleading information under the guise of independent analysis to artificially increase the stock price of the companies. Furthermore, the principal owner violated Standard V(A)—Diligence and Reasonable Basis by not having a reasonable and adequate basis for recommending the two companies and violated Standard VI(A)—Disclosure of Conflicts by not disclosing to investors the compensation agreements (which constituted a conflict of interest).

Example 2 (Personal Trading Practices and Price)

John Gray is a private investor in Belgium who bought a large position several years ago in Fame Pharmaceuticals, a German small-cap security with limited average trading volume. He has now decided to significantly reduce his holdings owing to the poor price performance. Gray is worried that the low trading volume for the stock may cause the price to decline further as he attempts to sell his large position.

Gray devises a plan to divide his holdings into multiple accounts in different brokerage firms and private banks in the names of family members, friends, and even a private religious institution. He then creates a rumor campaign on various blogs and social media outlets promoting the company.

Gray begins to buy and sell the stock using the accounts in hopes of raising the trading volume and the price. He conducts the trades through multiple brokers, selling slightly larger positions than he bought on a tactical schedule, and over time, he is able to reduce his holding as desired without negatively affecting the sale price.

Comment: Gray violated Standard II(B) by fraudulently creating the appearance that there was a greater investor interest in the stock through the online rumors. Additionally, through his trading strategy, he created the appearance that there was greater liquidity in the stock than actually existed. He was able to manipulate the price through both misinformation and trading practices.

Example 3 (Personal Trading and Volume)

Rajesh Sekar manages two funds—an equity fund and a balanced fund—whose equity components are supposed to be managed in accordance with the same model. According to that model, the funds' holdings in stock of Digital Design Inc. (DD) are excessive. Reduction of the DD holdings would not be easy, however, because the stock has low liquidity in the stock market. Sekar decides to start trading larger portions of DD stock back and forth between his two funds to slowly increase the price; he believes market participants will see growing volume and increasing price and become interested in the stock. If other investors are willing to buy the DD stock because of such interest, then Sekar will be able to get rid of at least some of his overweight position without inducing price decreases. In this way, the whole transaction will be for the benefit of fund participants, even if additional brokers' commissions are incurred.

Comment: Sekar's plan would be beneficial for his funds' participants but is based on artificial distortion of both trading volume and the price of the DD stock and thus constitutes a violation of Standard II(B).

Example 4 ("Pump-Priming" Strategy)

Sergei Gonchar is chairman of the ACME Futures Exchange, which is launching a new bond futures contract. To convince investors, traders, arbitrageurs, hedgers, and so on, to use its contract, the exchange attempts to demonstrate that it has the best liquidity. To do so, it enters into agreements with members in which they commit to a substantial minimum trading volume on the new contract over a specific period in exchange for substantial reductions of their regular commissions.

Comment: The formal liquidity of a market is determined by the obligations set on market makers, but the actual liquidity of a market is better estimated by the actual trading volume and bid–ask spreads. Attempts to mislead participants about the actual liquidity of the market constitute a violation of Standard II(B). In this example, investors have been intentionally misled to believe they chose the most liquid instrument for some specific purpose, but they could eventually see the actual liquidity of the contract significantly reduced after the term of the agreement expires. If the ACME Futures Exchange fully discloses its agreement with members to boost transactions over some initial launch period, it will not violate Standard II(B). ACME's intent is not to harm investors but, on the contrary, to give them a better service. For that purpose, it may engage in a liquidity-pumping strategy, but the strategy must be disclosed.

Example 5 (Pump and Dump Strategy)

In an effort to pump up the price of his holdings in Moosehead & Belfast Railroad Company, Steve Weinberg logs on to several investor chat rooms on the internet to start rumors that the company is about to expand its rail network in anticipation of receiving a large contract for shipping lumber.

Comment: Weinberg has violated Standard II(B) by disseminating false information about Moosehead & Belfast with the intent to mislead market participants.

Example 6 (Information Manipulation)

Allen King is a performance analyst for Torrey Investment Funds. King believes that the portfolio manager for the firm's small- and microcap equity fund dislikes him because the manager never offers him tickets to the local baseball team's games but does offer tickets to other employees. To incite a potential regulatory review of the manager, King creates user profiles on several online forums under the portfolio manager's name and starts rumors about potential mergers for several of the smaller companies in the portfolio. As the prices of these companies' stocks increase, the portfolio manager sells the position, which leads to an investigation by the regulator as King desired.

Comment: King has violated Standard II(B) even though he did not personally profit from the market's reaction to the rumor. In posting the false information, King misleads others into believing the companies were likely to be acquired. Although his intent was to create trouble for the portfolio manager, his actions clearly manipulated the factual information that was available to the market.

LESSON 3: STANDARD III: DUTIES TO CLIENTS

A. Loyalty, Prudence, and Care
B. Fair Dealing
C. Suitability
D. Performance Presentation
E. Preservation of Confidentiality

Standard III(A) Loyalty, Prudence, and Care

The Standard

Members and candidates have a duty of loyalty to their clients and must act with reasonable care and exercise prudent judgment. Members and candidates must act for the benefit of their clients and place their clients' interests before their employer's or their own interests.

Guidance

- Standard III(A) clarifies that client interests are paramount. A member's or candidate's responsibility to a client includes a duty of loyalty and a duty to exercise reasonable care. Investment actions must be carried out for the sole benefit of the client and in a manner the member or candidate believes, given the known facts and circumstances, to be in the best interest of the client. Members and candidates must exercise the same level of prudence, judgment, and care that they would apply in the management and disposition of their own interests in similar circumstances.
- Prudence requires caution and discretion. The exercise of prudence by investment professionals requires that they act with the care, skill, and diligence that a reasonable person acting in a like capacity and familiar with such matters would use. In the context of managing a client's portfolio, prudence requires following the investment parameters set forth by the client and balancing risk and return. Acting with care requires members and candidates to act in a prudent and judicious manner in avoiding harm to clients.
- Standard III(A), however, is not a substitute for a member's or candidate's legal or regulatory obligations. As stated in Standard I(A), members and candidates must abide by the most strict requirements imposed on them by regulators or the Code and Standards, including any legally imposed fiduciary duty.
- Members and candidates must also be aware of whether they have "custody" or effective control of client assets. If so, a heightened level of responsibility arises. Members and candidates are considered to have custody if they have any direct or indirect access to client funds. Members and candidates must manage any pool of assets in their control in accordance with the terms of the governing documents (such as trust documents and investment management agreements), which are the primary determinant of the manager's powers and duties.

Understanding the Application of Loyalty, Prudence, and Care

- Standard III(A) establishes a minimum benchmark for the duties of loyalty, prudence, and care that are required of all members and candidates regardless of whether a legal fiduciary duty applies. Although fiduciary duty often encompasses the principles of loyalty, prudence, and care, Standard III(A) does not render all members and candidates fiduciaries. The responsibilities of members and candidates for fulfilling their obligations under this standard depend greatly on the nature of their professional responsibilities and the relationships they have with clients.

- There is a large variety of professional relationships that members and candidates have with their clients. Standard III(A) requires them to fulfill the obligations outlined explicitly or implicitly in the client agreements to the best of their abilities and with loyalty, prudence, and care. Whether a member or candidate is structuring a new securitization transaction, completing a credit rating analysis, or leading a public company, he or she must work with prudence and care in delivering the agreed-on services.

Identifying the Actual Investment Client

- The first step for members and candidates in fulfilling their duty of loyalty to clients is to determine the identity of the "client" to whom the duty of loyalty is owed. In the context of an investment manager managing the personal assets of an individual, the client is easily identified. When the manager is responsible for the portfolios of pension plans or trusts, however, the client is not the person or entity who hires the manager but, rather, the beneficiaries of the plan or trust. The duty of loyalty is owed to the ultimate beneficiaries.
- Members and candidates managing a fund to an index or an expected mandate owe the duty of loyalty, prudence, and care to invest in a manner consistent with the stated mandate. The decisions of a fund's manager, although benefiting all fund investors, do not have to be based on an individual investor's requirements and risk profile. Client loyalty and care for those investing in the fund are the responsibility of members and candidates who have an advisory relationship with those individuals.

Developing the Client's Portfolio

- Professional investment managers should ensure that the client's objectives and expectations for the performance of the account are realistic and suitable to the client's circumstances and that the risks involved are appropriate. In most circumstances, recommended investment strategies should relate to the long-term objectives and circumstances of the client.
- When members and candidates cannot avoid potential conflicts between their firm and clients' interests, they must provide clear and factual disclosures of the circumstances to the clients.
- Members and candidates must follow any guidelines set by their clients for the management of their assets.
- Investment decisions must be judged in the context of the total portfolio rather than by individual investment within the portfolio. The member's or candidate's duty is satisfied with respect to a particular investment if the individual has thoroughly considered the investment's place in the overall portfolio, the risk of loss and opportunity for gains, tax implications, and the diversification, liquidity, cash flow, and overall return requirements of the assets or the portion of the assets for which the manager is responsible.

Soft Commission Policies

- An investment manager often has discretion over the selection of brokers executing transactions. Conflicts may arise when an investment manager uses client brokerage to purchase research services, a practice commonly called "soft dollars" or "soft commissions." A member or candidate who pays a higher brokerage commission than he or she would normally pay to allow for the purchase of goods or services, without corresponding benefit to the client, violates the duty of loyalty to the client.

- From time to time, a client will direct a manager to use the client's brokerage to purchase goods or services for the client, a practice that is commonly called "directed brokerage." Because brokerage commission is an asset of the client and is used to benefit that client, not the manager, such a practice does not violate any duty of loyalty. However, a member or candidate is obligated to seek "best price" and "best execution" and be assured by the client that the goods or services purchased from the brokerage will benefit the account beneficiaries. In addition, the member or candidate should disclose to the client that the client may not be getting best execution from the directed brokerage.
    - "Best execution" refers to a trading process that seeks to maximize the value of the client's portfolio within the client's stated investment objectives and constraints.

Proxy Voting Policies

- Part of a member's or candidate's duty of loyalty includes voting proxies in an informed and responsible manner. Proxies have economic value to a client, and members and candidates must ensure that they properly safeguard and maximize this value.
- An investment manager who fails to vote, casts a vote without considering the impact of the question, or votes blindly with management on non-routine governance issues (e.g., a change in company capitalization) may violate this standard. Voting of proxies is an integral part of the management of investments.
- A cost–benefit analysis may show that voting all proxies may not benefit the client, so voting proxies may not be necessary in all instances.
- Members and candidates should disclose to clients their proxy voting policies.

Recommended Procedures for Compliance

Regular Account Information

Members and candidates with control of client assets should:

- Submit to each client, at least quarterly, an itemized statement showing the funds and securities in the custody or possession of the member or candidate plus all debits, credits, and transactions that occurred during the period.
- Disclose to the client where the assets are to be maintained, as well as where or when they are moved.
- Separate the client's assets from any other party's assets, including the member's or candidate's own assets.

Client Approval

- If a member or candidate is uncertain about the appropriate course of action with respect to a client, the member or candidate should consider what he or she would expect or demand if the member or candidate were the client.
- If in doubt, a member or candidate should disclose the questionable matter in writing to the client and obtain client approval.

Firm Policies

Members and candidates should address and encourage their firms to address the following topics when drafting the statements or manuals containing their policies and procedures regarding responsibilities to clients:

- *Follow all applicable rules and laws:* Members and candidates must follow all legal requirements and applicable provisions of the Code and Standards.
- *Establish the investment objectives of the client:* Make a reasonable inquiry into a client's investment experience, risk and return objectives, and financial constraints prior to making investment recommendations or taking investment actions.
- *Consider all the information when taking actions:* When taking investment actions, members and candidates must consider the appropriateness and suitability of the investment relative to (1) the client's needs and circumstances, (2) the investment's basic characteristics, and (3) the basic characteristics of the total portfolio.
- *Diversify:* Members and candidates should diversify investments to reduce the risk of loss, unless diversification is not consistent with plan guidelines or is contrary to the account objectives.
- *Carry out regular reviews:* Members and candidates should establish regular review schedules to ensure that the investments held in the account adhere to the terms of the governing documents.
- *Deal fairly with all clients with respect to investment actions:* Members and candidates must not favor some clients over others and should establish policies for allocating trades and disseminating investment recommendations.
- *Disclose conflicts of interest:* Members and candidates must disclose all actual and potential conflicts of interest so that clients can evaluate those conflicts.
- *Disclose compensation arrangements:* Members and candidates should make their clients aware of all forms of manager compensation.
- *Vote proxies:* In most cases, members and candidates should determine who is authorized to vote shares and vote proxies in the best interests of the clients and ultimate beneficiaries.
- *Maintain confidentiality:* Members and candidates must preserve the confidentiality of client information.
- *Seek best execution:* Unless directed by the client as ultimate beneficiary, members and candidates must seek best execution for their clients. (Best execution is defined in the preceding text.)
- *Place client interests first:* Members and candidates must serve the best interests of clients.

Application of the Standard

Example 1 (Identifying the Client—Plan Participants)

First Country Bank serves as trustee for the Miller Company's pension plan. Miller is the target of a hostile takeover attempt by Newton, Inc. In attempting to ward off Newton, Miller's managers persuade Julian Wiley, an investment manager at First Country Bank, to purchase Miller common stock in the open market for the employee pension plan. Miller's officials indicate that such action would be favorably received and would probably result in other accounts being placed with the bank. Although Wiley believes the stock is overvalued and would not ordinarily buy it, he purchases the stock to support Miller's managers, to maintain Miller's good favor toward the bank, and to realize additional new business. The heavy stock purchases cause Miller's market price to rise to such a level that Newton retracts its takeover bid.

Comment: Standard III(A) requires that a member or candidate, in evaluating a takeover bid, act prudently and solely in the interests of plan participants and beneficiaries. To meet this requirement, a member or candidate must carefully evaluate the long-term prospects of the company against the short-term prospects presented by the takeover offer and by the ability to invest elsewhere. In this instance, Wiley, acting on behalf of his employer, which was the trustee for a pension plan, clearly violated Standard III(A). He used the pension plan to perpetuate existing management, perhaps to the detriment of plan participants and the company's shareholders, and to benefit himself. Wiley's responsibilities to the plan participants and beneficiaries should have taken precedence over any ties of his bank to corporate managers and over his self-interest. Wiley had a duty to examine the takeover offer on its own merits and to make an independent decision. The guiding principle is the appropriateness of the investment decision to the pension plan, not whether the decision benefited Wiley or the company that hired him.

Example 2 (Client Commission Practices)

JNI, a successful investment counseling firm, serves as investment manager for the pension plans of several large regionally based companies. Its trading activities generate a significant amount of commission-related business. JNI uses the brokerage and research services of many firms, but most of its trading activity is handled through a large brokerage company, Thompson, Inc., because the executives of the two firms have a close friendship. Thompson's commission structure is high in comparison with charges for similar brokerage services from other firms. JNI considers Thompson's research services and execution capabilities average. In exchange for JNI directing its brokerage to Thompson, Thompson absorbs a number of JNI overhead expenses, including those for rent.

Comment: JNI executives are breaching their responsibilities by using client brokerage for services that do not benefit JNI clients and by not obtaining best price and best execution for their clients. Because JNI executives are not upholding their duty of loyalty, they are violating Standard III(A).

Example 3 (Brokerage Arrangements)

Charlotte Everett, a struggling independent investment adviser, serves as investment manager for the pension plans of several companies. One of her brokers, Scott Company, is close to consummating management agreements with prospective new clients whereby Everett would manage the new client accounts and trade the accounts exclusively through Scott. One of Everett's existing clients, Crayton Corporation, has directed Everett to place securities transactions for Crayton's account exclusively through Scott. But to induce Scott to exert efforts to send more new accounts to her, Everett also directs transactions to Scott from other clients without their knowledge.

Comment: Everett has an obligation at all times to seek best price and best execution on all trades. Everett may direct new client trades exclusively through Scott Company as long as Everett receives best price and execution on the trades or receives a written statement from new clients that she is *not* to seek best price and execution and that they are aware of the consequence for their accounts. Everett may trade other accounts through Scott as a reward for directing clients to Everett only if the accounts receive best price and execution and the practice is disclosed to the accounts. Because Everett does not disclose the directed trading, Everett has violated Standard III(A).

Example 4 (Brokerage Arrangements)

Emilie Rome is a trust officer for Paget Trust Company. Rome's supervisor is responsible for reviewing Rome's trust account transactions and her monthly reports of personal stock transactions. Rome has been using Nathan Gray, a broker, almost exclusively for trust account brokerage transactions. When Gray makes a market in stocks, he has been giving Rome a lower price for personal purchases and a higher price for sales than he gives to Rome's trust accounts and other investors.

Comment: Rome is violating her duty of loyalty to the bank's trust accounts by using Gray for brokerage transactions simply because Gray trades Rome's personal account on favorable terms. Rome is placing her own interests before those of her clients.

Example 5 (Managing Family Accounts)

Adam Dill recently joined New Investments Asset Managers. To assist Dill in building a book of clients, both his father and brother opened new fee-paying accounts. Dill followed all the firm's procedures in noting his relationships with these clients and in developing their investment policy statements.

After several years, the number of Dill's clients has grown, but he still manages the original accounts of his family members. An IPO is coming to market that is a suitable investment for many of his clients, including his brother. Dill does not receive the amount of stock he requested, so to avoid any appearance of a conflict of interest, he does not allocate any shares to his brother's account.

Comment: Dill has violated Standard III(A) because he is not acting for the benefit of his brother's account as well as his other accounts. The brother's account is a regular fee-paying account comparable to the accounts of his other clients. By not allocating the shares proportionately across *all* accounts for which he thought the IPO was suitable, Dill is disadvantaging specific clients.

Dill would have been correct in not allocating shares to his brother's account if that account was being managed outside the normal fee structure of the firm.

Example 6 (Identifying the Client)

Donna Hensley has been hired by a law firm to testify as an expert witness. Although the testimony is intended to represent impartial advice, she is concerned that her work may have negative consequences for the law firm. If the law firm is Hensley's client, how does she ensure that her testimony will not violate the required duty of loyalty, prudence, and care to one's client?

Comment: In this situation, the law firm represents Hensley's employer and the aspect of "Who is the client?" is not well defined. When acting as an expert witness, Hensley is bound by the standard of independence and objectivity in the same manner as an independent research analyst would be bound. Hensley must not let the law firm influence the testimony she provides in the legal proceedings.

Example 7 (Client Loyalty)

After providing client account investment performance to the external-facing departments but prior to it being finalized for release to clients, Teresa Nguyen, an investment performance analyst, notices the reporting system missed a trade. Correcting the omission resulted in a large loss for a client that had previously placed the firm on "watch" for potential termination owing to underperformance in prior periods. Nguyen knows this news is unpleasant but informs the appropriate individuals that the report needs to be updated before releasing it to the client.

Comment: Nguyen's actions align with the requirements of Standard III(A). Even though the correction may to lead to the firm's termination by the client, withholding information on errors would not be in the best interest of the client.

Example 8 (Execution-Only Responsibilities)

Baftija Sulejman recently became a candidate in the CFA Program. He is a broker who executes client-directed trades for several high-net-worth individuals. Sulejman does not provide any investment advice and only executes the trading decisions made by clients. He is concerned that the Code and Standards impose a fiduciary duty on him in his dealing with clients and sends an e-mail to the CFA Ethics Helpdesk (ethics@cfainstitute.org) to seek guidance on this issue.

Comment: In this instance, Sulejman serves in an execution-only capacity and his duty of loyalty, prudence, and care is centered on the skill and diligence used when executing trades—namely, by seeking best execution and making trades within the parameters set by the clients (instructions on quantity, price, timing, etc.). Acting in the best interests of the client dictates that trades are executed on the most favorable terms that can be achieved for the client. Given this job function, the requirements of the Code and Standards for loyalty, prudence, and care clearly do not impose a fiduciary duty.

Standard III(B) Fair Dealing

The Standard

Members and candidates must deal fairly and objectively with all clients when providing investment analysis, making investment recommendations, taking investment action, or engaging in other professional activities.

Guidance

- Standard III(B) requires members and candidates to treat all clients fairly when disseminating investment recommendations or making material changes to prior investment recommendations, or when taking investment action with regard to general purchases, new issues, or secondary offerings.

- The term "fairly" implies that the member or candidate must take care not to discriminate against any clients when disseminating investment recommendations or taking investment action. Standard III(B) does not state "equally" because members and candidates could not possibly reach all clients at exactly the same time. Further, each client has unique needs, investment criteria, and investment objectives, so not all investment opportunities are suitable for all clients.
- Members and candidates may provide more personal, specialized, or in-depth service to clients who are willing to pay for premium services through higher management fees or higher levels of brokerage. Members and candidates may differentiate their services to clients, but different levels of service must not disadvantage or negatively affect clients. In addition, the different service levels should be disclosed to clients and prospective clients and should be available to everyone (i.e., different service levels should not be offered selectively).

Investment Recommendations

- An investment recommendation is any opinion expressed by a member or candidate in regard to purchasing, selling, or holding a given security or other investment. The opinion may be disseminated to customers or clients through an initial detailed research report, through a brief update report, by addition to or deletion from a list of recommended securities, or simply by oral communication. A recommendation that is distributed to anyone outside the organization is considered a communication for general distribution under Standard III(B).
- Each member or candidate is obligated to ensure that information is disseminated in such a manner that all clients have a fair opportunity to act on every recommendation. Members and candidates should encourage their firms to design an equitable system to prevent selective or discriminatory disclosure and should inform clients about what kind of communications they will receive.
- The duty to clients imposed by Standard III(B) may be more critical when members or candidates change their recommendations than when they make initial recommendations. Material changes in a member's or candidate's prior investment recommendations because of subsequent research should be communicated to all current clients; particular care should be taken that the information reaches those clients who the member or candidate knows have acted on or been affected by the earlier advice.
- Clients who do not know that the member or candidate has changed a recommendation and who, therefore, place orders contrary to a current recommendation should be advised of the changed recommendation before the order is accepted.

Investment Action

- Members or candidates must treat all clients fairly in light of their investment objectives and circumstances. For example, when making investments in new offerings or in secondary financings, members and candidates should distribute the issues to all customers for whom the investments are appropriate in a manner consistent with the policies of the firm for allocating blocks of stock. If the issue is oversubscribed, then the issue should be prorated to all subscribers. If the issue is oversubscribed, members and candidates should forgo any sales to themselves or their immediate families in order to free up additional shares for clients.
    - If the investment professional's family-member accounts are managed similarly to the accounts of other clients of the firm, however, the family-member accounts should not be excluded from buying such shares.

- Members and candidates must make every effort to treat all individual and institutional clients in a fair and impartial manner.
- Members and candidates should disclose to clients and prospective clients the documented allocation procedures they or their firms have in place and how the procedures would affect the client or prospect. The disclosure should be clear and complete so that the client can make an informed investment decision. Even when complete disclosure is made, however, members and candidates must put client interests ahead of their own. A member's or candidate's duty of fairness and loyalty to clients can never be overridden by client consent to patently unfair allocation procedures.
- Treating clients fairly also means that members and candidates should not take advantage of their position in the industry to the detriment of clients. For instance, in the context of IPOs, members and candidates must make bona fide public distributions of "hot issue" securities (defined as securities of a public offering that are trading at a premium in the secondary market whenever such trading commences because of the great demand for the securities). Members and candidates are prohibited from withholding such securities for their own benefit and must not use such securities as a reward or incentive to gain benefit.

Recommended Procedures for Compliance

Develop Firm Policies

- A member or candidate should recommend appropriate procedures to management if none are in place.
- A member or candidate should make management aware of possible violations of fair-dealing practices within the firm when they come to the attention of the member or candidate.
- Although a member or candidate need not communicate a recommendation to all customers, the selection process by which customers receive information should be based on suitability and known interest, not on any preferred or favored status.

A common practice to assure fair dealing is to communicate recommendations simultaneously within the firm and to customers. Members and candidates should consider the following points when establishing fair-dealing compliance procedures:

- Limit the number of people involved.
- Shorten the time frame between decision and dissemination.
- Publish guidelines for pre-dissemination behavior.
- Simultaneous dissemination.
- Maintain a list of clients and their holdings.
- Develop and document trade allocation procedures that ensure:
    - Fairness to advisory clients, both in priority of execution of orders and in the allocation of the price obtained in execution of block orders or trades.
    - Timeliness and efficiency in the execution of orders.
    - Accuracy of the member's or candidate's records as to trade orders and client account positions.

With these principles in mind, members and candidates should develop or encourage their firm to develop written allocation procedures, with particular attention to procedures for block trades and new issues. Procedures to consider are as follows:

- Requiring orders and modifications or cancellations of orders to be documented and time stamped.

- Processing and executing orders on a first-in, first-out basis with consideration of bundling orders for efficiency as appropriate for the asset class or the security.
- Developing a policy to address such issues as calculating execution prices and "partial fills" when trades are grouped, or in a block, for efficiency.
- Giving all client accounts participating in a block trade the same execution price and charging the same commission.
- When the full amount of the block order is not executed, allocating partially executed orders among the participating client accounts pro rata on the basis of order size while not going below an established minimum lot size for some securities (e.g., bonds).
- When allocating trades for new issues, obtaining advance indications of interest, allocating securities by client (rather than portfolio manager), and providing a method for calculating allocations.

Disclose Trade Allocation Procedures

- Members and candidates should disclose to clients and prospective clients how they select accounts to participate in an order and how they determine the amount of securities each account will buy or sell. Trade allocation procedures must be fair and equitable, and disclosure of inequitable allocation methods does not relieve the member or candidate of this obligation.

Establish Systematic Account Review

- Member and candidate supervisors should review each account on a regular basis to ensure that no client or customer is being given preferential treatment and that the investment actions taken for each account are suitable for each account's objectives.
- Because investments should be based on individual needs and circumstances, an investment manager may have good reasons for placing a given security or other investment in one account while selling it from another account and should fully document the reasons behind both sides of the transaction.
- Members and candidates should encourage firms to establish review procedures, however, to detect whether trading in one account is being used to benefit a favored client.

Disclose Levels of Service

- Members and candidates should disclose to all clients whether the organization offers different levels of service to clients for the same fee or different fees.
- Different levels of service should not be offered to clients selectively.

Application of the Standard

Example 1 (Selective Disclosure)

Bradley Ames, a well-known and respected analyst, follows the computer industry. In the course of his research, he finds that a small, relatively unknown company whose shares are traded over the counter has just signed significant contracts with some of the companies he follows. After a considerable amount of investigation, Ames decides to write a research report on the small company and recommend purchase of its shares. While the report is being reviewed by the company for factual accuracy, Ames schedules a luncheon with several of his best clients to discuss the company. At the luncheon, he mentions the purchase recommendation scheduled to be sent early the following week to all the firm's clients.

Comment: Ames has violated Standard III(B) by disseminating the purchase recommendation to the clients with whom he has lunch a week before the recommendation is sent to all clients.

Example 2 (Fair Dealing and IPO Distribution)

Dominic Morris works for a small regional securities firm. His work consists of corporate finance activities and investing for institutional clients. Arena, Ltd., is planning to go public. The partners have secured rights to buy an arena football league franchise and are planning to use the funds from the issue to complete the purchase. Because arena football is the current rage, Morris believes he has a hot issue on his hands. He has quietly negotiated some options for himself for helping convince Arena to do the financing through his securities firm. When he seeks expressions of interest, the institutional buyers oversubscribe the issue. Morris, assuming that the institutions have the financial clout to drive the stock up, then fills all orders (including his own) and decreases the institutional blocks.

Comment: Morris has violated Standard III(B) by not treating all customers fairly. He should not have taken any shares himself and should have prorated the shares offered among all clients. In addition, he should have disclosed to his firm and to his clients that he received options as part of the deal [see Standard VI(A)—Disclosure of Conflicts].

Example 3 (Fair Dealing and Transaction Allocation)

Eleanor Preston, the chief investment officer of Porter Williams Investments (PWI), a medium-size money management firm, has been trying to retain a client, Colby Company. Management at Colby, which accounts for almost half of PWI's revenues, recently told Preston that if the performance of its account did not improve, it would find a new money manager. Shortly after this threat, Preston purchases mortgage-backed securities (MBSs) for several accounts, including Colby's. Preston is busy with a number of transactions that day, so she fails to allocate the trades immediately or write up the trade tickets. A few days later, when Preston is allocating trades, she notes that some of the MBSs have significantly increased in price and some have dropped. Preston decides to allocate the profitable trades to Colby and spread the losing trades among several other PWI accounts.

Comment: Preston has violated Standard III(B) by failing to deal fairly with her clients in taking these investment actions. Preston should have allocated the trades prior to executing the orders, or she should have had a systematic approach to allocating the trades, such as pro rata, as soon as practical after they were executed. Among other things, Preston must disclose to the client that the adviser may act as broker for, receive commissions from, and have a potential conflict of interest regarding both parties in agency cross-transactions. After the disclosure, she should obtain from the client consent authorizing such transactions in advance.

Example 4 (Additional Services for Select Clients)

Jenpin Weng uses e-mail to issue a new recommendation to all his clients. He then calls his three largest institutional clients to discuss the recommendation in detail.

Comment: Weng has not violated Standard III(B) because he widely disseminated the recommendation and provided the information to all his clients prior to discussing it with a select few. Weng's largest clients received additional personal service because they presumably pay higher fees or because they have a large amount of assets under Weng's management. If Weng had discussed the report with a select group of clients prior to distributing it to all his clients, he would have violated Standard III(B).

Example 5 (Minimum Lot Allocations)

Lynn Hampton is a well-respected private wealth manager in her community with a diversified client base. She determines that a new 10-year bond being offered by Healthy Pharmaceuticals is appropriate for five of her clients. Three clients request to purchase US$10,000 each, and the other two request US$50,000 each. The minimum lot size is established at US$5,000, and the issue is oversubscribed at the time of placement. Her firm's policy is that odd-lot allocations, especially those below the minimum, should be avoided because they may affect the liquidity of the security at the time of sale.

Hampton is informed she will receive only US$55,000 of the offering for all accounts. Hampton distributes the bond investments as follows: The three accounts that requested US$10,000 are allocated US$5,000 each, and the two accounts that requested US$50,000 are allocated US$20,000 each.

Comment: Hampton has not violated Standard III(B), even though the distribution is not on a completely pro rata basis because of the required minimum lot size. With the total allocation being significantly below the amount requested, Hampton ensured that each client received at least the minimum lot size of the issue. This approach allowed the clients to efficiently sell the bond later if necessary.

Example 6 (Excessive Trading)

Ling Chan manages the accounts for many pension plans, including the plan of his father's employer. Chan developed similar but not identical investment policies for each client, so the investment portfolios are rarely the same. To minimize the cost to his father's pension plan, he intentionally trades more frequently in the accounts of other clients to ensure the required brokerage is incurred to continue receiving free research for use by all the pensions.

Comment: Chan is violating Standard III(B) because his trading actions are disadvantaging his clients to enhance a relationship with a preferred client. All clients are benefiting from the research being provided and should incur their fair portion of the costs. This does not mean that additional trading should occur if a client has not paid an equal portion of the commission; trading should occur only as required by the strategy.

Example 7 (Fair Dealing among Clients)

Paul Rove, performance analyst for Alpha-Beta Investment Management, is describing to the firm's chief investment officer (CIO) two new reports he would like to develop to assist the firm in meeting its obligations to treat clients fairly. Because many of the firm's clients have similar investment objectives and portfolios, Rove suggests a report detailing securities owned across several clients and the percentage of the portfolio the security represents. The second report would compare the monthly performance of portfolios with similar strategies. The outliers within each report would be submitted to the CIO for review.

Comment: As a performance analyst, Rove likely has little direct contact with clients and thus has limited opportunity to treat clients differently. The recommended reports comply with Standard III(B) while helping the firm conduct after-the-fact reviews of how effectively the firm's advisers are dealing with their clients' portfolios. Reports that monitor the fair treatment of clients are an important oversight tool to ensure that clients are treated fairly.

Standard III(C) Suitability

The Standard

1. When Members and candidates are in an advisory relationship with a client, they must:
   a. Make a reasonable inquiry into a client's or prospective client's investment experience, risk and return objectives, and financial constraints prior to making any investment recommendation or taking investment action and must reassess and update this information regularly.
   b. Determine that an investment is suitable to the client's financial situation and consistent with the client's written objectives, mandates, and constraints before making an investment recommendation or taking investment action.
   c. Judge the suitability of investments in the context of the client's total portfolio.
2. When members and candidates are responsible for managing a portfolio to a specific mandate, strategy, or style, they must make only investment recommendations or take only investment actions that are consistent with the stated objectives and constraints of the portfolio.

Guidance

- Standard III(C) requires that members and candidates who are in an investment advisory relationship with clients consider carefully the needs, circumstances, and objectives of the clients when determining the appropriateness and suitability of a given investment or course of investment action.
- In judging the suitability of a potential investment, the member or candidate should review many aspects of the client's knowledge, experience related to investing, and financial situation. These aspects include, but are not limited to, the risk profile of the investment as compared with the constraints of the client, the impact of the investment on the diversity of the portfolio, and whether the client has the means or net worth to assume the associated risk. The investment professional's determination of suitability should reflect only the investment recommendations or actions that a prudent person would be willing to undertake. Not every investment opportunity will be suitable for every portfolio, regardless of the potential return being offered.
- The responsibilities of members and candidates to gather information and make a suitability analysis prior to making a recommendation or taking investment action fall on those members and candidates who provide investment advice in the course of an advisory relationship with a client. Other members and candidates who are simply executing specific instructions for retail clients when buying or selling securities, may not have the opportunity to judge the suitability of a particular investment for the ultimate client.

Developing an Investment Policy

- When an advisory relationship exists, members and candidates must gather client information at the inception of the relationship. Such information includes the client's financial circumstances, personal data (such as age and occupation) that are relevant to investment decisions, attitudes toward risk, and objectives in investing. This information should be incorporated into a written investment policy statement (IPS) that addresses the client's risk tolerance, return requirements, and all investment constraints (including time horizon, liquidity needs, tax concerns, legal and regulatory factors, and unique circumstances).
- The IPS also should identify and describe the roles and responsibilities of the parties to the advisory relationship and investment process, as well as schedules for review and evaluation of the IPS.

- After formulating long-term capital market expectations, members and candidates can assist in developing an appropriate strategic asset allocation and investment program for the client, whether these are presented in separate documents or incorporated in the IPS or in appendices to the IPS.

Understanding the Client's Risk Profile

- The investment professional must consider the possibilities of rapidly changing investment environments and their likely impact on a client's holdings, both individual securities and the collective portfolio.
- The risk of many investment strategies can and should be analyzed and quantified in advance.
- Members and candidates should pay careful attention to the leverage inherent in many synthetic investment vehicles or products when considering them for use in a client's investment program.

Updating an Investment Policy

- Updating the IPS should be repeated at least annually and also prior to material changes to any specific investment recommendations or decisions on behalf of the client.
    - For an individual client, important changes might include the number of dependents, personal tax status, health, liquidity needs, risk tolerance, amount of wealth beyond that represented in the portfolio, and extent to which compensation and other income provide for current income needs.
    - For an institutional client, such changes might relate to the magnitude of unfunded liabilities in a pension fund, the withdrawal privileges in an employee savings plan, or the distribution requirements of a charitable foundation.
- If clients withhold information about their financial portfolios, the suitability analysis conducted by members and candidates cannot be expected to be complete; it must be based on the information provided.

The Need for Diversification

- The unique characteristics (or risks) of an individual investment may become partially or entirely neutralized when it is combined with other individual investments within a portfolio. Therefore, a reasonable amount of diversification is thus the norm for many portfolios.
- An investment with high relative risk on its own may be a suitable investment in the context of the entire portfolio or when the client's stated objectives contemplate speculative or risky investments.
- Members and candidates can be responsible for assessing the suitability of an investment only on the basis of the information and criteria actually provided by the client.

Addressing Unsolicited Trading Requests

- If an unsolicited request is expected to have only a minimum impact on the entire portfolio because the size of the requested trade is small or the trade would result in a limited change to the portfolio's risk profile, the member or candidate should focus on educating the investor on how the request deviates from the current policy statement, and then she may follow her firm's policies regarding the necessary client approval for executing unsuitable trades. At a minimum, the client should acknowledge the discussion and accept the conditions that make the recommendation unsuitable.
- If an unsolicited request is expected to have a material impact on the portfolio, the member or candidate should use this opportunity to update the investment policy statement. Doing so would allow the client to fully understand the potential effect of the requested trade on his or her current goals or risk levels.

- If the client declines to modify her policy statements while insisting an unsolicited trade be made, the member or candidate will need to evaluate the effectiveness of her services to the client. The options available to the members or candidates will depend on the services provided by their employer. Some firms may allow for the trade to be executed in a new unmanaged account. If alternative options are not available, members and candidates ultimately will need to determine whether they should continue the advisory arrangement with the client.

Managing to an Index or Mandate

Some members and candidates do not manage money for individuals but are responsible for managing a fund to an index or an expected mandate. The responsibility of these members and candidates is to invest in a manner consistent with the stated mandate.

Recommended Procedures for Compliance

Investment Policy Statement

In formulating an investment policy for the client, the member or candidate should take the following into consideration:

- *Client identification*—(1) type and nature of client, (2) the existence of separate beneficiaries, and (3) approximate portion of total client assets that the member or candidate is managing.
- *Investor objectives*—(1) return objectives (income, growth in principal, maintenance of purchasing power) and (2) risk tolerance (suitability, stability of values).
- *Investor constraints*—(1) liquidity needs, (2) expected cash flows (patterns of additions and/or withdrawals), (3) investable funds (assets and liabilities or other commitments), (4) time horizon, (5) tax considerations, (6) regulatory and legal circumstances, (7) investor preferences, prohibitions, circumstances, and unique needs, and (8) proxy voting responsibilities and guidance.
- *Performance measurement benchmarks.*

Regular Updates

- The investor's objectives and constraints should be maintained and reviewed periodically to reflect any changes in the client's circumstances.

Suitability Test Policies

- With the increase in regulatory required suitability tests, members and candidates should encourage their firms to develop related policies and procedures. The test procedures should require the investment professional to look beyond the potential return of the investment and include the following:
    - An analysis of the impact on the portfolio's diversification.
    - A comparison of the investment risks with the client's assessed risk tolerance.
    - The fit of the investment with the required investment strategy.

Application of the Standard

Example 1 (Investment Suitability—Risk Profile)

Caleb Smith, an investment adviser, has two clients: Larry Robertson, 60 years old, and Gabriel Lanai, 40 years old. Both clients earn roughly the same salary, but Robertson has a much higher risk tolerance because he has a large asset base. Robertson is willing to invest part of his assets very aggressively; Lanai wants only to achieve a steady rate of return with low volatility to pay for his children's education. Smith recommends investing 20% of both portfolios in zero-yield, small-cap, high-technology equity issues.

Comment: In Robertson's case, the investment may be appropriate because of his financial circumstances and aggressive investment position, but this investment is not suitable for Lanai. Smith is violating Standard III(C) by applying Robertson's investment strategy to Lanai because the two clients' financial circumstances and objectives differ.

Example 2 (Investment Suitability—Entire Portfolio)

Jessica McDowell, an investment adviser, suggests to Brian Crosby, a risk-averse client, that covered call options be used in his equity portfolio. The purpose would be to enhance Crosby's income and partially offset any untimely depreciation in the portfolio's value should the stock market or other circumstances affect his holdings unfavorably. McDowell educates Crosby about all possible outcomes, including the risk of incurring an added tax liability if a stock rises in price and is called away and, conversely, the risk of his holdings losing protection on the downside if prices drop sharply.

Comment: When determining suitability of an investment, the primary focus should be the characteristics of the client's entire portfolio, not the characteristics of single securities on an issue-by-issue basis. The basic characteristics of the entire portfolio will largely determine whether investment recommendations are taking client factors into account. Therefore, the most important aspects of a particular investment are those that will affect the characteristics of the total portfolio. In this case, McDowell properly considers the investment in the context of the entire portfolio and thoroughly explains the investment to the client.

Example 3 (Following an Investment Mandate)

Louis Perkowski manages a high-income mutual fund. He purchases zero-dividend stock in a financial services company because he believes the stock is undervalued and is in a potential growth industry, which makes it an attractive investment.

Comment: A zero-dividend stock does not seem to fit the mandate of the fund that Perkowski is managing. Unless Perkowski's investment fits within the mandate or is within the realm of allowable investments the fund has made clear in its disclosures, Perkowski has violated Standard III(C).

Example 4 (Submanager and IPS Reviews)

Paul Ostrowski's investment management business has grown significantly over the past couple of years, and some clients want to diversify internationally. Ostrowski decides to find a submanager to handle the expected international investments. Because this will be his first subadviser, Ostrowski uses the CFA Institute model "request for proposal" to design a questionnaire for his search. By his deadline, he receives seven completed questionnaires from a variety of domestic and international firms trying to gain his business. Ostrowski reviews all the applications in detail and decides to select the firm that charges the lowest fees because doing so will have the least impact on his firm's bottom line.

Comment: When selecting an external manager or subadviser, Ostrowski needs to ensure that the new manager's services are appropriate for his clients. This due diligence includes comparing the risk profile of the clients with the investment strategy of the manager. In basing the decision on the fee structure alone, Ostrowski may be violating Standard III(C).

When clients ask to diversify into international products, it is an appropriate time to review and update the clients' IPSs. Ostrowski's review may determine that the risk of international investments modifies the risk profiles of the clients or does not represent an appropriate investment.

See also Standard V(A)—Diligence and Reasonable Basis for further discussion of the review process needed in selecting appropriate submanagers.

Example 5 (Investment Suitability)

Andre Shrub owns and operates Conduit, an investment advisory firm. Prior to opening Conduit, Shrub was an account manager with Elite Investment, a hedge fund managed by his good friend Adam Reed. To attract clients to a new Conduit fund, Shrub offers lower-than-normal management fees. He can do so because the fund consists of two top-performing funds managed by Reed. Given his personal friendship with Reed and the prior performance record of these two funds, Shrub believes this new fund is a winning combination for all parties. Clients quickly invest with Conduit to gain access to the Elite funds. No one is turned away because Conduit is seeking to expand its assets under management.

Comment: Shrub has violated Standard III(C) because the risk profile of the new fund may not be suitable for every client. As an investment adviser, Shrub needs to establish an investment policy statement for each client and recommend only investments that match each client's risk and return profile in the IPS. Shrub is required to act as more than a simple sales agent for Elite.

Although Shrub cannot disobey the direct request of a client to purchase a specific security, he should fully discuss the risks of a planned purchase and provide reasons why it might not be suitable for a client. This requirement may lead members and candidates to decline new customers if those customers' requested investment decisions are significantly out of line with their stated requirements.

See also Standard V(A)—Diligence and Reasonable Basis.

Standard III(D) Performance Presentation

The Standard

When communicating investment performance information, members and candidates must make reasonable efforts to ensure that it is fair, accurate, and complete.

Guidance

- Members and candidates must provide credible performance information to clients and prospective clients and to avoid misstating performance or misleading clients and prospective clients about the investment performance of members or candidates or their firms.

- Standard III(D) covers any practice that would lead to misrepresentation of a member's or candidate's performance record, whether the practice involves performance presentation or performance measurement.
- Members and candidates should not state or imply that clients will obtain or benefit from a rate of return that was generated in the past.
- Research analysts promoting the success or accuracy of their recommendations must ensure that their claims are fair, accurate, and complete.
- If the presentation is brief, the member or candidate must make available to clients and prospects, on request, the detailed information supporting that communication. Best practice dictates that brief presentations include a reference to the limited nature of the information provided.

Recommended Procedures for Compliance

Apply the GIPS Standards

- Compliance with the GIPS standards is the best method to meet their obligations under Standard III(D).

Compliance without Applying GIPS Standards

Members and candidates can also meet their obligations under Standard III(D) by:

- Considering the knowledge and sophistication of the audience to whom a performance presentation is addressed.
- Presenting the performance of the weighted composite of similar portfolios rather than using a single representative account.
- Including terminated accounts as part of performance history with a clear indication of when the accounts were terminated.
- Including disclosures that fully explain the performance results being reported (for example, stating, when appropriate, that results are simulated when model results are used, clearly indicating when the performance record is that of a prior entity, or disclosing whether the performance is gross of fees, net of fees, or after tax).
- Maintaining the data and records used to calculate the performance being presented.

Application of the Standard

Example 1 (Performance Calculation and Length of Time)

Kyle Taylor of Taylor Trust Company, noting the performance of Taylor's common trust fund for the past two years, states in a brochure sent to his potential clients, "You can expect steady 25% annual compound growth of the value of your investments over the year." Taylor Trust's common trust fund did increase at the rate of 25% per year for the past year, which mirrored the increase of the entire market. The fund has never averaged that growth for more than one year, however, and the average rate of growth of all of its trust accounts for five years is 5% per year.

Comment: Taylor's brochure is in violation of Standard III(D). Taylor should have disclosed that the 25% growth occurred only in one year. Additionally, Taylor did not include client accounts other than those in the firm's common trust fund. A general claim of firm performance should take into account the performance of all categories of accounts. Finally, by stating that clients can expect a steady 25% annual compound growth rate, Taylor is also violating Standard I(C)—Misrepresentation, which prohibits assurances or guarantees regarding an investment.

Example 2 (Performance Calculation and Asset Weighting)

Anna Judd, a senior partner of Alexander Capital Management, circulates a performance report for the capital appreciation accounts for the years 1988 through 2004. The firm claims compliance with the GIPS standards. Returns are not calculated in accordance with the requirements of the GIPS standards, however, because the composites are not asset weighted.

Comment: Judd is in violation of Standard III(D). When claiming compliance with the GIPS standards, firms must meet *all* of the requirements, make mandatory disclosures, and meet any other requirements that apply to that firm's specific situation. Judd's violation is not from any misuse of the data but from a false claim of GIPS compliance.

Example 3 (Performance Calculation and Selected Accounts Only)

In a presentation prepared for prospective clients, William Kilmer shows the rates of return realized over a five-year period by a "composite" of his firm's discretionary accounts that have a "balanced" objective. This composite, however, consisted of only a few of the accounts that met the balanced criterion set by the firm, excluded accounts under a certain asset level without disclosing the fact of their exclusion, and included accounts that did not have the balanced mandate because those accounts would boost the investment results. In addition, to achieve better results, Kilmer manipulated the narrow range of accounts included in the composite by changing the accounts that made up the composite over time.

Comment: Kilmer violated Standard III(D) by misrepresenting the facts in the promotional material sent to prospective clients, distorting his firm's performance record, and failing to include disclosures that would have clarified the presentation.

Example 4 (Performance Attribution Changes)

Art Purell is reviewing the quarterly performance attribution reports for distribution to clients. Purell works for an investment management firm with a bottom-up, fundamentals-driven investment process that seeks to add value through stock selection. The attribution methodology currently compares each stock with its sector. The attribution report indicates that the value added this quarter came from asset allocation and that stock selection contributed negatively to the calculated return. Through running several different scenarios, Purell discovers that calculating attribution by comparing each stock with its industry and then rolling the effect to the sector level improves the appearance of the manager's stock selection activities. Because the firm defines the attribution terms and the results better reflect the stated strategy, Purell recommends that the client reports should use the revised methodology.

Comment: Modifying the attribution methodology without proper notifications to clients would fail to meet the requirements of Standard III(D). Purrell's recommendation is being done solely for the interest of the firm to improve its perceived ability to meet the stated investment strategy. Such changes are unfair to clients and obscure the facts regarding the firm's abilities. Had Purell believed the new methodology offered improvements to the original model, then he would have needed to report the results of both calculations to the client. The report should also include the reasons why the new methodology is preferred, which would allow the client to make a meaningful comparison to prior results and provide a basis for comparing future attributions.

Example 5 (Performance Calculation Methodology Disclosure)

While developing a new reporting package for existing clients, Alisha Singh, a performance analyst, discovers that her company's new system automatically calculates both time-weighted and money-weighted returns. She asks the head of client services and retention which value would be preferred given that the firm has various investment strategies that include bonds, equities, securities without leverage, and alternatives. Singh is told not to label the return value so that the firm may show whichever value is greatest for the period.

Comment: Following these instructions would lead to Singh violating Standard III(D). In reporting inconsistent return values, Singh would not be providing complete information to the firm's clients. Full information is provided when clients have sufficient information to judge the performance generated by the firm.

Example 6 (Performance Calculation Methodology Disclosure)

Richmond Equity Investors manages a long–short equity fund in which clients can trade once a week (on Fridays). For transparency reasons, a daily net asset value of the fund is calculated by Richmond. The monthly fact sheets of the fund report month-to-date and year-to-date performance. Richmond publishes the performance based on the higher of the last trading day of the month (typically, not the last business day) or the last business day of the month as determined by Richmond. The fact sheet mentions only that the data are as of the end of the month, without giving the exact date. Maggie Clark, the investment performance analyst in charge of the calculations, is concerned about the frequent changes and asks her supervisor whether they are appropriate.

Comment: Clark's actions in questioning the changing performance metric comply with Standard III(D). She has shown concern that these changes are not presenting an accurate and complete picture of the performance generated.

Standard III(E) Preservation of Confidentiality

The Standard

Members and candidates must keep information about current, former, and prospective clients confidential unless:

1. The information concerns illegal activities on the part of the client;
2. Disclosure is required by law; or
3. The client or prospective client permits disclosure of the information.

Guidance

- Members and candidates must preserve the confidentiality of information communicated to them by their clients, prospective clients, and former clients. This standard is applicable when (1) the member or candidate receives information because of his or her special ability to conduct a portion of the client's business or personal affairs and (2) the member or candidate receives information that arises from or is relevant to that portion of the client's business that is the subject of the special or confidential relationship.

- If disclosure of the information is required by law or the information concerns illegal activities by the client, however, the member or candidate may have an obligation to report the activities to the appropriate authorities.

Status of Client

- This standard protects the confidentiality of client information even if the person or entity is no longer a client of the member or candidate. Therefore, members and candidates must continue to maintain the confidentiality of client records even after the client relationship has ended.
- If a client or former client expressly authorizes the member or candidate to disclose information, however, the member or candidate may follow the terms of the authorization and provide the information.

Compliance with Laws

- As a general matter, members and candidates must comply with applicable law. If applicable law requires disclosure of client information in certain circumstances, members and candidates must comply with the law. Similarly, if applicable law requires members and candidates to maintain confidentiality, even if the information concerns illegal activities on the part of the client, members and candidates should not disclose such information.
- When in doubt, members and candidates should consult with their employer's compliance personnel or legal counsel before disclosing confidential information about clients.

Electronic Information and Security

- Standard III(E) does not require members or candidates to become experts in information security technology, but they should have a thorough understanding of the policies of their employer.
- Members and candidates should encourage their firm to conduct regular periodic training on confidentiality procedures for all firm personnel, including portfolio associates, receptionists, and other non-investment staff who have routine direct contact with clients and their records.

Professional Conduct Investigations by CFA Institute

- The requirements of Standard III(E) are not intended to prevent members and candidates from cooperating with an investigation by the CFA Institute Professional Conduct Program (PCP). When permissible under applicable law, members and candidates shall consider the PCP an extension of themselves when requested to provide information about a client in support of a PCP investigation into their own conduct.

Recommended Procedures for Compliance

The simplest, most conservative, and most effective way to comply with Standard III(E) is to avoid disclosing any information received from a client except to authorized fellow employees who are also working for the client. In some instances, however, a member or candidate may want to disclose information received from clients that is outside the scope of the confidential relationship and does not involve illegal activities. Before making such a disclosure, a member or candidate should ask the following:

- In what context was the information disclosed? If disclosed in a discussion of work being performed for the client, is the information relevant to the work?
- Is the information background material that, if disclosed, will enable the member or candidate to improve service to the client?

Communicating with Clients

- Members and candidates should make reasonable efforts to ensure that firm-supported communication methods and compliance procedures follow practices designed for preventing accidental distribution of confidential information.
- Members and candidates should be diligent in discussing with clients the appropriate methods for providing confidential information. It is important to convey to clients that not all firm-sponsored resources may be appropriate for such communications.

Application of the Standard

Example 1 (Possessing Confidential Information)

Sarah Connor, a financial analyst employed by Johnson Investment Counselors, Inc., provides investment advice to the trustees of City Medical Center. The trustees have given her a number of internal reports concerning City Medical's needs for physical plant renovation and expansion. They have asked Connor to recommend investments that would generate capital appreciation in endowment funds to meet projected capital expenditures. Connor is approached by a local businessman, Thomas Kasey, who is considering a substantial contribution either to City Medical Center or to another local hospital. Kasey wants to find out the building plans of both institutions before making a decision, but he does not want to speak to the trustees.

Comment: The trustees gave Connor the internal reports so she could advise them on how to manage their endowment funds. Because the information in the reports is clearly both confidential and within the scope of the confidential relationship, Standard III(E) requires that Connor refuse to divulge information to Kasey.

Example 2 (Disclosing Confidential Information)

Lynn Moody is an investment officer at the Lester Trust Company. She has an advisory customer who has talked to her about giving approximately US$50,000 to charity to reduce her income taxes. Moody is also treasurer of the Home for Indigent Widows (HIW), which is planning its annual giving campaign. HIW hopes to expand its list of prospects, particularly those capable of substantial gifts. Moody recommends that HIW's vice president for corporate gifts call on her customer and ask for a donation in the US$50,000 range.

Comment: Even though the attempt to help the Home for Indigent Widows was well intended, Moody violated Standard III(E) by revealing confidential information about her client.

Example 3 (Disclosing Possible Illegal Activity)

David Bradford manages money for a family-owned real estate development corporation. He also manages the individual portfolios of several of the family members and officers of the corporation, including the chief financial officer (CFO). Based on the financial records of the corporation and some questionable practices of the CFO that Bradford has observed, Bradford believes that the CFO is embezzling money from the corporation and putting it into his personal investment account.

Comment: Bradford should check with his firm's compliance department or appropriate legal counsel to determine whether applicable securities regulations require reporting the CFO's financial records.

Example 4 (Accidental Disclosure of Confidential Information)

Lynn Moody is an investment officer at the Lester Trust Company (LTC). She has stewardship of a significant number of individually managed taxable accounts. In addition to receiving quarterly written reports, about a dozen high-net-worth individuals have indicated to Moody a willingness to receive communications about overall economic and financial market outlooks directly from her by way of a social media platform. Under the direction of her firm's technology and compliance departments, she established a new group page on an existing social media platform specifically for her clients. In the instructions provided to clients, Moody asked them to "join" the group so they may be granted access to the posted content. The instructions also advised clients that all comments posted would be available to the public and thus the platform was not an appropriate method for communicating personal or confidential information.

Six months later, in early January, Moody posted LTC's year-end "Market Outlook." The report outlined a new asset allocation strategy that the firm is adding to its recommendations in the new year. Moody introduced the publication with a note informing her clients that she would be discussing the changes with them individually in their upcoming meetings.

One of Moody's clients responded directly on the group page that his family recently experienced a major change in their financial profile. The client described highly personal and confidential details of the event. Unfortunately, all clients that were part of the group were also able to read the detailed posting until Moody was able to have the comment removed.

Comment: Moody has taken reasonable steps for protecting the confidentiality of client information while using the social media platform. She provided instructions clarifying that all information posted to the site would be publicly viewable to all group members and warned against using this method for communicating confidential information. The accidental disclosure of confidential information by a client is not under Moody's control. Her actions to remove the information promptly once she became aware further align with Standard III(E).

In understanding the potential sensitivity clients express surrounding the confidentiality of personal information, this event highlights a need for further training. Moody might advocate for additional warnings or controls for clients when they consider using social media platforms for two-way communications.

LESSON 4: STANDARD IV: DUTIES TO EMPLOYERS

A. Loyalty
B. Additional Compensation Arrangements
C. Responsibilities of Supervisors

Standard IV(A) Loyalty

The Standard

In matters related to their employment, members and candidates must act for the benefit of their employer and not deprive their employer of the advantage of their skills and abilities, divulge confidential information, or otherwise cause harm to their employer.

Guidance

- Members and candidates should protect the interests of their firm by refraining from any conduct that would injure the firm, deprive it of profit, or deprive it of the member's or candidate's skills and ability.
- Members and candidates must always place the interests of clients above the interests of their employer but should also consider the effects of their conduct on the sustainability and integrity of the employer firm.
- In matters related to their employment, members and candidates must comply with the policies and procedures established by their employers that govern the employer–employee relationship—to the extent that such policies and procedures do not conflict with applicable laws, rules, or regulations or the Code and Standards.
- The standard does not require members and candidates to subordinate important personal and family obligations to their work.

Employer Responsibilities

- Employers must recognize the duties and responsibilities that they owe to their employees if they expect to have content and productive employees.
- Members and candidates are encouraged to provide their employer with a copy of the Code and Standards.
- Employers are not obligated to adhere to the Code and Standards. In expecting to retain competent employees who are members and candidates, however, they should not develop conflicting policies and procedures.

Independent Practice

- Members and candidates must abstain from independent competitive activity that could conflict with the interests of their employer.
- Members and candidates who plan to engage in independent practice for compensation must notify their employer and describe the types of services they will render to prospective independent clients, the expected duration of the services, and the compensation for the services.
- Members and candidates should not render services until they receive consent from their employer to all of the terms of the arrangement.
    - "Practice" means any service that the employer currently makes available for remuneration.
    - "Undertaking independent practice" means engaging in competitive business, as opposed to making preparations to begin such practice.

Leaving an Employer

- When members and candidates are planning to leave their current employer, they must continue to act in the employer's best interest. They must not engage in any activities that would conflict with this duty until their resignation becomes effective.
- Activities that might constitute a violation, especially in combination, include the following:
  - Misappropriation of trade secrets.
  - Misuse of confidential information.
  - Solicitation of the employer's clients prior to cessation of employment.
  - Self-dealing (appropriating for one's own property a business opportunity or information belonging to one's employer).
  - Misappropriation of clients or client lists.
- A departing employee is generally free to make arrangements or preparations to go into a competitive business before terminating the relationship with his or her employer as long as such preparations do not breach the employee's duty of loyalty.
- A member or candidate who is contemplating seeking other employment must not contact existing clients or potential clients prior to leaving his or her employer for purposes of soliciting their business for the new employer. Once notice is provided to the employer of the intent to resign, the member or candidate must follow the employer's policies and procedures related to notifying clients of his or her planned departure. In addition, the member or candidate must not take records or files to a new employer without the written permission of the previous employer.
- Once an employee has left the firm, the skills and experience that an employee obtained while employed are not "confidential" or "privileged" information. Similarly, simple knowledge of the names and existence of former clients is generally not confidential information unless deemed such by an agreement or by law.
- Standard IV(A) does not prohibit experience or knowledge gained at one employer from being used at another employer. Firm records or work performed on behalf of the firm that is stored in paper copy or electronically for the member's or candidate's convenience while employed, however, should be erased or returned to the employer unless the firm gives permission to keep those records after employment ends.
- The standard does not prohibit former employees from contacting clients of their previous firm as long as the contact information does not come from the records of the former employer or violate an applicable "non-compete agreement." Members and candidates are free to use public information after departing to contact former clients without violating Standard IV(A) as long as there is no specific agreement not to do so.

Use of Social Media

- Members and candidates should understand and abide by all applicable firm policies and regulations as to the acceptable use of social media platforms to interact with clients and prospective clients.
- Specific accounts and user profiles of members and candidates may be created for solely professional reasons, including firm-approved accounts for client engagements. Such firm-approved business-related accounts would be considered part of the firm's assets, thus requiring members and candidates to transfer or delete the accounts as directed by their firm's policies and procedures.
- Best practice for members and candidates is to maintain separate accounts for their personal and professional social media activities. Members and candidates should discuss with their employers how profiles should be treated when a single account includes personal connections and also is used to conduct aspects of their professional activities.

Whistleblowing

Sometimes, circumstances may arise (e.g., when an employer is engaged in illegal or unethical activity) in which members and candidates must act contrary to their employer's interests in order to comply with their duties to the market and clients. In such instances, activities that would normally violate a member's or candidate's duty to his or her employer (such as contradicting employer instructions, violating certain policies and procedures, or preserving a record by copying employer records) may be justified. However, such action would be permitted only if the intent is clearly aimed at protecting clients or the integrity of the market, not for personal gain.

Nature of Employment

- Members and candidates must determine whether they are employees or independent contractors in order to determine the applicability of Standard IV(A). This issue will be decided largely by the degree of control exercised by the employing entity over the member or candidate. Factors determining control include whether the member's or candidate's hours, work location, and other parameters of the job are set; whether facilities are provided to the member or candidate; whether the member's or candidate's expenses are reimbursed; whether the member or candidate seeks work from other employers; and the number of clients or employers the member or candidate works for.
- A member's or candidate's duties within an independent contractor relationship are governed by the oral or written agreement between the member and the client. Members and candidates should take care to define clearly the scope of their responsibilities and the expectations of each client within the context of each relationship. Once a member or candidate establishes a relationship with a client, the member or candidate has a duty to abide by the terms of the agreement.

Recommended Procedures for Compliance

Competition Policy

- A member or candidate must understand any restrictions placed by the employer on offering similar services outside the firm while employed by the firm.
- If a member's or candidate's employer elects to have its employees sign a non-compete agreement as part of the employment agreement, the member or candidate should ensure that the details are clear and fully explained prior to signing the agreement.

Termination Policy

- Members and candidates should clearly understand the termination policies of their employer. Termination policies should:
  - Establish clear procedures regarding the resignation process, including addressing how the termination will be disclosed to clients and staff and whether updates posted through social media platforms will be allowed.
  - Outline the procedures for transferring ongoing research and account management responsibilities.
  - Address agreements that allow departing employees to remove specific client-related information upon resignation.

Incident-Reporting Procedures

- Members and candidates should be aware of their firm's policies related to whistleblowing and encourage their firm to adopt industry best practices in this area.

Employee Classification

- Members and candidates should understand their status within their employer firm.

Application of the Standard

Example 1 (Soliciting Former Clients)

Samuel Magee manages pension accounts for Trust Assets, Inc., but has become frustrated with the working environment and has been offered a position with Fiduciary Management. Before resigning from Trust Assets, Magee asks four big accounts to leave that firm and open accounts with Fiduciary. Magee also persuades several prospective clients to sign agreements with Fiduciary Management. Magee had previously made presentations to these prospects on behalf of Trust Assets.

Comment: Magee violated the employee–employer principle requiring him to act solely for his employer's benefit. Magee's duty is to Trust Assets as long as he is employed there. The solicitation of Trust Assets' current clients and prospective clients is unethical and violates Standard IV(A).

Example 2 (Addressing Rumors)

Reuben Winston manages all-equity portfolios at Target Asset Management (TAM), a large, established investment counselor. Ten years previously, Philpott & Company, which manages a family of global bond mutual funds, acquired TAM in a diversification move. After the merger, the combined operations prospered in the fixed-income business but the equity management business at TAM languished. Lately, a few of the equity pension accounts that had been with TAM before the merger have terminated their relationships with TAM. One day, Winston finds on his voice mail the following message from a concerned client: "Hey! I just heard that Philpott is close to announcing the sale of your firm's equity management business to Rugged Life. What is going on?" Not being aware of any such deal, Winston and his associates are stunned. Their internal inquiries are met with denials from Philpott management, but the rumors persist. Feeling left in the dark, Winston contemplates leading an employee buyout of TAM's equity management business.

Comment: An employee-led buyout of TAM's equity asset management business would be consistent with Standard IV(A) because it would rest on the permission of the employer and, ultimately, the clients. In this case, however, in which employees suspect the senior managers or principals are not truthful or forthcoming, Winston should consult legal counsel to determine appropriate action.

Example 3 (Ownership of Completed Prior Work)

Emma Madeline, a recent college graduate and a candidate in the CFA Program, spends her summer as an unpaid intern at Murdoch and Lowell. The senior managers at Murdoch are attempting to bring the firm into compliance with the GIPS standards, and Madeline is assigned to assist in its efforts. Two months into her internship, Madeline applies for a job at McMillan & Company, which has plans to become GIPS compliant. Madeline accepts the job with McMillan. Before leaving Murdoch, she copies the firm's software that she helped develop because she believes this software will assist her in her new position.

Comment: Even though Madeline does not receive monetary compensation for her services at Murdoch, she has used firm resources in creating the software and is considered an employee because she receives compensation and benefits in the form of work experience and knowledge. By copying the software, Madeline violated Standard IV(A) because she misappropriated Murdoch's property without permission.

Example 4 (Starting a New Firm)

Geraldine Allen currently works at a registered investment company as an equity analyst. Without notice to her employer, she registers with government authorities to start an investment company that will compete with her employer, but she does not actively seek clients. Does registration of this competing company with the appropriate regulatory authorities constitute a violation of Standard IV(A)?

Comment: Allen's preparation for the new business by registering with the regulatory authorities does not conflict with the work for her employer if the preparations have been done on Allen's own time outside the office and if Allen will not be soliciting clients for the business or otherwise operating the new company until she has left her current employer.

Example 5 (Competing with Current Employer)

Several employees are planning to depart their current employer within a few weeks and have been careful to not engage in any activities that would conflict with their duty to their current employer. They have just learned that one of their employer's clients has undertaken a request for proposal (RFP) to review and possibly hire a new investment consultant. The RFP has been sent to the employer and all of its competitors. The group believes that the new entity to be formed would be qualified to respond to the RFP and be eligible for the business. The RFP submission period is likely to conclude before the employees' resignations are effective. Is it permissible for the group of departing employees to respond to the RFP for their anticipated new firm?

Comment: A group of employees responding to an RFP that their employer is also responding to would lead to direct competition between the employees and the employer. Such conduct violates Standard IV(A) unless the group of employees receives permission from their employer as well as the entity sending out the RFP.

Example 6 (Externally Compensated Assignments)

Alfonso Mota is a research analyst with Tyson Investments. He works part time as a mayor for his hometown, a position for which he receives compensation. Must Mota seek permission from Tyson to serve as mayor?

Comment: If Mota's mayoral duties are so extensive and time-consuming that they might detract from his ability to fulfill his responsibilities at Tyson, he should discuss his outside activities with his employer and come to a mutual agreement regarding how to manage his personal commitments with his responsibilities to his employer.

Example 7 (Soliciting Former Clients)

After leaving her employer, Shawna McQuillen establishes her own money management business. While with her former employer, she did not sign a non-compete agreement that would have prevented her from soliciting former clients. Upon her departure, she does not take any of her client lists or contact information and she clears her personal computer of any employer records, including client contact information. She obtains the phone numbers of her former clients through public records and contacts them to solicit their business.

Comment: McQuillen is not in violation of Standard IV(A) because she has not used information or records from her former employer and is not prevented by an agreement with her former employer from soliciting her former clients.

Example 8 (Leaving an Employer)

Laura Webb just left her position as portfolio analyst at Research Systems, Inc. (RSI). Her employment contract included a non-solicitation agreement that requires her to wait two years before soliciting RSI clients for any investment-related services. Upon leaving, Webb was informed that RSI would contact clients immediately about her departure and introduce her replacement.

While working at RSI, Webb connected with clients, other industry associates, and friends through her LinkedIn network. Her business and personal relationships were intermingled because she considered many of her clients to be personal friends. Realizing that her LinkedIn network would be a valuable resource for new employment opportunities, she updated her profile several days following her departure from RSI. LinkedIn automatically sent a notification to Webb's entire network that her employment status had been changed in her profile.

Comment: Prior to her departure, Webb should have discussed any client information contained in her social media networks. By updating her LinkedIn profile after RSI notified clients and after her employment ended, she has appropriately placed her employer's interests ahead of her own personal interests. In addition, she has not violated the non-solicitation agreement with RSI, unless it prohibited any contact with clients during the two-year period.

Example 9 (Confidential Firm Information)

Sam Gupta is a research analyst at Naram Investment Management (NIM). NIM uses a team-based research process to develop recommendations on investment opportunities covered by the team members. Gupta, like others, provides commentary for NIM's clients through the company blog, which is posted weekly on the NIM password-protected website. According to NIM's policy, every contribution to the website must be approved by the company's compliance department before posting. Any opinions expressed on the website are disclosed as representing the perspective of NIM.

Gupta also writes a personal blog to share his experiences with friends and family. As with most blogs, Gupta's personal blog is widely available to interested readers through various internet search engines. Occasionally, when he disagrees with the team-based research opinions of NIM, Gupta uses his personal blog to express his own opinions as a counterpoint to the commentary posted on the NIM website. Gupta believes this provides his readers with a more complete perspective on these investment opportunities.

Comment: Gupta is in violation of Standard IV(A) for disclosing confidential firm information through his personal blog. The recommendations on the firm's blog to clients are not freely available across the internet, but his personal blog post indirectly provides the firm's recommendations.

Additionally, by posting research commentary on his personal blog, Gupta is using firm resources for his personal advantage. To comply with Standard IV(A), members and candidates must receive consent from their employer prior to using company resources.

Example 10 (Notification of Code and Standards)

Krista Smith is a relatively new assistant trader for the fixed-income desk of a major investment bank. She is on a team responsible for structuring collateralized debt obligations (CDOs) made up of securities in the inventory of the trading desk. At a meeting of the team, senior executives explain the opportunity to eventually separate the CDO into various risk-rated tranches to be sold to the clients of the firm. After the senior executives leave the meeting, the head trader announces various responsibilities of each member of the team and then says, "This is a good time to unload some of the junk we have been stuck with for a while and disguise it with ratings and a thick, unreadable prospectus, so don't be shy in putting this CDO together. Just kidding." Smith is worried by this remark and asks some of her colleagues what the head trader meant. They all respond that he was just kidding but that there is some truth in the remark because the CDO is seen by management as an opportunity to improve the quality of the securities in the firm's inventory.

Concerned about the ethical environment of the workplace, Smith decides to talk to her supervisor about her concerns and provides the head trader with a copy of the Code and Standards. Smith discusses the principle of placing the client above the interest of the firm and the possibility that the development of the new CDO will not adhere to this responsibility. The head trader assures Smith that the appropriate analysis will be conducted when determining the appropriate securities for collateral. Furthermore, the ratings are assigned by an independent firm and the prospectus will include full and factual disclosures. Smith is reassured by the meeting, but she also reviews the company's procedures and requirements for reporting potential violations of company policy and securities laws.

Comment: Smith's review of the company policies and procedures for reporting violations allows her to be prepared to report through the appropriate whistleblower process if she decides that the CDO development process involves unethical actions by others. Smith's actions comply with the Code and Standards principles of placing the client's interests first and being loyal to her employer. In providing her supervisor with a copy of the Code and Standards, Smith is highlighting the high level of ethical conduct she is required to adhere to in her professional activities.

Standard IV(B) Additional Compensation Arrangements

The Standard

Members and candidates must not accept gifts, benefits, compensation, or consideration that competes with or might reasonably be expected to create a conflict of interest with their employer's interest unless they obtain written consent from all parties involved.

Guidance

- Members and candidates must obtain permission from their employer before accepting compensation or other benefits from third parties for the services rendered to the employer or for any services that might create a conflict with their employer's interest.
  - Compensation and benefits include direct compensation by the client and any indirect compensation or other benefits received from third parties.
  - "Written consent" includes any form of communication that can be documented (for example, communication via e-mail that can be retrieved and documented).

Recommended Procedures for Compliance

- Members and candidates should make an immediate written report to their supervisor and compliance officer specifying any compensation they propose to receive for services in addition to the compensation or benefits received from their employer.
- The details of the report should be confirmed by the party offering the additional compensation, including performance incentives offered by clients.
- This written report should state the terms of any agreement under which a member or candidate will receive additional compensation; "terms" include the nature of the compensation, the approximate amount of compensation, and the duration of the agreement.

Application of the Standard

Example 1 (Notification of Client Bonus Compensation)

Geoff Whitman, a portfolio analyst for Adams Trust Company, manages the account of Carol Cochran, a client. Whitman is paid a salary by his employer, and Cochran pays the trust company a standard fee based on the market value of assets in her portfolio. Cochran proposes to Whitman that "any year that my portfolio achieves at least a 15% return before taxes, you and your wife can fly to Monaco at my expense and use my condominium during the third week of January." Whitman does not inform his employer of the arrangement and vacations in Monaco the following January as Cochran's guest.

Comment: Whitman violated Standard IV(B) by failing to inform his employer in writing of this supplemental, contingent compensation arrangement. The nature of the arrangement could have resulted in partiality to Cochran's account, which could have detracted from Whitman's performance with respect to other accounts he handles for Adams Trust. Whitman must obtain the consent of his employer to accept such a supplemental benefit.

Example 2 (Notification of Outside Compensation)

Terry Jones sits on the board of directors of Exercise Unlimited, Inc. In return for his services on the board, Jones receives unlimited membership privileges for his family at all Exercise Unlimited facilities. Jones purchases Exercise Unlimited stock for the client accounts for which it is appropriate. Jones does not disclose this arrangement to his employer because he does not receive monetary compensation for his services to the board.

Comment: Jones has violated Standard IV(B) by failing to disclose to his employer benefits received in exchange for his services on the board of directors. The nonmonetary compensation may create a conflict of interest in the same manner as being paid to serve as a director.

Example 3 (Prior Approval for Outside Compensation)

Jonathan Hollis is an analyst of oil-and-gas companies for Specialty Investment Management. He is currently recommending the purchase of ABC Oil Company shares and has published a long, well-thought-out research report to substantiate his recommendation. Several weeks after publishing the report, Hollis receives a call from the investor-relations office of ABC Oil saying that Thomas Andrews, CEO of the company, saw the report and really liked the analyst's grasp of the business and his company. The investor-relations officer invites Hollis to visit ABC Oil to discuss the industry further. ABC Oil offers to send a company plane to pick Hollis up and arrange for his accommodations while visiting. Hollis, after gaining the appropriate approvals, accepts the meeting with the CEO but declines the offered travel arrangements.

Several weeks later, Andrews and Hollis meet to discuss the oil business and Hollis's report. Following the meeting, Hollis joins Andrews and the investment relations officer for dinner at an upscale restaurant near ABC Oil's headquarters.

Upon returning to Specialty Investment Management, Hollis provides a full review of the meeting to the director of research, including a disclosure of the dinner attended.

Comment: Hollis's actions did not violate Standard IV(B). Through gaining approval before accepting the meeting and declining the offered travel arrangements, Hollis sought to avoid any potential conflicts of interest between his company and ABC Oil. Because the location of the dinner was not available prior to arrival and Hollis notified his company of the dinner upon his return, accepting the dinner should not impair his objectivity. By disclosing the dinner, Hollis has enabled Specialty Investment Management to assess whether it has any impact on future reports and recommendations by Hollis related to ABC Oil.

Standard IV(C) Responsibilities of Supervisors

The Standard

Members and candidates must make reasonable efforts to ensure that anyone subject to their supervision or authority complies with applicable laws, rules, regulations, and the Code and Standards.

Guidance

- Members and candidates must promote actions by all employees under their supervision and authority to comply with applicable laws, rules, regulations, and firm policies and the Code and Standards.
- A member's or candidate's responsibilities under Standard IV(C) include instructing those subordinates to whom supervision is delegated about methods to promote compliance, including preventing and detecting violations of laws, rules, regulations, firm policies, and the Code and Standards.
- At a minimum, Standard IV(C) requires that members and candidates with supervisory responsibility make reasonable efforts to prevent and detect violations by ensuring

the establishment of effective compliance systems. However, an effective compliance system goes beyond enacting a code of ethics, establishing policies and procedures to achieve compliance with the code and applicable law, and reviewing employee actions to determine whether they are following the rules.

- To be effective supervisors, members and candidates should implement education and training programs on a recurring or regular basis for employees under their supervision. Further, establishing incentives—monetary or otherwise—for employees not only to meet business goals but also to reward ethical behavior offers supervisors another way to assist employees in complying with their legal and ethical obligations.
- A member or candidate with supervisory responsibility should bring an inadequate compliance system to the attention of the firm's senior managers and recommend corrective action. If the member or candidate clearly cannot discharge supervisory responsibilities because of the absence of a compliance system or because of an inadequate compliance system, the member or candidate should decline in writing to accept supervisory responsibility until the firm adopts reasonable procedures to allow adequate exercise of supervisory responsibility.

System for Supervision

- Members and candidates with supervisory responsibility must understand what constitutes an adequate compliance system for their firms and make reasonable efforts to see that appropriate compliance procedures are established, documented, communicated to covered personnel, and followed.
    - "Adequate" procedures are those designed to meet industry standards, regulatory requirements, the requirements of the Code and Standards, and the circumstances of the firm.
    - To be effective, compliance procedures must be in place prior to the occurrence of a violation of the law or the Code and Standards.
- Once a supervisor learns that an employee has violated or may have violated the law or the Code and Standards, the supervisor must promptly initiate an assessment to determine the extent of the wrongdoing. Relying on an employee's statements about the extent of the violation or assurances that the wrongdoing will not reoccur is not enough. Reporting the misconduct up the chain of command and warning the employee to cease the activity are also not enough. Pending the outcome of the investigation, a supervisor should take steps to ensure that the violation will not be repeated, such as placing limits on the employee's activities or increasing the monitoring of the employee's activities.

Supervision Includes Detection

- Members and candidates with supervisory responsibility must also make reasonable efforts to detect violations of laws, rules, regulations, firm policies, and the Code and Standards. If a member or candidate has adopted reasonable procedures and taken steps to institute an effective compliance program, then the member or candidate may not be in violation of Standard IV(C) if he or she does not detect violations that occur despite these efforts. The fact that violations do occur may indicate, however, that the compliance procedures are inadequate.
- In addition, in some cases, merely enacting such procedures may not be sufficient to fulfill the duty required by Standard IV(C). A member or candidate may be in violation of Standard IV(C) if he or she knows or should know that the procedures designed to promote compliance, including detecting and preventing violations, are not being followed.

Recommended Procedures for Compliance

Codes of Ethics or Compliance Procedures

- Members and candidates are encouraged to recommend that their employers adopt a code of ethics, and put in place specific policies and procedures needed to ensure compliance with the codes and with securities laws and regulations
- Members and candidates should encourage their employers to provide their codes of ethics to clients.

Adequate Compliance Procedures

Adequate compliance procedures should:

- Be contained in a clearly written and accessible manual that is tailored to the firm's operations.
- Be drafted so that the procedures are easy to understand.
- Designate a compliance officer whose authority and responsibility are clearly defined and who has the necessary resources and authority to implement the firm's compliance procedures.
- Describe the hierarchy of supervision and assign duties among supervisors.
- Implement a system of checks and balances.
- Outline the scope of the procedures.
- Outline procedures to document the monitoring and testing of compliance procedures.
- Outline permissible conduct.
- Delineate procedures for reporting violations and sanctions.

Once a compliance program is in place, a supervisor should:

- Disseminate the contents of the program to appropriate personnel.
- Periodically update procedures to ensure that the measures are adequate under the law.
- Continually educate personnel regarding the compliance procedures.
- Issue periodic reminders of the procedures to appropriate personnel.
- Incorporate a professional conduct evaluation as part of an employee's performance review.
- Review the actions of employees to ensure compliance and identify violators.
- Take the necessary steps to enforce the procedures once a violation has occurred.

Once a violation is discovered, a supervisor should:

- Respond promptly.
- Conduct a thorough investigation of the activities to determine the scope of the wrongdoing.
- Increase supervision or place appropriate limitations on the wrongdoer pending the outcome of the investigation.
- Review procedures for potential changes necessary to prevent future violations from occurring.

Implementation of Compliance Education and Training

- Regular ethics and compliance training, in conjunction with the adoption of a code of ethics, is critical to investment firms seeking to establish a strong culture of integrity and to provide an environment in which employees routinely engage in ethical conduct in compliance with the law.

Establish an Appropriate Incentive Structure

- Supervisors and firms must look closely at their incentive structure to determine whether the structure encourages profits and returns at the expense of ethically appropriate conduct. Only when compensation and incentives are firmly tied to client interests and *how* outcomes are achieved, rather than *how much* is generated for the firm, will employees work to achieve a culture of integrity.

Application of the Standard

Example 1 (Supervising Research Activities)

Jane Mattock, senior vice president and head of the research department of H&V, Inc., a regional brokerage firm, has decided to change her recommendation for Timber Products from buy to sell. In line with H&V's procedures, she orally advises certain other H&V executives of her proposed actions before the report is prepared for publication. As a result of Mattock's conversation with Dieter Frampton, one of the H&V executives accountable to Mattock, Frampton immediately sells Timber's stock from his own account and from certain discretionary client accounts. In addition, other personnel inform certain institutional customers of the changed recommendation before it is printed and disseminated to all H&V customers who have received previous Timber reports.

Comment: Mattock has violated Standard IV(C) by failing to reasonably and adequately supervise the actions of those accountable to her. She did not prevent or establish reasonable procedures designed to prevent dissemination of or trading on the information by those who knew of her changed recommendation. She must ensure that her firm has procedures for reviewing or recording any trading in the stock of a corporation that has been the subject of an unpublished change in recommendation. Adequate procedures would have informed the subordinates of their duties and detected sales by Frampton and selected customers.

Example 2 (Supervising Trading Activities)

David Edwards, a trainee trader at Wheeler & Company, a major national brokerage firm, assists a customer in paying for the securities of Highland, Inc., by using anticipated profits from the immediate sale of the same securities. Despite the fact that Highland is not on Wheeler's recommended list, a large volume of its stock is traded through Wheeler in this manner. Roberta Ann Mason is a Wheeler vice president responsible for supervising compliance with the securities laws in the trading department. Part of her compensation from Wheeler is based on commission revenues from the trading department. Although she notices the increased trading activity, she does nothing to investigate or halt it.

Comment: Mason's failure to adequately review and investigate purchase orders in Highland stock executed by Edwards and her failure to supervise the trainee's activities violate Standard IV(C). Supervisors should be especially sensitive to actual or potential conflicts between their own self-interests and their supervisory responsibilities.

Example 3 (Supervising Trading Activities and Record Keeping)

Samantha Tabbing is senior vice president and portfolio manager for Crozet, Inc., a registered investment advisory and registered broker/dealer firm. She reports to Charles Henry, the president of Crozet. Crozet serves as the investment adviser and principal underwriter for ABC and XYZ public mutual funds. The two funds' prospectuses allow Crozet to trade financial futures for the funds for the limited purpose of hedging against market risks. Henry, extremely impressed by Tabbing's performance in the past two years, directs Tabbing to act as portfolio manager for the funds. For the benefit of its employees, Crozet has also organized the Crozet Employee Profit-Sharing Plan (CEPSP), a defined contribution retirement plan. Henry assigns Tabbing to manage 20% of the assets of CEPSP. Tabbing's investment objective for her portion of CEPSP's assets is aggressive growth. Unbeknownst to Henry, Tabbing frequently places S&P 500 Index purchase and sale orders for the funds and the CEPSP without providing the futures commission merchants (FCMs) who take the orders with any prior or simultaneous designation of the account for which the trade has been placed. Frequently, neither Tabbing nor anyone else at Crozet completes an internal trade ticket to record the time an order was placed or the specific account for which the order was intended. FCMs often designate a specific account only after the trade, when Tabbing provides such designation. Crozet has no written operating procedures or compliance manual concerning its futures trading, and its compliance department does not review such trading. After observing the market's movement, Tabbing assigns to CEPSP the S&P 500 positions with more favorable execution prices and assigns positions with less favorable execution prices to the funds.

Comment: Henry violated Standard IV(C) by failing to adequately supervise Tabbing with respect to her S&P 500 trading. Henry further violated Standard IV(C) by failing to establish record-keeping and reporting procedures to prevent or detect Tabbing's violations. Henry must make a reasonable effort to determine that adequate compliance procedures covering all employee trading activity are established, documented, communicated, and followed.

Example 4 (Supervising Research Activities)

Mary Burdette was recently hired by Fundamental Investment Management (FIM) as a junior auto industry analyst. Burdette is expected to expand the social media presence of the firm because she is active with various networks, including Facebook, LinkedIn, and Twitter. Although Burdette's supervisor, Joe Graf, has never used social media, he encourages Burdette to explore opportunities to increase FIM's online presence and ability to share content, communicate, and broadcast information to clients. In response to Graf's encouragement, Burdette is working on a proposal detailing the advantages of getting FIM onto Twitter in addition to launching a company Facebook page.

As part of her auto industry research for FIM, Burdette is completing a report on the financial impact of Sun Drive Auto Ltd.'s new solar technology for compact automobiles. This research report will be her first for FIM, and she believes Sun Drive's technology could revolutionize the auto industry. In her excitement, Burdette sends a quick tweet to FIM Twitter followers summarizing her "buy" recommendation for Sun Drive Auto stock.

Comment: Graf has violated Standard IV(C) by failing to reasonably supervise Burdette with respect to the contents of her tweet. He did not establish reasonable procedures to prevent the unauthorized dissemination of company research through social media networks. Graf must make sure all employees receive regular training about FIM's policies and procedures, including the appropriate business use of personal social media networks.

See Standard III(B) for additional guidance.

Example 5 (Supervising Research Activities)

Chen Wang leads the research department at YYRA Retirement Planning Specialists. Chen supervises a team of 10 analysts in a fast-paced and understaffed organization. He is responsible for coordinating the firm's approved process to review all reports before they are provided to the portfolio management team for use in rebalancing client portfolios.

One of Chen's direct reports, Huang Mei, covers the banking industry. Chen must submit the latest updates to the portfolio management team tomorrow morning. Huang has yet to submit her research report on ZYX Bank because she is uncomfortable providing a "buy" or "sell" opinion of ZYX on the basis of the completed analysis. Pressed for time and concerned that Chen will reject a "hold" recommendation, she researches various websites and blogs on the banking sector for whatever she can find on ZYX. One independent blogger provides a new interpretation of the recently reported data Huang has analyzed and concludes with a strong "sell" recommendation for ZYX. She is impressed by the originality and resourcefulness of this blogger's report.

Very late in the evening, Huang submits her report and "sell" recommendation to Chen without any reference to the independent blogger's report. Given the late time of the submission and the competence of Huang's prior work, Chen compiles this report with the recommendations from each of the other analysts and meets with the portfolio managers to discuss implementation.

Comment: Chen has violated Standard IV(C) by neglecting to reasonably and adequately follow the firm's approved review process for Huang's research report. The delayed submission and the quality of prior work do not remove Chen's requirement to uphold the designated review process. A member or candidate with supervisory responsibility must make reasonable efforts to see that appropriate procedures are established, documented, communicated to covered personnel, and followed.

LESSON 5: STANDARD V: INVESTMENT ANALYSIS, RECOMMENDATIONS, AND ACTIONS

A. Diligence and Reasonable Basis
B. Communication with Clients and Prospective Clients
C. Record Retention

Standard V(A) Diligence and Reasonable Basis

The Standard

Members and candidates must:

1. Exercise diligence, independence, and thoroughness in analyzing investments, making investment recommendations, and taking investment actions.
2. Have a reasonable and adequate basis, supported by appropriate research and investigation, for any investment analysis, recommendation, or action.

Guidance

- The requirements for issuing conclusions based on research will vary in relation to the member's or candidate's role in the investment decision-making process, but the member or candidate must make reasonable efforts to cover all pertinent issues when arriving at a recommendation.
- Members and candidates enhance transparency by providing or offering to provide supporting information to clients when recommending a purchase or sale or when changing a recommendation.

Defining Diligence and Reasonable Basis

- As with determining the suitability of an investment for the client, the necessary level of research and analysis will differ with the product, security, or service being offered. The following list provides some, but definitely not all, examples of attributes to consider while forming the basis for a recommendation:
  - Global, regional, and country macroeconomic conditions.
  - A company's operating and financial history.
  - The industry's and sector's current conditions and the stage of the business cycle.
  - A mutual fund's fee structure and management history.
  - The output and potential limitations of quantitative models.
  - The quality of the assets included in a securitization.
  - The appropriateness of selected peer-group comparisons.
- The steps taken in developing a diligent and reasonable recommendation should minimize unexpected downside events.

Using Secondary or Third-Party Research

- If members and candidates rely on secondary or third-party research, they must make reasonable and diligent efforts to determine whether such research is sound.
  - Secondary research is defined as research conducted by someone else in the member's or candidate's firm.
  - Third-party research is research conducted by entities outside the member's or candidate's firm, such as a brokerage firm, bank, or research firm.
- Members and candidates should make reasonable inquiries into the source and accuracy of all data used in completing their investment analysis and recommendations.

- Criteria that a member or candidate can use in forming an opinion on whether research is sound include the following:
  - Assumptions used.
  - Rigor of the analysis performed.
  - Date/timeliness of the research.
  - Evaluation of the objectivity and independence of the recommendations.
- A member or candidate may rely on others in his or her firm to determine whether secondary or third-party research is sound and use the information in good faith unless the member or candidate has reason to question its validity or the processes and procedures used by those responsible for the research.
- A member or candidate should verify that the firm has a policy about the timely and consistent review of approved research providers to ensure that the quality of the research continues to meet the necessary standards. If such a policy is not in place at the firm, the member or candidate should encourage the development and adoption of a formal review practice.

Using Quantitatively Oriented Research

- Members and candidates must have an understanding of the parameters used in models and quantitative research that are incorporated into their investment recommendations. Although they are not required to become experts in every technical aspect of the models, they must understand the assumptions and limitations inherent in any model and how the results were used in the decision-making process.
- Members and candidates should make reasonable efforts to test the output of investment models and other pre-programmed analytical tools they use. Such validation should occur before incorporating the process into their methods, models, or analyses.
- Although not every model can test for every factor or outcome, members and candidates should ensure that their analyses incorporate a broad range of assumptions sufficient to capture the underlying characteristics of investments. The omission from the analysis of potentially negative outcomes or of levels of risk outside the norm may misrepresent the true economic value of an investment. The possible scenarios for analysis should include factors that are likely to have a substantial influence on the investment value and may include extremely positive and negative scenarios.

Developing Quantitatively Oriented Techniques

- Members and candidates involved in the development and oversight of quantitatively oriented models, methods, and algorithms must understand the technical aspects of the products they provide to clients. A thorough testing of the model and resulting analysis should be completed prior to product distribution.
- In reviewing the computer models or the resulting output, members and candidates need to pay particular attention to the assumptions used in the analysis and the rigor of the analysis to ensure that the model incorporates a wide range of possible input expectations, including negative market events.

Selecting External Advisers and Sub-Advisers

- Members and candidates must review managers as diligently as they review individual funds and securities.
- Members and candidates who are directly involved with the use of external advisers need to ensure that their firms have standardized criteria for reviewing these selected external

advisers and managers. Such criteria would include, but would not be limited to, the following:

- Reviewing the adviser's established code of ethics,
- Understanding the adviser's compliance and internal control procedures,
- Assessing the quality of the published return information, and
- Reviewing the adviser's investment process and adherence to its stated strategy.

Group Research and Decision Making

In some instances, a member or candidate will not agree with the view of the group. If, however, the member or candidate believes that the consensus opinion has a reasonable and adequate basis and is independent and objective, the member or candidate need not decline to be identified with the report. If the member or candidate is confident in the process, the member or candidate does not need to dissociate from the report even if it does not reflect his or her opinion.

Recommended Procedures for Compliance

Members and candidates should encourage their firms to consider the following policies and procedures to support the principles of Standard V(A):

- Establish a policy requiring that research reports, credit ratings, and investment recommendations have a basis that can be substantiated as reasonable and adequate.
- Develop detailed, written guidance for analysts (research, investment, or credit), supervisory analysts, and review committees that establishes the due diligence procedures for judging whether a particular recommendation has a reasonable and adequate basis.
- Develop measurable criteria for assessing the quality of research, the reasonableness and adequacy of the basis for any recommendation or rating, and the accuracy of recommendations over time.
- Develop detailed, written guidance that establishes minimum levels of scenario testing of all computer-based models used in developing, rating, and evaluating financial instruments.
- Develop measurable criteria for assessing outside providers, including the quality of information being provided, the reasonableness and adequacy of the provider's collection practices, and the accuracy of the information over time.
- Adopt a standardized set of criteria for evaluating the adequacy of external advisers.

Application of the Standard

Example 1 (Sufficient Due Diligence)

Helen Hawke manages the corporate finance department of Sarkozi Securities, Ltd. The firm is anticipating that the government will soon close a tax loophole that currently allows oil-and-gas exploration companies to pass on drilling expenses to holders of a certain class of shares. Because market demand for this tax-advantaged class of stock is currently high, Sarkozi convinces several companies to undertake new equity financings at once, before the loophole closes. Time is of the essence, but Sarkozi lacks sufficient resources to conduct adequate research on all the prospective issuing companies. Hawke decides to estimate the IPO prices on the basis of the relative size of each company and to justify the pricing later when her staff has time.

Comment: Sarkozi should have taken on only the work that it could adequately handle. By categorizing the issuers by general size, Hawke has bypassed researching all the other relevant aspects that should be considered when pricing new issues and thus has not performed sufficient due diligence. Such an omission can result in investors purchasing shares at prices that have no actual basis. Hawke has violated Standard V(A).

Example 2 (Sufficient Scenario Testing)

Babu Dhaliwal works for Heinrich Brokerage in the corporate finance group. He has just persuaded Feggans Resources, Ltd., to allow his firm to do a secondary equity financing at Feggans Resources' current stock price. Because the stock has been trading at higher multiples than similar companies with equivalent production, Dhaliwal presses the Feggans Resources managers to project what would be the maximum production they could achieve in an optimal scenario. Based on these numbers, he is able to justify the price his firm will be asking for the secondary issue. During a sales pitch to the brokers, Dhaliwal then uses these numbers as the base-case production levels that Feggans Resources will achieve.

Comment: When presenting information to the brokers, Dhaliwal should have given a range of production scenarios and the probability of Feggans Resources achieving each level. By giving the maximum production level as the likely level of production, he has misrepresented the chances of achieving that production level and seriously misled the brokers. Dhaliwal has violated Standard V(A).

Example 3 (Reliance on Third-Party Research)

Gary McDermott runs a two-person investment management firm. McDermott's firm subscribes to a service from a large investment research firm that provides research reports. McDermott's firm makes investment recommendations on the basis of these reports.

Comment: Members and candidates can rely on third-party research but must make reasonable and diligent efforts to determine that such research is sound. If McDermott undertakes due diligence efforts on a regular basis to ensure that the research produced by the large firm is objective and reasonably based, McDermott can rely on that research when making investment recommendations to clients.

Example 4 (Quantitative Model Diligence)

Barry Cannon is the lead quantitative analyst at CityCenter Hedge Fund. He is responsible for the development, maintenance, and enhancement of the proprietary models the fund uses to manage its investors' assets. Cannon reads several high-level mathematical publications and blogs to stay informed of current developments. One blog, run by Expert CFA, presents some intriguing research that may benefit one of CityCenter's current models. Cannon is under pressure from firm executives to improve the model's predictive abilities, and he incorporates the factors discussed in the online research. The updated output recommends several new investments to the fund's portfolio managers.

Comment: Cannon has violated Standard V(A) by failing to have a reasonable basis for the new recommendations made to the portfolio managers. He needed to diligently research the effect of incorporating the new factors before offering the output recommendations. Cannon may use the blog for ideas, but it is his responsibility to determine the effect on the firm's proprietary models.

See Standard VII(B) regarding the violation by "Expert CFA" in the use of the CFA designation.

Example 5 (Selecting a Service Provider)

Ellen Smith is a performance analyst at Artic Global Advisors, a firm that manages global equity mandates for institutional clients. She was asked by her supervisor to review five new performance attribution systems and recommend one that would more appropriately explain the firm's investment strategy to clients. On the list was a system she recalled learning about when visiting an exhibitor booth at a recent conference. The system is highly quantitative and something of a "black box" in how it calculates the attribution values. Smith recommended this option without researching the others because the sheer complexity of the process was sure to impress the clients.

Comment: Smith's actions do not demonstrate a sufficient level of diligence in reviewing this product to make a recommendation for selecting the service. Besides not reviewing or considering the other four potential systems, she did not determine whether the "black box" attribution process aligns with the investment practices of the firm, including its investments in different countries and currencies. Smith must review and understand the process of any software or system before recommending its use as the firm's attribution system.

Example 6 (Subadviser Selection)

Craig Jackson is working for Adams Partners, Inc., and has been assigned to select a hedge fund subadviser to improve the diversification of the firm's large fund-of-funds product. The allocation must be in place before the start of the next quarter. Jackson uses a consultant database to find a list of suitable firms that claim compliance with the GIPS standards. He calls more than 20 firms on the list to confirm their potential interest and to determine their most recent quarterly and annual total return values. Because of the short turnaround, Jackson recommends the firm with the greatest total return values for selection.

Comment: By considering only performance and GIPS compliance, Jackson has not conducted sufficient review of potential firms to satisfy the requirements of Standard V(A). A thorough investigation of the firms and their operations should be conducted to ensure that their addition would increase the diversity of clients' portfolios and that they are suitable for the fund-of-funds product.

Example 7 (Manager Selection)

Timothy Green works for Peach Asset Management, where he creates proprietary models that analyze data from the firm request for proposal questionnaires to identify managers for possible inclusion in the firm's fund-of-funds investment platform. Various criteria must be met to be accepted to the platform. Because of the number of respondents to the questionnaires, Green uses only the data submitted to make a recommendation for adding a new manager.

Comment: By failing to conduct any additional outside review of the information to verify what was submitted through the request for proposal, Green has likely not satisfied the requirements of Standard V(A). The amount of information requested from outside managers varies among firms. Although the requested information may be comprehensive, Green should ensure sufficient effort is undertaken to verify the submitted information before recommending a firm for inclusion. This requires that he go beyond the information provided by the manager on the request for proposal questionnaire and may include interviews with interested managers, reviews of regulatory filings, and discussions with the managers' custodian or auditor.

Example 8 (Technical Model Requirements)

Jérôme Dupont works for the credit research group of XYZ Asset Management, where he is in charge of developing and updating credit risk models. In order to perform accurately, his models need to be regularly updated with the latest market data.

Dupont does not interact with or manage money for any of the firm's clients. He is in contact with the firm's U.S. corporate bond fund manager, John Smith, who has only very superficial knowledge of the model and who from time to time asks very basic questions regarding the output recommendations. Smith does not consult Dupont with respect to finalizing his clients' investment strategies.

Dupont's recently assigned objective is to develop a new emerging market corporate credit risk model. The firm is planning to expand into emerging credit, and the development of such a model is a critical step in this process. Because Smith seems to follow the model's recommendations without much concern for its quality as he develops his clients' investment strategies, Dupont decides to focus his time on the development of the new emerging market model and neglects to update the U.S. model.

After several months without regular updates, Dupont's diagnostic statistics start to show alarming signs with respect to the quality of the U.S. credit model. Instead of conducting the long and complicated data update, Dupont introduces new codes into his model with some limited new data as a quick "fix." He thinks this change will address the issue without needing to complete the full data update, so he continues working on the new emerging market model.

Several months following the quick "fix," another set of diagnostic statistics reveals nonsensical results and Dupont realizes that his earlier change contained an error. He quickly corrects the error and alerts Smith. Smith realizes that some of the prior trades he performed were due to erroneous model results. Smith rebalances the portfolio to remove the securities purchased on the basis of the questionable results without reporting the issue to anyone else.

Comment: Smith violated Standard V(A) because exercising "diligence, independence, and thoroughness in analyzing investments, making investment recommendations, and taking investment actions" means that members and candidates must understand the technical aspects of the products they provide to clients. Smith does not understand the model he is relying on to manage money. Members and candidates should also make reasonable inquiries into the source and accuracy of all data used in completing their investment analysis and recommendations.

Dupont violated Standard V(A) even if he does not trade securities or make investment decisions. Dupont's models give investment recommendations, and Dupont is accountable for the quality of those recommendations. Members and candidates should make reasonable efforts to test the output of pre-programed analytical tools they use. Such validation should occur before incorporating the tools into their decision-making process.

See also Standard V(B)—Communication with Clients and Prospective Clients.

Standard V(B) Communication with Clients and Prospective Clients

The Standard

Members and candidates must:

1. Disclose to clients and prospective clients the basic format and general principles of the investment processes they use to analyze investments, select securities, and construct portfolios, and must promptly disclose any changes that might materially affect those processes.
2. Disclose to clients and prospective clients significant limitations and risks associated with the investment process.
3. Use reasonable judgment in identifying which factors are important to their investment analyses, recommendations, or actions, and include those factors in communications with clients and prospective clients.
4. Distinguish between fact and opinion in the presentation of investment analyses and recommendations.

Guidance

- Members and candidates should communicate in a recommendation the factors that were instrumental in making the investment recommendation. A critical part of this requirement is to distinguish clearly between opinions and facts.
- Follow-up communication of significant changes in the risk characteristics of a security or asset strategy is required.
- Providing regular updates to any changes in the risk characteristics is recommended.

Informing Clients of the Investment Process

- Members and candidates must adequately describe to clients and prospective clients the manner in which they conduct the investment decision-making process. Such disclosure should address factors that have positive and negative influences on the recommendations, including significant risks and limitations of the investment process used.
- The member or candidate must keep clients and other interested parties informed on an ongoing basis about changes to the investment process, especially newly identified significant risks and limitations.
- Members and candidates should inform the clients about the specialization or diversification expertise provided by the external adviser(s).

Different Forms of Communication

- Members and candidates using any social media service to communicate business information must be diligent in their efforts to avoid unintended problems because these services may not be available to all clients. When providing information to clients through new technologies, members and candidates should take reasonable steps to ensure that such delivery would treat all clients fairly and, if necessary, be considered publicly disseminated.
- If recommendations are contained in capsule form (such as a recommended stock list), members and candidates should notify clients that additional information and analyses are available from the producer of the report.

Identifying Risks and Limitations

- Members and candidates must outline to clients and prospective clients significant risks and limitations of the analysis contained in their investment products or recommendations.
- The appropriateness of risk disclosure should be assessed on the basis of what was known at the time the investment action was taken (often called an *ex ante* basis). Members and candidates must disclose significant risks known to them at the time of the disclosure.

Members and candidates cannot be expected to disclose risks they are unaware of at the time recommendations or investment actions are made.
- Having no knowledge of a risk or limitation that subsequently triggers a loss may reveal a deficiency in the diligence and reasonable basis of the research of the member or candidate but may not reveal a breach of Standard V(B).

Report Presentation

- A report writer who has done adequate investigation may emphasize certain areas, touch briefly on others, and omit certain aspects deemed unimportant.
- Investment advice based on quantitative research and analysis must be supported by readily available reference material and should be applied in a manner consistent with previously applied methodology. If changes in methodology are made, they should be highlighted.

Distinction between Facts and Opinions in Reports

- Violations often occur when reports fail to separate the past from the future by not indicating that earnings estimates, changes in the outlook for dividends, or future market price information are *opinions* subject to future circumstances.
- In the case of complex quantitative analyses, members and candidates must clearly separate fact from statistical conjecture and should identify the known limitations of an analysis.
- Members and candidates should explicitly discuss with clients and prospective clients the assumptions used in the investment models and processes to generate the analysis. Caution should be used in promoting the perceived accuracy of any model or process to clients because the ultimate output is merely an estimate of future results and not a certainty.

Recommended Procedures for Compliance

- Members and candidates should encourage their firms to have a rigorous methodology for reviewing research that is created for publication and dissemination to clients.
- To assist in the after-the-fact review of a report, the member or candidate must maintain records indicating the nature of the research and should, if asked, be able to supply additional information to the client (or any user of the report) covering factors not included in the report.

Application of the Standard

Example 1 (Sufficient Disclosure of Investment System)

Sarah Williamson, director of marketing for Country Technicians, Inc., is convinced that she has found the perfect formula for increasing Country Technicians' income and diversifying its product base. Williamson plans to build on Country Technicians' reputation as a leading money manager by marketing an exclusive and expensive investment advice letter to high-net-worth individuals. One hitch in the plan is the complexity of Country Technicians' investment system—a combination of technical trading rules (based on historical price and volume fluctuations) and portfolio construction rules designed to minimize risk. To simplify the newsletter, she decides to include only each week's top five "buy" and "sell" recommendations and to leave out details of the valuation models and the portfolio structuring scheme.

Comment: Williamson's plans for the newsletter violate Standard V(B). Williamson need not describe the investment system in detail in order to implement the advice effectively, but she must inform clients of Country Technicians' basic process and logic. Without understanding the basis for a recommendation, clients cannot possibly understand its limitations or its inherent risks.

Example 2 (Proper Description of a Security)

Olivia Thomas, an analyst at Government Brokers, Inc., which is a brokerage firm specializing in government bond trading, has produced a report that describes an investment strategy designed to benefit from an expected decline in U.S. interest rates. The firm's derivative products group has designed a structured product that will allow the firm's clients to benefit from this strategy. Thomas's report describing the strategy indicates that high returns are possible if various scenarios for declining interest rates are assumed. Citing the proprietary nature of the structured product underlying the strategy, the report does not describe in detail how the firm is able to offer such returns or the related risks in the scenarios, nor does the report address the likely returns of the strategy if, contrary to expectations, interest rates rise.

Comment: Thomas has violated Standard V(B) because her report fails to describe properly the basic characteristics of the actual and implied risks of the investment strategy, including how the structure was created and the degree to which leverage was embedded in the structure. The report should include a balanced discussion of how the strategy would perform in the case of rising as well as falling interest rates, preferably illustrating how the strategies might be expected to perform in the event of a reasonable variety of interest rate and credit risk–spread scenarios. If liquidity issues are relevant with regard to the valuation of either the derivatives or the underlying securities, provisions the firm has made to address those risks should also be disclosed.

Example 3 (Notification of Changes to the Investment Process)

RJZ Capital Management is an active value-style equity manager that selects stocks by using a combination of four multifactor models. The firm has found favorable results when back testing the most recent 10 years of available market data in a new dividend discount model (DDM) designed by the firm. This model is based on projected inflation rates, earnings growth rates, and interest rates. The president of RJZ decides to replace its simple model that uses price to trailing 12-month earnings with the new DDM.

Comment: Because the introduction of a new and different valuation model represents a material change in the investment process, RJZ's president must communicate the change to the firm's clients. RJZ is moving away from a model based on hard data toward a new model that is at least partly dependent on the firm's forecasting skills. Clients would likely view such a model as a significant change rather than a mere refinement of RJZ's process.

Example 4 (Notification of Changes to the Investment Process)

RJZ Capital Management loses the chief architect of its multifactor valuation system. Without informing its clients, the president of RJZ decides to redirect the firm's talents and resources toward developing a product for passive equity management—a product that will emulate the performance of a major market index.

Comment: By failing to disclose to clients a substantial change to its investment process, the president of RJZ has violated Standard V(B).

Example 5 (Sufficient Disclosure of Investment System)

Amanda Chinn is the investment director for Diversified Asset Management, which manages the endowment of a charitable organization. Because of recent staff departures, Diversified has decided to limit its direct investment focus to large-cap securities and supplement the needs for small-cap and mid-cap management by hiring outside fund managers. In describing the planned strategy change to the charity, Chinn's update letter states, "As investment director, I will directly oversee the investment team managing the endowment's large-capitalization allocation. I will coordinate the selection and ongoing review of external managers responsible for allocations to other classes." The letter also describes the reasons for the change and the characteristics external managers must have to be considered.

Comment: Standard V(B) requires the disclosure of the investment process used to construct the portfolio of the fund. Changing the investment process from managing all classes of investments within the firm to the use of external managers is one example of information that needs to be communicated to clients. Chinn and her firm have embraced the principles of Standard V(B) by providing their client with relevant information. The charity can now make a reasonable decision about whether Diversified Asset Management remains the appropriate manager for its fund.

Example 6 (Notification of Risks and Limitations)

Quantitative analyst Yuri Yakovlev has developed an investment strategy that selects small-cap stocks on the basis of quantitative signals. Yakovlev's strategy typically identifies only a small number of stocks (10–20) that tend to be illiquid, but according to his backtests, the strategy generates significant risk-adjusted returns. The partners at Yakovlev's firm, QSC Capital, are impressed by these results. After a thorough examination of the strategy's risks, stress testing, historical back testing, and scenario analysis, QSC decides to seed the strategy with US$10 million of internal capital in order for Yakovlev to create a track record for the strategy.

After two years, the strategy has generated performance returns greater than the appropriate benchmark and the Sharpe ratio of the fund is close to 1.0. On the basis of these results, QSC decides to actively market the fund to large institutional investors. While creating the offering materials, Yakovlev informs the marketing team that the capacity of the strategy is limited. The extent of the limitation is difficult to ascertain with precision; it depends on market liquidity and other factors in his model that can evolve over time. Yakovlev indicates that given the current market conditions, investments in the fund beyond US$100 million of capital could become more difficult and negatively affect expected fund returns.

Alan Wellard, the manager of the marketing team, is a partner with 30 years of marketing experience and explains to Yakovlev that these are complex technical issues that will muddy the marketing message. According to Wellard, the offering material should focus solely on the great track record of the fund. Yakovlev does not object because the fund has only US$12 million of capital, very far from the US$100 million threshold.

Comment: Yakovlev and Wellard have not appropriately disclosed a significant limitation associated with the investment product. Yakovlev believes this limitation, once reached, will materially affect the returns of the fund. Although the fund is currently far from the US$100 million mark, current and prospective investors must be made aware of this capacity issue. If significant limitations are complicated to grasp and clients do not have the technical background required to understand them, Yakovlev and Wellard should either educate the clients or ascertain whether the fund is suitable for each client.

Example 7 (Notification of Risks and Limitations)

Brickell Advisers offers investment advisory services mainly to South American clients. Julietta Ramon, a risk analyst at Brickell, describes to clients how the firm uses value at risk (VaR) analysis to track the risk of its strategies. Ramon assures clients that calculating a VaR at a 99% confidence level, using a 20-day holding period, and applying a methodology based on an *ex ante* Monte Carlo simulation is extremely effective. The firm has never had losses greater than those predicted by this VaR analysis.

Comment: Ramon has not sufficiently communicated the risks associated with the investment process to satisfy the requirements of Standard V(B). The losses predicted by a VaR analysis depend greatly on the inputs used in the model. The size and probability of losses can differ significantly from what an individual model predicts. Ramon must disclose how the inputs were selected and the potential limitations and risks associated with the investment strategy.

Example 8 (Notification of Risks and Limitations)

Lily Smith attended an industry conference and noticed that John Baker, an investment manager with Baker Associates, attracted a great deal of attention from the conference participants. On the basis of her knowledge of Baker's reputation and the interest he received at the conference, Smith recommends adding Baker Associates to the approved manager platform. Her recommendation to the approval committee includes the statement "John Baker is well respected in the industry, and his insights are consistently sought after by investors. Our clients are sure to benefit from investing with Baker Associates."

Comment: Smith is not appropriately separating facts from opinions in her recommendation to include the manager within the platform. Her actions conflict with the requirements of Standard V(B). Smith is relying on her opinions about Baker's reputation and the fact that many attendees were talking with him at the conference. Smith should also review the requirements of Standard V(A) regarding reasonable basis to determine the level of review necessary to recommend Baker Associates.

Standard V(C) Record Retention

The Standard

Members and candidates must develop and maintain appropriate records to support their investment analyses, recommendations, actions, and other investment-related communications with clients and prospective clients.

Guidance

- Members and candidates must retain records that substantiate the scope of their research and reasons for their actions or conclusions. The retention requirement applies to decisions to buy or sell a security as well as reviews undertaken that do not lead to a change in position.
- Records may be maintained either in hard copy or electronic form.

New Media Records

- Members and candidates should understand that although employers and local regulators are developing digital media retention policies, these policies may lag behind the advent of new communication channels. Such lag places greater responsibility on the individual for ensuring that all relevant information is retained. Examples of non-print media formats that should be retained include, but are not limited to e-mails, text messages, blog posts, and Twitter posts.

Records Are Property of the Firm

- As a general matter, records created as part of a member's or candidate's professional activity on behalf of his or her employer are the property of the firm.
- When a member or candidate leaves a firm to seek other employment, the member or candidate cannot take the property of the firm, including original forms or copies of supporting records of the member's or candidate's work, to the new employer without the express consent of the previous employer.
- The member or candidate cannot use historical recommendations or research reports created at the previous firm because the supporting documentation is unavailable.
- For future use, the member or candidate must re-create the supporting records at the new firm with information gathered through public sources or directly from the covered company and not from memory or sources obtained at the previous employer.

Local Requirements

- Local regulators and firms may also implement policies detailing the applicable time frame for retaining research and client communication records. Fulfilling such regulatory and firm requirements satisfies the requirements of Standard V(C).
- In the absence of regulatory guidance or firm policies, CFA Institute recommends maintaining records for at least seven years.

Recommended Procedures for Compliance

The responsibility to maintain records that support investment action generally falls with the firm rather than individuals. Members and candidates must, however, archive research notes and other documents, either electronically or in hard copy, that support their current investment-related communications.

Application of the Standard

Example 1 (Record Retention and Research Process)

Malcolm Young is a research analyst who writes numerous reports rating companies in the luxury retail industry. His reports are based on a variety of sources, including interviews with company managers, manufacturers, and economists; on-site company visits; customer surveys; and secondary research from analysts covering related industries.

Comment: Young must carefully document and keep copies of all the information that goes into his reports, including the secondary or third-party research of other analysts. Failure to maintain such files would violate Standard V(C).

Example 2 (Records as Firm, Not Employee, Property)

Martin Blank develops an analytical model while he is employed by Green Partners Investment Management, LLP (GPIM). While at the firm, he systematically documents the assumptions that make up the model as well as his reasoning behind the assumptions. As a result of the success of his model, Blank is hired to be the head of the research department of one of GPIM's competitors. Blank takes copies of the records supporting his model to his new firm.

Comment: The records created by Blank supporting the research model he developed at GPIM are the records of GPIM. Taking the documents with him to his new employer without GPIM's permission violates Standard V(C). To use the model in the future, Blank must re-create the records supporting his model at the new firm.

LESSON 6: STANDARD VI: CONFLICTS OF INTEREST

A. Disclosure of Conflicts
B. Priority of Transactions
C. Referral Fees

Standard VI(A) Disclosure of Conflicts

The Standard

Members and candidates must make full and fair disclosure of all matters that could reasonably be expected to impair their independence and objectivity or interfere with respective duties to their clients, prospective clients, and employer. Members and candidates must ensure that such disclosures are prominent, are delivered in plain language, and communicate the relevant information effectively.

Guidance

- Best practice is to avoid actual conflicts or the appearance of conflicts of interest when possible. Conflicts of interest often arise in the investment profession.
- When conflicts cannot be reasonably avoided, clear and complete disclosure of their existence is necessary.
- In making and updating disclosures of conflicts of interest, members and candidates should err on the side of caution to ensure that conflicts are effectively communicated.

Disclosure of Conflicts to Employers

- When reporting conflicts of interest to employers, members and candidates must give their employers enough information to assess the impact of the conflict.
- Members and candidates must take reasonable steps to avoid conflicts and, if they occur inadvertently, must report them promptly so that the employer and the member or candidate can resolve them as quickly and effectively as possible.
- Any potential conflict situation that could prevent clear judgment about or full commitment to the execution of a member's or candidate's duties to the employer should be reported to the member's or candidate's employer and promptly resolved.

Disclosure to Clients

- The most obvious conflicts of interest, which should always be disclosed, are relationships between an issuer and the member, the candidate, or his or her firm (such as a directorship or consultancy by a member; investment banking, underwriting, and financial relationships; broker/dealer market-making activities; and material beneficial ownership of stock).
- Disclosures should be made to clients regarding fee arrangements, sub-advisory agreements, or other situations involving nonstandard fee structures. Equally important is the disclosure of arrangements in which the firm benefits directly from investment recommendations. An obvious conflict of interest is the rebate of a portion of the service fee some classes of mutual funds charge to investors.

Cross-Departmental Conflicts

- Other circumstances can give rise to actual or potential conflicts of interest. For instance:
    - A sell-side analyst working for a broker/dealer may be encouraged, not only by members of her or his own firm but by corporate issuers themselves, to write research reports about particular companies.

  - A buy-side analyst is likely to be faced with similar conflicts as banks exercise their underwriting and security-dealing powers.
  - The marketing division may ask an analyst to recommend the stock of a certain company in order to obtain business from that company.
- Members, candidates, and their firms should attempt to resolve situations presenting potential conflicts of interest or disclose them in accordance with the principles set forth in Standard VI(A).

Conflicts with Stock Ownership

- The most prevalent conflict requiring disclosure under Standard VI(A) is a member's or candidate's ownership of stock in companies that he or she recommends to clients or that clients hold. Clearly, the easiest method for preventing a conflict is to prohibit members and candidates from owning any such securities, but this approach is overly burdensome and discriminates against members and candidates. Therefore:
  - Sell-side members and candidates should disclose any materially beneficial ownership interest in a security or other investment that the member or candidate is recommending.
  - Buy-side members and candidates should disclose their procedures for reporting requirements for personal transactions.

Conflicts as a Director

- Service as a director poses three basic conflicts of interest.
  - A conflict may exist between the duties owed to clients and the duties owed to shareholders of the company.
  - Investment personnel who serve as directors may receive the securities or options to purchase securities of the company as compensation for serving on the board, which could raise questions about trading actions that might increase the value of those securities.
  - Board service creates the opportunity to receive material nonpublic information involving the company.
- When members or candidates providing investment services also serve as directors, they should be isolated from those making investment decisions by the use of firewalls or similar restrictions.

Recommended Procedures for Compliance

- Members or candidates should disclose special compensation arrangements with the employer that might conflict with client interests, such as bonuses based on short-term performance criteria, commissions, incentive fees, performance fees, and referral fees.
- Members' and candidates' firms are encouraged to include information on compensation packages in firms' promotional literature.

Application of the Standard

Example 1 (Conflict of Interest and Business Relationships)

Hunter Weiss is a research analyst with Farmington Company, a broker and investment banking firm. Farmington's merger and acquisition department has represented Vimco, a conglomerate, in all of Vimco's acquisitions for 20 years. From time to time, Farmington officers sit on the boards of directors of various Vimco subsidiaries. Weiss is writing a research report on Vimco.

Comment: Weiss must disclose in his research report Farmington's special relationship with Vimco. Broker/dealer management of and participation in public offerings must be disclosed in research reports. Because the position of underwriter to a company entails a special past and potential future relationship with a company that is the subject of investment advice, it threatens the independence and objectivity of the report writer and must be disclosed.

Example 2 (Conflict of Interest and Business Stock Ownership)

The investment management firm of Dover & Roe sells a 25% interest in its partnership to a multinational bank holding company, First of New York. Immediately after the sale, Margaret Hobbs, president of Dover & Roe, changes her recommendation for First of New York's common stock from "sell" to "buy" and adds First of New York's commercial paper to Dover & Roe's approved list for purchase.

Comment: Hobbs must disclose the new relationship with First of New York to all Dover & Roe clients. This relationship must also be disclosed to clients by the firm's portfolio managers when they make specific investment recommendations or take investment actions with respect to First of New York's securities.

Example 3 (Conflict of Interest and Personal Stock Ownership)

Carl Fargmon, a research analyst who follows firms producing office equipment, has been recommending purchase of Kincaid Printing because of its innovative new line of copiers. After his initial report on the company, Fargmon's wife inherits from a distant relative US$3 million of Kincaid stock. He has been asked to write a follow-up report on Kincaid.

Comment: Fargmon must disclose his wife's ownership of the Kincaid stock to his employer and in his follow-up report. Best practice would be to avoid the conflict by asking his employer to assign another analyst to draft the follow-up report.

Example 4 (Conflict of Interest and Personal Stock Ownership)

Betty Roberts is speculating in penny stocks for her own account and purchases 100,000 shares of Drew Mining, Inc., for US$0.30 a share. She intends to sell these shares at the sign of any substantial upward price movement of the stock. A week later, her employer asks her to write a report on penny stocks in the mining industry to be published in two weeks. Even without owning the Drew stock, Roberts would recommend it in her report as a "buy." A surge in the price of the stock to the US$2 range is likely to result once the report is issued.

Comment: Although this holding may not be material, Roberts must disclose it in the report and to her employer before writing the report because the gain for her will be substantial if the market responds strongly to her recommendation. The fact that she has only recently purchased the stock adds to the appearance that she is not entirely objective.

Example 5 (Conflict of Interest and Compensation Arrangements)

Gary Carter is a representative with Bengal International, a registered broker/dealer. Carter is approached by a stock promoter for Badger Company, who offers to pay Carter additional compensation for sales of Badger Company's stock to Carter's clients. Carter accepts the stock promoter's offer but does not disclose the arrangements to his clients or to his employer. Carter sells shares of the stock to his clients.

Comment: Carter has violated Standard VI(A) by failing to disclose to clients that he is receiving additional compensation for recommending and selling Badger stock. Because he did not disclose the arrangement with Badger to his clients, the clients were unable to evaluate whether Carter's recommendations to buy Badger were affected by this arrangement. Carter's conduct also violated Standard VI(A) by failing to disclose to his employer monetary compensation received in addition to the compensation and benefits conferred by his employer. Carter was required by Standard VI(A) to disclose the arrangement with Badger to his employer so that his employer could evaluate whether the arrangement affected Carter's objectivity and loyalty.

Example 6 (Conflict of Interest and Directorship)

Carol Corky, a senior portfolio manager for Universal Management, recently became involved as a trustee with the Chelsea Foundation, a large not-for-profit foundation in her hometown. Universal is a small money manager (with assets under management of approximately US$100 million) that caters to individual investors. Chelsea has assets in excess of US$2 billion. Corky does not believe informing Universal of her involvement with Chelsea is necessary.

Comment: By failing to inform Universal of her involvement with Chelsea, Corky violated Standard VI(A). Given the large size of the endowment at Chelsea, Corky's new role as a trustee can reasonably be expected to be time consuming, to the possible detriment of Corky's portfolio responsibilities with Universal. Also, as a trustee, Corky may become involved in the investment decisions at Chelsea. Therefore, Standard VI(A) obligates Corky to discuss becoming a trustee at Chelsea with her compliance officer or supervisor at Universal before accepting the position, and she should have disclosed the degree to which she would be involved in investment decisions at Chelsea.

Example 7 (Conflict of Interest and Requested Favors)

Michael Papis is the chief investment officer of his state's retirement fund. The fund has always used outside advisers for the real estate allocation, and this information is clearly presented in all fund communications. Thomas Nagle, a recognized sell-side research analyst and Papis's business school classmate, recently left the investment bank he worked for to start his own asset management firm, Accessible Real Estate. Nagle is trying to build his assets under management and contacts Papis about gaining some of the retirement fund's allocation. In the previous few years, the performance of the retirement fund's real estate investments was in line with the fund's benchmark but was not extraordinary. Papis decides to help out his old friend and also to seek better returns by moving the real estate allocation to Accessible. The only notice of the change in adviser appears in the next annual report in the listing of associated advisers.

Comment: Papis has violated Standard VI(A) by not disclosing to his employer his personal relationship with Nagle. Disclosure of his past history with Nagle would allow his firm to determine whether the conflict may have impaired Papis's independence in deciding to change managers.

See also Standard IV(C)—Responsibilities of Supervisors, Standard V(A)—Diligence and Reasonable Basis, and Standard V(B)—Communication with Clients and Prospective Clients.

Example 8 (Conflict of Interest and Business Relationships)

Bob Wade, trust manager for Central Midas Bank, was approached by Western Funds about promoting its family of funds, with special interest in the service-fee class. To entice Central to promote this class, Western Funds offered to pay the bank a service fee of 0.25%. Without disclosing the fee being offered to the bank, Wade asked one of the investment managers to review the Western Funds family of funds to determine whether they were suitable for clients of Central. The manager completed the normal due diligence review and determined that the funds were fairly valued in the market with fee structures on a par with their competitors. Wade decided to accept Western's offer and instructed the team of portfolio managers to exclusively promote these funds and the service-fee class to clients seeking to invest new funds or transfer from their current investments. So as to not influence the investment managers, Wade did not disclose the fee offer and allowed that income to flow directly to the bank.

Comment: Wade is violating Standard VI(A) by not disclosing the portion of the service fee being paid to Central. Although the investment managers may not be influenced by the fee, neither they nor the client have the proper information about Wade's decision to exclusively market this fund family and class of investments. Central may come to rely on the new fee as a component of the firm's profitability and may be unwilling to offer other products in the future that could affect the fees received.

(See also Standard I(B)—Independence and Objectivity.)

Example 9 (Disclosure of Conflicts to Employers)

Yehudit Dagan is a portfolio manager for Risk Management Bank (RMB), whose clients include retirement plans and corporations. RMB provides a defined contribution retirement plan for its employees that offers 20 large diversified mutual fund investment options, including a mutual fund managed by Dagan's RMB colleagues. After being employed for six months, Dagan became eligible to participate in the retirement plan, and she intends to allocate her retirement plan assets in six of the investment options, including the fund managed by her RMB colleagues. Dagan is concerned that joining the plan will lead to a potentially significant amount of paperwork for her (e.g., disclosure of her retirement account holdings and needing preclearance for her transactions), especially with her investing in the in-house fund.

Comment: Standard VI(A) would not require Dagan to disclosure her personal or retirement investments in large diversified mutual funds, unless specifically required by her employer. For practical reasons, the standard does not require Dagan to gain preclearance for ongoing payroll deduction contributions to retirement plan account investment options.

Dagan should ensure that her firm does not have a specific policy regarding investment—whether personal or in the retirement account—for funds managed by the company's employees. These mutual funds may be subject to the company's disclosure, preclearance, and trading restriction procedures to identify possible conflicts prior to the execution of trades.

Standard VI(B) Priority of Transactions

The Standard

Investment transactions for clients and employers must have priority over investment transactions in which a member or candidate is the beneficial owner.

Guidance

- This standard is designed to prevent any potential conflict of interest or the appearance of a conflict of interest with respect to personal transactions.
- Client interests have priority. Client transactions must take precedence over transactions made on behalf of the member's or candidate's firm or personal transactions.

Avoiding Potential Conflicts

- Although conflicts of interest exist, nothing is inherently unethical about individual managers, advisers, or mutual fund employees making money from personal investments as long as (1) the client is not disadvantaged by the trade, (2) the investment professional does not benefit personally from trades undertaken for clients, and (3) the investment professional complies with applicable regulatory requirements.
- Some situations occur in which a member or candidate may need to enter a personal transaction that runs counter to current recommendations or what the portfolio manager is doing for client portfolios. In these situations, the same three criteria given in the preceding paragraph should be applied in the transaction so as to not violate Standard VI(B).

Personal Trading Secondary to Trading for Clients

- The objective of the standard is to prevent personal transactions from adversely affecting the interests of clients or employers. A member or candidate having the same investment positions or being co-invested with clients does not always create a conflict.
- Personal investment positions or transactions of members or candidates or their firm should never, however, adversely affect client investments.

Standards for Nonpublic Information

- Standard VI(B) covers the activities of members and candidates who have knowledge of pending transactions that may be made on behalf of their clients or employers, who have access to nonpublic information during the normal preparation of research recommendations, or who take investment actions.
- Members and candidates are prohibited from conveying nonpublic information to any person whose relationship to the member or candidate makes the member or candidate a beneficial owner of the person's securities.
- Members and candidates must not convey this information to any other person if the nonpublic information can be deemed material.

Impact on All Accounts with Beneficial Ownership

- Members or candidates may undertake transactions in accounts for which they are a beneficial owner only after their clients and employers have had adequate opportunity to act on a recommendation.
- Personal transactions include those made for the member's or candidate's own account, for family (including spouse, children, and other immediate family members) accounts, and for accounts in which the member or candidate has a direct or indirect pecuniary interest, such as a trust or retirement account.

- Family accounts that are client accounts should be treated like any other firm account and should neither be given special treatment nor be disadvantaged because of the family relationship. If a member or candidate has a beneficial ownership in the account, however, the member or candidate may be subject to preclearance or reporting requirements of the employer or applicable law.

Recommended Procedures for Compliance

- Members and candidates should urge their firms to establish such policies and procedures.
- The specific provisions of each firm's standards will vary, but all firms should adopt certain basic procedures to address the conflict areas created by personal investing. These procedures include the following:
    - Limited participation in equity IPOs.
    - Restrictions on private placements.
    - Establish blackout/restricted periods.
    - Reporting requirements, including:
        - Disclosure of holdings in which the employee has a beneficial interest.
        - Providing duplicate confirmations of transactions.
        - Preclearance procedures.
    - Disclosure of policies to investors.

Application of the Standard

Example 1 (Personal Trading)

Research analyst Marlon Long does not recommend purchase of a common stock for his employer's account because he wants to purchase the stock personally and does not want to wait until the recommendation is approved and the stock is purchased by his employer.

Comment: Long has violated Standard VI(B) by taking advantage of his knowledge of the stock's value before allowing his employer to benefit from that information.

Example 2 (Trading for Family Member Account)

Carol Baker, the portfolio manager of an aggressive growth mutual fund, maintains an account in her husband's name at several brokerage firms with which the fund and a number of Baker's other individual clients do a substantial amount of business. Whenever a hot issue becomes available, she instructs the brokers to buy it for her husband's account. Because such issues normally are scarce, Baker often acquires shares in hot issues but her clients are not able to participate in them.

Comment: To avoid violating Standard VI(B), Baker must acquire shares for her mutual fund first and acquire them for her husband's account only after doing so, even though she might miss out on participating in new issues via her husband's account. She also must disclose the trading for her husband's account to her employer because this activity creates a conflict between her personal interests and her employer's interests.

Example 3 (Trading Prior to Report Dissemination)

A brokerage's insurance analyst, Denise Wilson, makes a closed-circuit TV report to her firm's branches around the country. During the broadcast, she includes negative comments about a major company in the insurance industry. The following day, Wilson's report is printed and distributed to the sales force and public customers. The report recommends that both short-term traders and intermediate investors take profits by selling that insurance company's stock. Seven minutes after the broadcast, however, Ellen Riley, head of the firm's trading department, had closed out a long "call" position in the stock. Shortly thereafter, Riley established a sizable "put" position in the stock. When asked about her activities, Riley claimed she took the actions to facilitate anticipated sales by institutional clients.

Comment: Riley did not give customers an opportunity to buy or sell in the options market before the firm itself did. By taking action before the report was disseminated, Riley's firm may have depressed the price of the calls and increased the price of the puts. The firm could have avoided a conflict of interest if it had waited to trade for its own account until its clients had an opportunity to receive and assimilate Wilson's recommendations. As it is, Riley's actions violated Standard VI(B).

Standard VI(C) Referral Fees

The Standard

Members and candidates must disclose to their employer, clients, and prospective clients, as appropriate, any compensation, consideration, or benefit received from or paid to others for the recommendation of products or services.

Guidance

- Members and candidates must inform their employer, clients, and prospective clients of any benefit received for referrals of customers and clients.
- Members and candidates must disclose when they pay a fee or provide compensation to others who have referred prospective clients to the member or candidate.
- Appropriate disclosure means that members and candidates must advise the client or prospective client, before entry into any formal agreement for services, of any benefit given or received for the recommendation of any services provided by the member or candidate. In addition, the member or candidate must disclose the nature of the consideration or benefit

Recommended Procedures for Compliance

- Members and candidates should encourage their employers to develop procedures related to referral fees. The firm may completely restrict such fees. If the firm does not adopt a strict prohibition of such fees, the procedures should indicate the appropriate steps for requesting approval.
- Employers should have investment professionals provide to the clients notification of approved referral fee programs and provide the employer regular (at least quarterly) updates on the amount and nature of compensation received.

Application of the Standard

Example 1 (Disclosure of Interdepartmental Referral Arrangements)

James Handley works for the trust department of Central Trust Bank. He receives compensation for each referral he makes to Central Trust's brokerage department and personal financial management department that results in a sale. He refers several of his clients to the personal financial management department but does not disclose the arrangement within Central Trust to his clients.

Comment: Handley has violated Standard VI(C) by not disclosing the referral arrangement at Central Trust Bank to his clients. Standard VI(C) does not distinguish between referral payments paid by a third party for referring clients to the third party and internal payments paid within the firm to attract new business to a subsidiary. Members and candidates must disclose all such referral fees. Therefore, Handley is required to disclose, at the time of referral, any referral fee agreement in place among Central Trust Bank's departments. The disclosure should include the nature and the value of the benefit and should be made in writing.

Example 2 (Disclosure of Referral Arrangements and Informing Firm)

Katherine Roberts is a portfolio manager at Katama Investments, an advisory firm specializing in managing assets for high-net-worth individuals. Katama's trading desk uses a variety of brokerage houses to execute trades on behalf of its clients. Roberts asks the trading desk to direct a large portion of its commissions to Naushon, Inc., a small broker/dealer run by one of Roberts's business school classmates. Katama's traders have found that Naushon is not very competitive on pricing, and although Naushon generates some research for its trading clients, Katama's other analysts have found most of Naushon's research to be not especially useful. Nevertheless, the traders do as Roberts asks, and in return for receiving a large portion of Katama's business, Naushon recommends the investment services of Roberts and Katama to its wealthiest clients. This arrangement is not disclosed to either Katama or the clients referred by Naushon.

Comment: Roberts is violating Standard VI(C) by failing to inform her employer of the referral arrangement.

Example 3 (Disclosure of Referral Arrangements and Outside Organizations)

Alex Burl is a portfolio manager at Helpful Investments, a local investment advisory firm. Burl is on the advisory board of his child's school, which is looking for ways to raise money to purchase new playground equipment for the school. Burl discusses a plan with his supervisor in which he will donate to the school a portion of his service fee from new clients referred by the parents of students at the school. Upon getting the approval from Helpful, Burl presents the idea to the school's advisory board and directors. The school agrees to announce the program at the next parent event and asks Burl to provide the appropriate written materials to be distributed. A week following the distribution of the fliers, Burl receives the first school-related referral. In establishing the client's investment policy statement, Burl clearly discusses the school's referral and outlines the plans for distributing the donation back to the school.

Comment: Burl has not violated Standard VI(C) because he secured the permission of his employer, Helpful Investments, and the school prior to beginning the program and because he discussed the arrangement with the client at the time the investment policy statement was designed.

Example 4 (Disclosure of Referral Arrangements and Outside Parties)

The sponsor of a state employee pension is seeking to hire a firm to manage the pension plan's emerging market allocation. To assist in the review process, the sponsor has hired Thomas Arrow as a consultant to solicit proposals from various advisers. Arrow is contracted by the sponsor to represent its best interest in selecting the most appropriate new manager. The process runs smoothly, and Overseas Investments is selected as the new manager.

The following year, news breaks that Arrow is under investigation by the local regulator for accepting kickbacks from investment managers after they are awarded new pension allocations. Overseas Investments is included in the list of firms allegedly making these payments. Although the sponsor is happy with the performance of Overseas since it has been managing the pension plan's emerging market funds, the sponsor still decides to have an independent review of the proposals and the selection process to ensure that Overseas was the appropriate firm for its needs. This review confirms that, even though Arrow was being paid by both parties, the recommendation of Overseas appeared to be objective and appropriate.

Comment: Arrow has violated Standard VI(C) because he did not disclose the fee being paid by Overseas. Withholding this information raises the question of a potential lack of objectivity in the recommendations Overseas is making; this aspect is in addition to questions about the legality of having firms pay to be considered for an allocation.

Regulators and governmental agencies may adopt requirements concerning allowable consultant activities. Local regulations sometimes include having a consultant register with the regulatory agency's ethics board. Regulator policies may include a prohibition on acceptance of payments from investment managers receiving allocations and require regular reporting of contributions made to political organizations and candidates. Arrow would have to adhere to these requirements as well as the Code and Standards.

LESSON 7: STANDARD VII: RESPONSIBILITIES AS A CFA INSTITUTE MEMBER OR CFA CANDIDATE

A. Conduct as Participants in the CFA Institute Program
B. Reference to CFA Institute, the CFA Designation, and the CFA Program

Standard VII(A) Conduct as Participants in CFA Institute Programs

The Standard

Members and candidates must not engage in any conduct that compromises the reputation or integrity of CFA Institute or the CFA designation or the integrity, validity, or security of CFA Institute programs.

Guidance

- Standard VII(A) prohibits any conduct that undermines the public's confidence that the CFA charter represents a level of achievement based on merit and ethical conduct.
- Conduct covered includes but is not limited to:
    - Giving or receiving assistance (cheating) on any CFA Institute examinations.
    - Violating the rules, regulations, and testing policies of CFA Institute programs,
    - Providing confidential program or exam information to candidates or the public,
    - Disregarding or attempting to circumvent security measures established for any CFA Institute examinations,
    - Improperly using an association with CFA Institute to further personal or professional goals, and
    - Misrepresenting information on the Professional Conduct Statement or in the CFA Institute Continuing Education Program.

Confidential Program Information

- Examples of information that cannot be disclosed by candidates sitting for an exam include but are not limited to:
    - Specific details of questions appearing on the exam and
    - Broad topical areas and formulas tested or not tested on the exam.
- All aspects of the exam, including questions, broad topical areas, and formulas, tested or not tested, are considered confidential until such time as CFA Institute elects to release them publicly.

Additional CFA Program Restrictions

- Violating any of the testing policies, such as the calculator policy, personal belongings policy, or the Candidate Pledge, constitutes a violation of Standard VII(A).
- Examples of information that cannot be shared by members involved in developing, administering, or grading the exams include but are not limited to:
    - Questions appearing on the exam or under consideration.
    - Deliberation related to the exam process.
    - Information related to the scoring of questions.

Expressing an Opinion

- Standard VII(A) does *not* cover expressing opinions regarding CFA Institute, the CFA Program, or other CFA Institute programs.
- However, when expressing a personal opinion, a candidate is prohibited from disclosing content-specific information, including any actual exam question and the information as to subject matter covered or not covered in the exam.

Application of the Standard

Example 1 (Sharing Exam Questions)

Travis Nero serves as a proctor for the administration of the CFA examination in his city. In the course of his service, he reviews a copy of the Level II exam on the evening prior to the exam's administration and provides information concerning the exam questions to two candidates who use it to prepare for the exam.

Comment: Nero and the two candidates have violated Standard VII(A). By giving information about the exam questions to two candidates, Nero provided an unfair advantage to the two candidates and undermined the integrity and validity of the Level II exam as an accurate measure of the knowledge, skills, and abilities necessary to earn the right to use the CFA designation. By accepting the information, the candidates also compromised the integrity and validity of the Level II exam and undermined the ethical framework that is a key part of the designation.

Example 2 (Sharing Exam Content)

After completing Level II of the CFA exam, Annabelle Rossi posts on her blog about her experience. She posts the following: "Level II is complete! I think I did fairly well on the exam. It was really difficult, but fair. I think I did especially well on the derivatives questions. And there were tons of them! I think I counted 18! The ethics questions were really hard. I'm glad I spent so much time on the Code and Standards. I was surprised to see there were no questions at all about IPO allocations. I expected there to be a couple. Well, off to celebrate getting through it. See you tonight?"

Comment: Rossi did not violate Standard VII(A) when she wrote about how difficult she found the exam or how well she thinks she may have done. By revealing portions of the CBOK covered on the exam and areas not covered, however, she did violate Standard VII(A) and the Candidate Pledge. Depending on the time frame in which the comments were posted, Rossi not only may have assisted future candidates but also may have provided an unfair advantage to candidates yet to sit for the same exam, thereby undermining the integrity and validity of the Level II exam.

Example 3 (Sharing Exam Content)

Level I candidate Etienne Gagne has been a frequent visitor to an internet forum designed specifically for CFA Program candidates. The week after completing the Level I examination, Gagne and several others begin a discussion thread on the forum about the most challenging questions and attempt to determine the correct answers.

Comment: Gagne has violated Standard VII(A) by providing and soliciting confidential exam information, which compromises the integrity of the exam process and violates the Candidate Pledge. In trying to determine correct answers to specific questions, the group's discussion included question-specific details considered to be confidential to the CFA Program.

Example 4 (Sharing Exam Content)

CFA4Sure is a company that produces test-preparation materials for CFA Program candidates. Many candidates register for and use the company's products. The day after the CFA examination, CFA4Sure sends an e-mail to all its customers asking them to share with the company the hardest questions from the exam so that CFA4Sure can better prepare its customers for the next exam administration. Marisol Pena e-mails a summary of the questions she found most difficult on the exam.

Comment: Pena has violated Standard VII(A) by disclosing a portion of the exam questions. The information provided is considered confidential until publicly released by CFA Institute. CFA4Sure is likely to use such feedback to refine its review materials for future candidates. Pena's sharing of the specific questions undermines the integrity of the exam while potentially making the exam easier for future candidates.

If the CFA4Sure employees who participated in the solicitation of confidential CFA Program information are CFA Institute members or candidates, they also have violated Standard VII(A).

Example 5 (Compromising CFA Institute Integrity as a Volunteer)

Jose Ramirez is an investor-relations consultant for several small companies that are seeking greater exposure to investors. He is also the program chair for the CFA Institute society in the city where he works. Ramirez schedules only companies that are his clients to make presentations to the society and excludes other companies.

Comment: Ramirez, by using his volunteer position at CFA Institute to benefit himself and his clients, compromises the reputation and integrity of CFA Institute and thus violates Standard VII(A).

Example 6 (Compromising CFA Institute Integrity as a Volunteer)

Marguerite Warrenski is a member of the CFA Institute GIPS Executive Committee, which oversees the creation, implementation, and revision of the GIPS standards. As a member of the Executive Committee, she has advance knowledge of confidential information regarding the GIPS standards, including any new or revised standards the committee is considering. She tells her clients that her Executive Committee membership will allow her to better assist her clients in keeping up with changes to the Standards and facilitating their compliance with the changes.

Comment: Warrenski is using her association with the GIPS Executive Committee to promote her firm's services to clients and potential clients. In defining her volunteer position at CFA Institute as a strategic business advantage over competing firms and implying to clients that she would use confidential information to further their interests, Warrenski is compromising the reputation and integrity of CFA Institute and thus violating Standard VII(A). She may factually state her involvement with the Executive Committee but cannot infer any special advantage to her clients from such participation.

Standard VII(B) Reference to CFA Institute, the CFA Designation, and the CFA Program

The Standard

When referring to CFA Institute, CFA Institute membership, the CFA designation, or candidacy in the CFA Program, members and candidates must not misrepresent or exaggerate the meaning or implications of membership in CFA Institute, holding the CFA designation, or candidacy in the CFA Program.

Guidance

- Standard VII(B) is intended to prevent promotional efforts that make promises or guarantees that are tied to the CFA designation. Individuals may refer to their CFA designation, CFA Institute membership, or candidacy in the CFA Program but must not exaggerate the meaning or implications of membership in CFA Institute, holding the CFA designation, or candidacy in the CFA Program.
- Standard VII(B) is not intended to prohibit factual statements related to the positive benefit of earning the CFA designation. However, statements referring to CFA Institute, the CFA designation, or the CFA Program that overstate the competency of an individual or imply, either directly or indirectly, that superior performance can be expected from someone with the CFA designation are not allowed under the standard.
- Statements that highlight or emphasize the commitment of CFA Institute members, CFA charterholders, and CFA candidates to ethical and professional conduct or mention the thoroughness and rigor of the CFA Program are appropriate.
- Members and candidates may make claims about the relative merits of CFA Institute, the CFA Program, or the Code and Standards as long as those statements are implicitly or explicitly stated as the opinion of the speaker.
- Standard VII(B) applies to any form of communication, including but not limited to communications made in electronic or written form (such as on firm letterhead, business cards, professional biographies, directory listings, printed advertising, firm brochures, or personal resumes), and oral statements made to the public, clients, or prospects.

CFA Institute Membership

The term “CFA Institute member” refers to “regular” and “affiliate” members of CFA Institute who have met the membership requirements as defined in the CFA Institute Bylaws. Once accepted as a CFA Institute member, the member must satisfy the following requirements to maintain his or her status:

- Remit annually to CFA Institute a completed Professional Conduct Statement, which renews the commitment to abide by the requirements of the Code and Standards and the CFA Institute Professional Conduct Program.
- Pay applicable CFA Institute membership dues on an annual basis.

If a CFA Institute member fails to meet any of these requirements, the individual is no longer considered an active member. Until membership is reactivated, individuals must not present themselves to others as active members. They may state, however, that they were CFA Institute members in the past or refer to the years when their membership was active.

Using the CFA Designation

- Those who have earned the right to use the Chartered Financial Analyst designation may use the trademarks or registered marks "Chartered Financial Analyst" or "CFA" and are encouraged to do so but only in a manner that does not misrepresent or exaggerate the meaning or implications of the designation.
- The use of the designation may be accompanied by an accurate explanation of the requirements that have been met to earn the right to use the designation.
- "CFA charterholders" are those individuals who have earned the right to use the CFA designation granted by CFA Institute. These people have satisfied certain requirements, including completion of the CFA Program and required years of acceptable work experience. Once granted the right to use the designation, individuals must also satisfy the CFA Institute membership requirements (see above) to maintain their right to use the designation.
- If a CFA charterholder fails to meet any of the membership requirements, he or she forfeits the right to use the CFA designation. Until membership is reactivated, individuals must not present themselves to others as CFA charterholders. They may state, however, that they were charterholders in the past.
- Given the growing popularity of social media, where individuals may anonymously express their opinions, pseudonyms or online profile names created to hide a member's identity should not be tagged with the CFA designation.

Referring to Candidacy in the CFA Program

- Candidates in the CFA Program may refer to their participation in the CFA Program, but such references must clearly state that an individual is a *candidate* in the CFA Program and must not imply that the candidate has achieved any type of partial designation. A person is a candidate in the CFA Program if:
    - The person's application for registration in the CFA Program has been accepted by CFA Institute, as evidenced by issuance of a notice of acceptance, and the person is enrolled to sit for a specified examination; or
    - The registered person has sat for a specified examination but exam results have not yet been received.
- If an individual is registered for the CFA Program but declines to sit for an exam or otherwise does not meet the definition of a candidate as described in the CFA Institute Bylaws, then that individual is no longer considered an active candidate. Once the person is enrolled to sit for a future examination, his or her CFA candidacy resumes.
- CFA candidates must never state or imply that they have a partial designation as a result of passing one or more levels, or cite an expected completion date of any level of the CFA Program. Final award of the charter is subject to meeting the CFA Program requirements and approval by the CFA Institute Board of Governors.
- If a candidate passes each level of the exam in consecutive years and wants to state that he or she did so, that is not a violation of Standard VII(B) because it is a statement of fact. If the candidate then goes on to claim or imply superior ability by obtaining the designation in only three years, however, he or she is in violation of Standard VII(B).

Proper and Improper References to the CFA Designation

Proper References	Improper References
"Completion of the CFA Program has enhanced my portfolio management skills."	"CFA charterholders achieve better performance results."
"John Smith passed all three CFA examinations in three consecutive years."	"John Smith is among the elite, having passed all three CFA examinations in three consecutive attempts."
"The CFA designation is globally recognized and attests to a charterholder's success in a rigorous and comprehensive study program in the field of investment management and research analysis."	"As a CFA charterholder, I am the most qualified to manage client investments."
"The credibility that the CFA designation affords and the skills the CFA Program cultivates are key assets for my future career development."	"As a CFA charterholder, Jane White provides the best value in trade execution."
"I enrolled in the CFA Program to obtain the highest set of credentials in the global investment management industry."	"Enrolling as a candidate in the CFA Program ensures one of becoming better at valuing debt securities."
"I passed Level I of the CFA exam."	"CFA, Level II"
"I am a 2010 Level III candidate in the CFA Program."	"CFA, Expected 2011" "Level III CFA Candidate"
"I passed all three levels of the CFA Program and will be eligible for the CFA charter upon completion of the required work experience."	"CFA, Expected 2011" "John Smith, Charter Pending"
"As a CFA charterholder, I am committed to the highest ethical standards."	

Proper Usage of the CFA Marks

- Upon obtaining the CFA charter from CFA Institute, charterholders are given the right to use the CFA marks, including Chartered Financial Analyst®, CFA®, and the CFA logo (a certification mark)
- The Chartered Financial Analyst and CFA marks must always be used either after a charterholder's name or as adjectives (never as nouns) in written documents or oral conversations. For example, to refer to oneself as "a CFA" or "a Chartered Financial Analyst" is improper.
- Members and candidates must not use a pseudonym or fictitious phrase meant to hide their identity in conjunction with the CFA designation. CFA Institute can verify only that a specific individual has earned the designation according to the name that is maintained in the membership database.
- The CFA logo certification mark is used by charterholders as a distinctive visual symbol of the CFA designation that can be easily recognized by employers, colleagues, and clients. As a certification mark, it must be used only to directly refer to an individual charterholder or group of charterholders.

Correct and Incorrect Use of the Chartered Financial Analyst and CFA Marks

Correct	Incorrect	Principle
He is one of two CFA charterholders in the company.	He is one of two CFAs in the company.	The CFA and Chartered Financial Analyst designations must always be used as adjectives, never as nouns or common names.
He earned the right to use the Chartered Financial Analyst designation.	He is a Chartered Financial Analyst.	
Jane Smith, CFA	Jane Smith, C.F.A. John Doe, cfa	No periods. Always capitalize the letters "CFA."
	John, a CFA-type portfolio manager.	
John Jones, CFA	The focus is on Chartered Financial Analysis.	Do not alter the designation to create new words or phrases.
	CFA-equivalent program. Swiss-CFA.	
John Jones, Chartered Financial Analyst	Jones Chartered Financial Analysts, Inc.	The designation must not be used as part of the name of a firm.
Jane Smith, CFA John Doe, Chartered Financial Analyst	Jane Smith, **CFA** John Doe, **Chartered Financial Analyst**	The CFA designation should not be given more prominence (e.g., larger or bold font) than the charterholder's name.
Level I candidate in the CFA Program.	Chartered Financial Analyst (CFA), September 2011.	Candidates in the CFA Program must not cite the expected date of exam completion and award of charter.
Passed Level I of the CFA examination in 2010.	CFA Level I. CFA degree expected in 2011.	No designation exists for someone who has passed Level I, Level II, or Level III of the exam. The CFA designation should not be referred to as a degree.
I have passed all three levels of the CFA Program and may be eligible for the CFA charter upon completion of the required work experience.	CFA (Passed Finalist) CFA Charter Pending Pending CFA Charterholder	A candidate who has passed Level III but has not yet received his or her charter cannot use the CFA or Chartered Financial Analyst designation.

Correct	Incorrect	Principle
CFA Charter, 2009, CFA Institute (optional: Charlottesville, Virginia, USA)	CFA Charter, 2009, CFA Society of the UK	In citing the designation in a resume, a charterholder should use the date that he or she received the designation and should cite CFA Institute as the conferring body.
John Smith, CFA	Crazy Bear CFA (Online social media user name)	Charterholders should not attach the CFA designation to anonymous or fictitious names meant to conceal their identity.

Application of the Standard

Example 1 (Passing Exams in Consecutive Years)

An advertisement for AZ Investment Advisors states that all the firm's principals are CFA charterholders and all passed the three examinations on their first attempt. The advertisement prominently links this fact to the notion that AZ's mutual funds have achieved superior performance.

Comment: AZ may state that all principals passed the three examinations on the first try as long as this statement is true, but it must not be linked to performance or imply superior ability. Implying that (1) CFA charterholders achieve better investment results and (2) those who pass the exams on the first try may be more successful than those who do not violates Standard VII(B).

Example 2 (Right to Use CFA Designation)

Five years after receiving his CFA charter, Louis Vasseur resigns his position as an investment analyst and spends the next two years traveling abroad. Because he is not actively engaged in the investment profession, he does not file a completed Professional Conduct Statement with CFA Institute and does not pay his CFA Institute membership dues. At the conclusion of his travels, Vasseur becomes a self-employed analyst accepting assignments as an independent contractor. Without reinstating his CFA Institute membership by filing his Professional Conduct Statement and paying his dues, he prints business cards that display "CFA" after his name.

Comment: Vasseur has violated Standard VII(B) because his right to use the CFA designation was suspended when he failed to file his Professional Conduct Statement and stopped paying dues. Therefore, he no longer is able to state or imply that he is an active CFA charterholder. When Vasseur files his Professional Conduct Statement, resumes paying CFA Institute dues to activate his membership, and completes the CFA Institute reinstatement procedures, he will be eligible to use the CFA designation.

Example 3 (Order of Professional and Academic Designations)

Tatiana Prittima has earned both her CFA designation and a PhD in finance. She would like to cite both her accomplishments on her business card but is unsure of the proper method for doing so.

Comment: The order of designations cited on such items as resumes and business cards is a matter of personal preference. Prittima is free to cite the CFA designation either before or after citing her PhD.

Example 4 (Use of Fictitious Name)

Barry Glass is the lead quantitative analyst at CityCenter Hedge Fund. Glass is responsible for the development, maintenance, and enhancement of the proprietary models the fund uses to manage its investors' assets. Glass reads several high-level mathematical publications and blogs to stay informed on current developments. One blog, run by Expert CFA, presents some intriguing research that may benefit one of CityCenter's current models. Glass is under pressure from firm executives to improve the model's predictive abilities, and he incorporates the factors discussed in the online research. The updated output recommends several new investments to the fund's portfolio managers.

Comment: "Expert CFA" has violated Standard VII(B) by using the CFA designation inappropriately. As with any research report, authorship of online comments must include the charterholder's full name along with any reference to the CFA designation.

See also Standard V(A)—Diligence and Reasonable Basis, which Glass has violated for guidance on diligence and reasonable basis.

READING 3: CFA INSTITUTE RESEARCH OBJECTIVITY STANDARDS

LESSON 1: CFA INSTITUTE RESEARCH OBJECTIVITY STANDARDS

LOS 3a: Explain the objectives of the Research Objectivity Standards.
Vol 1, pp 210–212

When designing policies and procedures for implementing the CFA Institute Research Objectivity Standards, firms should strive to achieve the following objectives:

A. To prepare research reports, make investment recommendations, and take investment actions; and develop policies, procedures, and disclosures that always place the interests of investing clients before their employees' or the firm's interests.
B. To facilitate full, fair, meaningful, and specific disclosures of potential and actual conflicts of interest of the firm or its employees to its current and prospective clients.
C. To promote the creation and maintenance of effective policies and procedures that would minimize and manage conflicts of interest that may jeopardize the independence and objectivity of research.
D. To support self-regulation through voluntary industry development of, and adherence to, specific, measurable, and demonstrable standards that promote and reward independent and objective research.
E. To provide a work environment for all investment professionals that supports, encourages, and rewards ethical behavior and supports CFA Institute members, CFA charterholders, and CFA candidates in their adherence to the CFA Institute Code and Standards.

LOS 3b: Evaluate company policies and practices related to research objectivity, and distinguish between changes required and changes recommended for compliance with the Research Objectivity Standards. **Vol 1, pp 213–221**

Definitions

- Covered employee: An employee of the firm who:
    - Conducts research, writes research reports, and/or makes investment recommendations;
    - Takes investment action on behalf of clients or the firm, or is involved in the decision-making process; or
    - May benefit, either personally or professionally, from influencing research reports or recommendations.
- Investment manager: An employee of an investment management firm who conducts investment research and/or takes investment action for client accounts or for the firm's own account, whether or not such person has the title of "investment manager."

CFA Institute Research Objectivity Standards

1.0 Research Objectivity Policy

Requirements

Firms must have:

a. A formal written policy on the independence and objectivity of research (Policy) that must be:
    i. made available to clients and prospective clients (both investing and corporate); and
    ii. disseminated to all firm employees;

b. Supervisory procedures that reasonably ensure that the firm and its covered employees comply with the provisions of the policy and all applicable laws and regulations; and

c. A senior officer of the firm who attests annually to clients and prospective clients to the firm's implementation of, and adherence to, the Policy.

Recommended Procedures for Compliance

Firms should:

> Research analyst: An employee who is primarily responsible for, contributes to, or is connected with, the preparation of a research report, whether or not such person has the title of "research analyst."

- Identify and describe the job title, function, and department of covered employees.
- Specify whether covered employees are subject to a code of ethics and standards of professional conduct, and provide the code and standards, if applicable.
- Train covered employees regularly regarding their responsibilities under the Policy and require them to attest annually in writing that they understand and adhere to the Policy.
- Fully disclose any conflicts of interest that covered employees may face.
- The Policy should clearly describe the factors on which a research analyst's compensation is based.
- Disclose the conditions under which a research report may be purchased or acquired by clients, prospective clients, and investors in general.

> Public appearances: Participation in any public forum, including seminars, open forums, radio, television, or other media interview, or other public speaking activity in which a research analyst or investment manager makes a recommendation or offers an opinion.

2.0 Public Appearances

Requirements

Firms that permit research analysts and other covered employees to present and discuss their research and recommendations in public appearances must require these employees to fully disclose personal and firm conflicts of interest to the host or interviewer and, whenever possible, to the audience.

Recommended Procedures for Compliance

Firms that allow covered employees to make public appearances should:

- Ensure that the audience has sufficient information to:
  - Make informed judgments about the objectivity of the research and recommendations.
  - Assess the suitability of the investment in light of their specific circumstances and constraints.
- Ensure that covered employees who make public appearances are prepared to disclose all conflicts of interest that they or their firm might have. Such disclosures may include:
  - Whether the subject company is an investment banking or other corporate finance client of the firm; and
  - Whether the research analyst has participated, or is participating, in marketing activities for the subject company.
- Provide full research reports on the subject companies discussed to members of the audience at a reasonable price. (Note that standards do not define a "reasonable price".)

> Subject company: A corporate issuer whose securities are the subject of a research report or recommendation.

3.0 Reasonable and Adequate Basis

Requirements

Firms must require research reports and recommendations to have a basis that can be substantiated as reasonable and adequate. An individual employee (supervisory analyst who is someone other than the author) or a group of employees (review committee) must be appointed to review and approve all research reports and recommendations.

> Supervisory analyst: A designated person responsible for reviewing research reports to assess and maintain the quality and integrity of research reports.

Recommended Procedures for Compliance

- Firms should provide detailed written guidance to determine what constitutes reasonable and adequate basis for a particular recommendation.
- When recommending a purchase, sale, or a change in recommendation, firms should provide, or offer to provide, supporting information to investing clients. When making a recommendation, the current market price of the security should be disclosed.

4.0 Investment Banking

Requirements

Firms that engage in, or collaborate on, investment banking activities must:

a. Establish and implement effective policies and procedures that:
   - i. segregate research analysts from the investment banking department; and
   - ii. ensure that investment banking objectives or employees do not have the ability to influence or affect research or recommendations;

b. Implement reporting structures and review procedures that ensure that research analysts do not report to, and are not supervised or controlled by, the investment banking or another department of the firm that could compromise the independence of the analyst; and

c. Implement procedures that prevent investment banking or corporate finance departments from reviewing, modifying, approving, or rejecting research reports and recommendations on their own authority.

Recommended Procedures for Compliance

- Firms should prohibit research analysts from sharing with, or communicating to, members of the investment banking or corporate finance departments, prior to publication, any section of the research report that might indicate the analyst's proposed recommendations.
- All communications between the research analyst and the investment banking or corporate finance departments should take place through the firm's compliance or legal department.
- The investment banking and corporate finance departments should only be permitted to review a research report to verify factual information or to identify potential conflicts of interest.
- Firms should have quiet periods for IPOs and secondary offerings of sufficient length to ensure that research reports and recommendations are not based on inside information acquired by the analyst through investment banking sources.
- Firms should prohibit research analysts from participating in marketing activities (such as road shows) for IPOs and secondary offerings. If such participation is allowed, then the research analyst should disclose any participation in all interviews and public appearances.

> Quiet period: Period during which covered employees are prohibited from issuing research reports or recommendations on, and speaking publicly about, a specific subject company.

5.0 Research Analyst Compensation

Requirements

Firms must establish and implement salary, bonus, and other compensation for research analysts that:

a. Compensation is aligned with the quality of the research and the accuracy of the recommendations over time; and
b. Compensation is not linked to investment banking or other corporate finance activities on which the analyst collaborated (either individually or in the aggregate).

Recommended Procedures for Compliance

- Compensation arrangements should be based on measurable criteria for assessing the quality of research and should be applied consistently to all research analysts.
- Firms should disclose the extent to which analyst compensation is dependent upon the firm's investment banking revenues.

6.0 Relationships with Subject Companies

Requirements

Firms must implement policies and procedures that manage the working relationships that research analysts develop with the management of subject companies.

Research analysts must be prohibited from:

a. Sharing with, or communicating to, a subject company, prior to publication, any section of a research report that might communicate the research analyst's proposed recommendation, rating, or price target; and
b. Directly or indirectly promising a subject company or other corporate issuer a favorable report or a specific price target, or from threatening to change reports, recommendations, or price targets.

> Corporate issuer: A company obtaining funding from public capital markets.

Recommended Procedures for Compliance

- Firms should have policies and procedures that govern the relationships of research analysts with subject companies, including policies regarding material gifts, company-sponsored trips, communications with the company management, and so on.
- Prior to publication, subject companies should only be permitted to review and verify sections of the research report that contain facts.
- A draft research report should be submitted to the firm's compliance or legal department before it is shared with the subject company.
- Any changes to the research report that occur as a consequence of verification by the subject company should be approved by the compliance or legal department. Furthermore, the research analyst should provide written justifications for any changes that occur after verification by the subject company.

7.0 Personal Investments and Trading

Requirements

Firms must have policies and procedures that:

a. Manage covered employees' "personal investments and trading activities" effectively.
b. Ensure that covered employees do not share information about the subject company or security with any person who could have the ability to trade in advance of ("front run") or otherwise disadvantage investing clients.
c. Ensure that covered employees and members of their immediate families do not have the ability to trade in advance of or otherwise disadvantage investing clients relative to themselves or the firm;
d. Prohibit covered employees and members of their immediate families from trading in a manner that is contrary to, or inconsistent with, the employees' or the firm's most recent, published recommendations or ratings, except in circumstances of extreme financial hardship; and
e. Prohibit covered employees and members of their immediate families from purchasing or receiving securities prior to an IPO for subject companies and other companies in the industry or industries assigned.

> Personal investments and trading: Conducting purchases and sales of a particular security in which an individual has a financial interest.

Recommended Procedures for Compliance

- Precautions should be taken to ensure that the interests of clients are placed before the interests of employees, members of their immediate families, and the firm.
- Covered employees should obtain approval from the firm's compliance or legal department prior to trading in any securities of subject companies in industries that they are assigned.

Restricted period: Period during which covered employees are prohibited from trading specified securities.

- Firms should have procedures in place to prevent covered employees from trading in advance of client trades (front running). Restricted periods of at least 30 calendar days before and 5 calendar days after the issuance of research reports are recommended.
- Covered employees should be prohibited from trading contrary to published recommendations of the firm unless they would suffer "extreme financial hardship" if they were unable to liquidate their investments.
- Covered employees should be required to provide to the firm or its legal or compliance department a complete list of all personal investments in which they or their immediate family members have a financial interest. This list should be provided at least annually.
- Firms should establish policies and procedures that prevent short-term trading of securities by covered employees. Covered employees should be required to hold securities for at least 60 calendar days, except in cases of extreme financial hardship.

8.0 Timeliness of Research Reports and Recommendations

Requirements

Firms must issue research reports on subject companies on a timely and regular basis.

Recommended Procedures for Compliance

- Firms should update research reports and recommendations on a regular (ideally quarterly) basis. Additional updates are recommended when there is an announcement of significant news or events by, or that might impact, the subject company.
- A "final" research report should be issued on a subject company if its coverage is being discontinued. This report should explain reasons for discontinuing coverage.

9.0 Compliance and Enforcement

Requirements

Firms must:

a. Have effective enforcement of their policies and compliance procedures to ensure research objectivity;
b. Implement appropriate disciplinary sanctions for covered employees, up to and including dismissal from the firm, for violations;
c. Monitor and audit the effectiveness of compliance procedures; and
d. Maintain records of the results of internal audits.

Recommended Procedures for Compliance

A list of activities that would be considered violations along with resulting disciplinary sanctions should be provided to all covered employees, as well as current and prospective clients of the firm.

10.0 Disclosure

Requirements

Firms must provide full and fair disclosure of all conflicts of interest to which the firm or its covered employees are subject.

Recommended Procedures for Compliance

- Disclosures should be comprehensive and complete, prominent, and easily understood by an average reader.
- In addition to disclosures in research reports, firms should determine the appropriate communication method(s) to inform investing clients of the following:
  - Whether the firm makes a market in securities of a subject company.
  - Whether the firm managed or co-managed a recent initial public or secondary offering of a subject company.
  - Whether the research analyst or firm owns securities or any financial instrument that might reasonably be expected to benefit from the recommendation; or
  - Whether the firm, an allied or affiliated firm, or the covered employee or a member of that employee's immediate family is a director, officer, or advisory board member of the subject company.
- It is recommended that firms disclose the following in the research reports of all subject companies:
  - Whether the subject company is a corporate client;
  - Whether the firm or any of its affiliates holds 1% or more of any class of the outstanding common equity of the subject company as of five (5) business days prior to the issuance of the research report;
  - Whether the firm makes a market in the securities of the subject company;
  - Whether the firm permits the author(s) or members of their immediate families to invest or trade in the securities of the subject company;
  - Whether the author(s) or members of their immediate families have a financial interest in any financial instrument that might reasonably be expected to benefit from the recommendation.

> Immediate family: Includes people who have the same principal residence as the subject person.

- When the subject company is also a corporate client, it is recommended that firms also disclose the following in research reports and on their website:
  - The nature of the corporate client relationship (e.g., initial public offering, merger and acquisition, etc.).
  - Whether the firm received fees or revenues from the subject company in the previous 12 months or is expected to receive fees or revenues in the next 3 months.
  - Whether the author(s) of the report assisted the firm in nonresearch activities and the specific nature of those activities (e.g., evaluated a subject company for acceptability as a corporate client, marketing activities).
  - Whether the compensation of the author(s) was dependent upon participation in investment banking or corporate finance activities.
- Firms should provide appropriate statistical or qualitative basis for their recommendations and ratings.
- Firms should disclose the valuation methods used by them to determine price targets along with a description of the risk associated with achieving those targets.

11.0 Rating System

Requirements

Firms must establish a rating system that:

a. Is useful for investors and for investment decision-making; and
b. Provides investors with information for assessing the suitability of the security to their own unique circumstances and constraints.

Recommended Procedures for Compliance

- Firms should avoid one-dimensional rating systems as they do not provide sufficient information to investors to make informed investment decisions.
- Rating systems should include the following categories:
    - Recommendation or rating categories may be absolute (e.g., buy, hold, sell) or relative (e.g., market outperform, neutral, or underperform). If the recommendation categories are relative, the firm should clearly identify the relevant benchmark, index, or objective.
    - Time horizon categories should clearly identify whether the time horizon measures the period over which the expected price target would be achieved or sustained.
    - Risk categories.
- Firms should require that communications of a firm's rating or recommendation, including discussions in public appearances, always include all three elements of the rating.
- Firms should prohibit covered employees from communicating a rating or recommendation that is different from the current published rating or recommendation.
- Firms should provide clients and prospective clients with a complete description of the firm's rating system on request. Firms should regularly inform clients and prospective clients of the availability of this description and how a client or prospective client can acquire this description.

Study Session 2: Ethical and Professional Standards—Application

Reading 4: The Glenarm Company

LESSON 1: THE GLENARM COMPANY

LOS 4a: Evaluate the practices and policies presented. Vol 1, pp 227–231

LOS 4b: Explain the appropriate action to take in response to conduct that violates the CFA Institute Code of Ethics and Standards of Professional Conduct. Vol 1, pp 227–231

Case Facts

Peter Sherman, CFA, worked for 5 years at Pearl Investment Management as an emerging market analyst. At the same time, he provided consulting services to several third-world companies in which Pearl did not own any stock. This arrangement was fully disclosed to Pearl. Sherman recently switched jobs and is now a portfolio manager at Glenarm Company.

Glenarm is a small investment management firm that was recently investigated, censured, and fined by the U.S. Securities and Exchange Commission (SEC). Its partners were eager to rehabilitate the firm's reputation and believed that hiring a CFA charterholder would demonstrate their commitment to professionalism.

Glenarm had offered Sherman a large portion of the first-year investment management fee for any Pearl clients that he would be able to bring across to Glenarm. While he was still employed at Pearl, Sherman:

- Paid social calls to several local Pearl clients after business hours to persuade them to switch to Glenarm.
- Contacted a number of Pearl's potential clients to encourage them to hire Glenarm.
- Contacted a number of clients that Pearl had rejected in the past to determine if they would be interested in hiring Glenarm.

Sherman was successful in convincing several of Pearl's current and prospective clients to hire Glenarm as their investment manager. Further, he took the following items from Pearl to his new job:

- Sample marketing presentations that he had prepared for Pearl.
- Computer stock selection and asset allocation models that he had developed.
- Research materials on several companies that he had been following.
- News articles that contained potential research ideas.
- A list of companies that he had recommended for further research but had been rejected by Pearl.

Sherman has not informed Glenarm about his consulting services on the side.

Case Results

The following standards have been violated in the stated scenario:

Standard IV(A) – Loyalty

Solicitation of current and prospective clients of Pearl is a violation of Standard IV(A). The fact that Sherman did it after office hours is irrelevant. Note that solicitation of clients that Pearl had rejected in the past is not a violation of this standard.

Departing employees may not take the employer's property unless the employer consents. All the items that Sherman took were the property of Pearl and taking that property was a violation of this standard.

Appropriate Actions

In order to avoid violations of this Standard, Sherman should not have solicited any of Pearl's current and prospective clients while he was still an employee of Pearl. Further, he should have sought permission for taking copies of any work that he had prepared for Pearl during the course of his employment there.

Standard IV(B) – Additional Compensation Arrangements; Standard VI(A) – Disclosure of Conflicts; and Standard I(B) – Independence and Objectivity

By not disclosing his consulting services to Glenarm, Sherman violated Standards IV(B), VI(A), and I(B). Although such services might benefit Glenarm, they are likely to divert Sherman's energies away from managing Glenarm's clients. Further, his independent consulting services might also affect Sherman's ability to offer objective advice.

Appropriate Actions

Sherman should have informed Glenarm in writing about his independent consulting services to enable the company to make an informed determination about his ability to perform his responsibilities with the firm. He should have made full and fair disclosure of all matters that could reasonably be expected to impair his ability to offer independent and objective advice. Such disclosures must be prominent and delivered in plain language.

Reading 5: Preston Partners

LESSON 1: PRESTON PARTNERS

LOS 5a: Evaluate the practices and policies presented. Vol 1, pp 233–237

LOS 5b: Explain the appropriate action to take in response to conduct that violates the CFA Institute Code of Ethics and Standards of Professional Conduct. Vol 1, pp 233–237

Case Facts

Sheldon Preston, CFA, is the senior partner and President of Preston Partners (PP), a medium-sized investment management firm that specializes in managing large-cap portfolios of U.S. equities for individuals and pension funds. PP has adopted the CFA Institute Code of Ethics and Standards of Professional Conduct as part of its compliance manual.

The manual was written by Preston himself. However, due to time constraints, he concentrated on the key elements and could not address all policies in detail. He ensures that every person who joins the firm receives a copy of the manual.

Every day Preston reviews all the trades made by PP and monitors major price changes. In one of his daily reviews, Preston finds out that several weeks ago, while he was on vacation, Gerald Smithson, a portfolio manager at PP, had added the stock of Utah BioChemical Company and Norgood PLC to all his clients' portfolios.

Utah BioChemical is a client of PP and Preston knows that Smithson and Arne Okapuu, President and CEO of Utah BioChemical, have known each other for a long time. In fact, Smithson manages Okapuu's personal portfolio and Utah BioChemical's pension fund.

Smithson explained that while he was on vacation in Britain, he had seen Okapuu in a restaurant dining with the chairman of Norgood PLC. To obtain more information on Norgood, he had gotten in touch with Andrew Jones, an old analyst friend in London. Jones's latest research report on Norgood recommended a "hold" on Norgood stock.

Upon his return to the United States, Smithson conducted his own research on both companies and concluded that both stocks were trading at attractive prices. He also determined that while Norgood was a relatively stable stock, Utah BioChemical had exhibited considerable volatility in the past. Further research on the two companies revealed that they were in complementary businesses. This information, coupled with the fact that he saw Okapuu and the chairman of Norgood dining together, led Smithson to deduce that the two companies might be planning a merger.

Smithson put in a block trade for 50,000 shares of each firm. He reviewed the procedures for allocating shares from a block trade in the firm's compliance manual, but found it to be very vague on the matter. Therefore, he decided to allocate shares based on account size, with the largest accounts receiving shares first, and gradually working down to the smaller accounts. The objectives and constraints of Smithson's clients varied widely.

Utah BioChemical and Norgood PLC soon announced that they were going to merge. The announcement prompted a 40% rise in the share prices of both companies.

Case Results

Smithson complied with Standard V(A) – Diligence and Reasonable Basis as far as his research and decision-making were concerned. He conducted proper research and did not base his decision merely on the fact that Okapuu and the chairman of Norgood were dining together. Smithson did not overhear their conversation, so he neither possessed nor acted on inside information.

Smithson, however, did violate standards relating to the suitability of investments and fair dealing. Furthermore, Preston violated the standard related to the duties of supervisors.

Standard III(C) – Suitability

Norgood was a relatively conservative investment, while Utah BioChemical was a more aggressive investment. Further, Smithson's clients had different objectives and constraints. Therefore, purchasing shares of the two companies for all his clients violated Standard III(C).

Appropriate Actions

Smithson should have allocated shares based on each client's objectives and constraints. If shares have been included in accounts for which they are unsuitable, they should be sold and PP should reimburse any loss.

Standard III(B) – Fair Dealing

Standard III(B) requires members and candidates to deal fairly with all clients. Smithson discriminated against smaller clients by first allocating shares from the block trade to larger clients (presumably at more favorable prices).

Appropriate Actions

PP should form detailed guidelines regarding the trade allocation procedures that should ensure:

- Fairness to clients.
- Timely and efficient execution of trades.
- Accurate records for trade orders.

Standard IV(C) – Responsibilities of Supervisors

PP did not have appropriate procedures described in its compliance manual to prevent improper allocation of shares by Smithson. Preston should have made reasonable efforts to detect and prevent violations of applicable laws, rules, and regulations. It was his responsibility to ensure that compliance policies were clear and well developed.

Appropriate Actions

PP should establish proper trade allocation procedures. Further, there should be a designated compliance officer responsible for ensuring that all policies, procedures, laws, and regulations are being followed by the employees.

Reading 6: Super Selection

LESSON 1: SUPER SELECTION

LOS 6a: Evaluate the practices and policies presented. Vol 1, pp 239–244

LOS 6b: Explain the appropriate action to take in response to conduct that violates the CFA Institute Code of Ethics and Standards of Professional Conduct. Vol 1, pp 239–244

Case Facts

Super Selection (SS) is a rapidly growing, medium-sized money manager. It is registered with the U.S. Securities and Exchange Commission (SEC) to manage both separate accounts and mutual funds. The company has incorporated the CFA Institute Code and Standards into its compliance manual.

Patricia Cuff is the chief financial officer and compliance officer for SS. She is also a member of CFA Institute. Recently, a board member of Atlantis Medical Devices (AMD) informed Patricia of Karen Trader's (a portfolio manager at SS) possible misconduct, so she is now reviewing Trader's brokerage statements. Trader had previously not submitted her statements to Cuff. She had recently bought the stock of AMD for all of her portfolios.

Trader's friend, Josey James, is the president of AMD. Over the past few years James has provided Trader with information regarding attractive investment opportunities in biotech firms. Trader has benefited from that information by placing orders for her personal account as well as for her clients' portfolios. On several occasions, she has purchased a stock for her personal account before purchasing it for her clients' portfolios.

Three years ago James had asked Trader to serve as an outside director for AMD, and Trader had agreed. Due to the uncertain prospects at that time, the company compensated its directors with stock options (which were essentially worthless at the time) instead of cash payments. Trader did not disclose her relationship with AMD to SS.

AMD's sales and earnings are currently at record levels and the company has started paying its directors a quarterly fee of $5,000. Since the market for IPOs was very attractive, AMD's directors recently voted to take the company public. Trader also voted in favor of the IPO as she was in need of cash and wanted to exercise her stock options.

Shortly before the IPO date, James informed Trader that the IPO market had reversed and that valuations of biotech companies were falling. She was concerned that low investor interest may threaten AMD's IPO and asked Trader to commit to purchase a block of AMD shares for her clients' portfolios.

Trader had previously determined that AMD shares were not good investments for her clients' portfolios, but proceeded to purchase the shares for them anyway.

Case Results

Several violations of the Code and Standards have occurred in this scenario. Although she is neither a CFA charterholder nor a member of CFA Institute, Trader is bound by the CFA Institute Code and Standards to the extent that they are incorporated in SS's compliance procedures.

Standard IV(C) – Responsibilities of Supervisors

Although Trader does not report directly to Cuff, as a compliance officer, Cuff is assumed to be the supervisor and, hence, must comply with this standard. Cuff has a responsibility to take appropriate steps to prevent violations of applicable statutes, regulations, and CFA Institute Standards by those under her supervision. Further, she should ensure that the firm's compliance policies are being followed by employees and that any violations are addressed.

Appropriate Actions

Cuff should:

- Report the violations to senior management and work with them to address the misconduct.
- Initiate a thorough investigation of Trader's actions and place limitations on her activities if required.
- If senior management fails to act on this information, Cuff should consider reporting the incident to SS's board of directors and to appropriate regulatory authorities. She may also need to consider resigning from the firm.

Standard VI(A) – Disclosure of Conflicts

Trader violated Standard VI(A) by not disclosing the conflict of interest that arose from her ownership of AMD stock options. She also violated her duty to disclose the compensation (both the stock options and the quarterly $5,000) that she received as a director of AMD to her employer.

Appropriate Actions

Trader should have disclosed all compensation received as an AMD director to SS. Further, she should have disclosed her ownership of AMD stock options and her directorship so that her employer and clients could evaluate the objectivity of her investment advice and actions.

Cuff should ensure that proper disclosure is made to clients. She should also review Trader's clients' accounts and her personal account to determine whether any conflicts have occurred in addition to the IPO violation. Cuff should take appropriate action if other conflicts are discovered.

Standard V(A) – Diligence and Reasonable Basis

Trader had previously determined that AMD shares were not a good investment for her clients' portfolios, but proceeded to purchase the shares for them due to pressure from James. Hence, she violated Standard V(A).

Appropriate Actions

Trader should have conducted due diligence and thorough research on AMD prior to investing in the security for her clients' accounts. She should not have changed her opinion without a reasonable basis. Further, she should have disclosed to her clients her directorship of AMD and ownership of AMD stock options.

Cuff should review investment actions taken for clients by SS employees at least annually.

Standard III(A) – Loyalty, Prudence, and Care

By investing in AMD's stock, Trader placed her interests before those of her clients and, therefore, violated Standard III(A).

Appropriate Actions

Any investment decision should have been taken for the sole benefit of clients.

It is Cuff's responsibility to:

- Thoroughly investigate Trader's activities to determine whether any conflicts have occurred in addition to the IPO violation. Limitations should be placed on Trader's activities if any other conflicts are discovered.
- Implement proper procedures to prevent and detect future occurrences of such violations.
- Follow up to ensure that her recommendations are carried out.

Standard III(C.1) – Suitability

Trader purchased AMD stock for all her clients' accounts without considering their individual needs and circumstances. Therefore, she violated Standard III(C.1).

Appropriate Actions

Trader should have considered clients' needs and circumstances before taking investment action. She should not have purchased the shares for her clients just so that she could liquidate her options.

Cuff should establish at least an annual review to ensure that investment actions taken for clients confirm to their investment policy statements.

Standard VI(B) – Priority of Transactions

Trader carried out personal trades prior to her clients' trades, thereby violating Standard VI(B).

Appropriate Actions

Trader failed to follow her firm's procedures by not reporting trades and brokerage accounts. Even so, it was Cuff's responsibility to ensure that SS's policies and procedures were being followed. Cuff should:

- Investigate Trader's personal transactions and recommend proper sanctions.
- Review her firm's policies and procedures to ensure that they are adequate and determine whether any adjustments are required.
- Carry out any adjustments if necessary.
- Ensure that the firm's employees are periodically informed of the Code and Standards.

Reading 7: Trade Allocation: Fair Dealing and Disclosure

LESSON 1: TRADE ALLOCATION: FAIR DEALING AND DISCLOSURE

LOS 7a: Evaluate trade allocation practices and determine whether they comply with the CFA Institute Standards of Professional Conduct addressing fair dealing and client loyalty. Vol 1, pp 245–247

McKenzie Walker Investment Management

McKenzie Walker was censured and fined by the U.S. Securities and Exchange Commission (SEC) for failing to disclose its trade allocation practices. Further, the company's trade allocation procedures were found to be unsatisfactory.

- The company did not prescribe any objective procedures or formulas for allocating trades among clients or maintain any internal control mechanism to ensure that portfolio managers allocated trades fairly.
- The firm allocated trades on an ad hoc basis according to clients' needs and objectives, the profitability of the trade, the type of client account, and in some instances, the client's relationship with the firm or its principal.
  - The company significantly favored the firm's performance-based fee accounts over its asset-based fee accounts in allocating trades.
  - The firm used profitable equity trades as well as hot initial public offerings (IPOs) to boost the performance of performance-based accounts in general and certain accounts in particular.
  - Asset-based accounts were also allocated all of the trading losses for poorly performing IPOs.
  - Among the performance-based fee accounts, the firm favored certain clients.
- The firm did not appoint anyone to review trade allocation practices to assess whether all accounts received an equitable allocation of trades consistent with their internal objectives.

LOS 7b: Describe appropriate actions to take in response to trade allocation practices that do not adequately respect client interests. Vol 1, pp 245–247

The CFA Institute Standards of Professional Conduct require members not only to disclose trade allocation procedures fully, but also to adopt such trade allocation procedures that treat clients in an equitable manner. This means that members should adhere to allocation procedures that ensure that investment opportunities are allocated to all clients in an appropriate and fair manner.

Members' adherence to trade allocation procedures helps maintain the trust of clients in investment professionals. To ensure that adequate trade allocation practices are followed, the CFA Institute Standards of Practice Handbook suggests that members and their firms should:

- Obtain advance indications of clients' interest for new issues.
- Allocate new shares by client rather than by portfolio manager.
- Adopt a pro rata or similar objective method or formula for allocating trades.
- Treat clients fairly in terms of both trade execution order and price.
- Execute orders timely and efficiently.
- Keep accurate records of trades and client accounts.
- Periodically review all accounts to ensure that all clients are being treated fairly.

Reading 8: Changing Investment Objectives

LESSON 1: CHANGING INVESTMENT OBJECTIVES

LOS 8a: Evaluate the disclosure of investment objectives and basic policies and determine whether they comply with the CFA Institute Standards of Professional Conduct. Vol 1, pp 249–250

The U.S. Securities and Exchange Commission (SEC) sanctioned Mitchell Hutchins Asset Management (Mitchell Hutchins), a registered broker-dealer and investment advisor, for the failure to trade securities for an investment fund within the limits of the stated fund objectives.

Mitchell Hutchins commenced management of the PaineWebber Short-Term U.S. Government Income Fund (the Fund) in 1993, marketing it as a higher-yield and somewhat higher-risk alternative to money market funds and bank certificates of deposit. The prospectus disclosed that the Fund's investment objective was to achieve the highest level of income consistent with preservation of capital and low volatility of net asset value. The appendix to the prospectus also disclosed that the Fund had "no present intention" of investing in certain classes of interest-only (IO) and principal-only (PO) stripped mortgage-backed securities.

Contrary to the Fund's low-volatility investment objective and "no present intention" statement, the Fund's portfolio manager began investing in certain IO and PO securities in the fall of 1993. When interest rates increased sharply in February 1994, the Fund incurred significant losses, performing well below comparable funds.

The SEC found that the fund manager improperly deviated from the investment policy recited in its registration statement without shareholder approval. The SEC also found that Mitchell Hutchins violated the antifraud provisions of the Federal Securities Laws by marketing the Fund as a low-volatility investment, when ultimately it was not.

LOS 8b: Describe appropriate actions needed to ensure adequate disclosure of the investment process. Vol 1, pp 249–250

When managing pooled investment funds, it is extremely important for portfolio managers to adhere to the investment strategy stated in the fund's prospectus. This enables investors:

- To judge the appropriateness and suitability of the fund for themselves; and
- Protects them from style drift and exposure to investment strategies, asset classes, and risks other than those explicitly stated.

A material deviation from the fund's stated objectives, if not approved by shareholders, is a violation of Standard III(C.2) – Suitability, which states that when members and candidates are responsible for managing a portfolio to a specific mandate, strategy, or style, they must only make investment recommendations or take investment actions that are consistent with the stated objectives and constraints of the portfolio.

Further, Standard V(B.1) – Communication with Clients and Prospective Clients states that members and candidates must disclose to clients and prospective clients the basic format and general principles of the investment processes by which securities are selected and portfolios are constructed, and must promptly disclose any changes that might materially affect those processes. Therefore, any deviation from the fund's stated strategy without disclosure to clients and prospective clients amounts to a violation of Standard V(B.1).

In order to abide by the CFA Institute Standards, portfolio managers should take the following steps:

- Determine the client's financial situation, investment experience, and investment objectives. This information should be updated at least annually.
- Adequately disclose to clients the basic format and general principles of the investment processes by which securities are selected and portfolios are constructed.
- Conduct regular internal checks to ensure that portfolio characteristics meet the account's investment mandate, or the stated investment strategy in the case of pooled funds.
- Notify clients and investors of any potential changes in the investment objectives or strategies of the managed portfolios, including the impact of the change on the portfolio, and secure documented authorization of the change in strategy from the client.

STUDY SESSION 3: QUANTITATIVE METHODS FOR VALUATION

READING 9: CORRELATION AND REGRESSION

LESSON 1: CORRECTION ANALYSIS

LOS 9a: Calculate and interpret a sample covariance and a sample correlation coefficient and interpret a scatter plot. Vol 1, pp 256–262

Two of the most popular methods for examining how two sets of data are related are scatter plots and correlation analysis.

Scatter Plots

A scatter plot is a graph that illustrates the relationship between observations of two data series in two dimensions. See Example 1-1.

Example 1-1: Scatter Plot

The following table lists average observations of annual money supply growth and inflation rates for 6 countries over the period 1990 to 2010. Illustrate the data on a scatter plot and comment on the relationship.

Country	Money Supply Growth Rate (X_i)	Inflation Rate (Y_i)
A	0.0685	0.0545
B	0.1160	0.0776
C	0.0575	0.0349
D	0.1050	0.0735
E	0.1250	0.0825
F	0.1350	0.1076

Figure 1-1: Scatter Plot

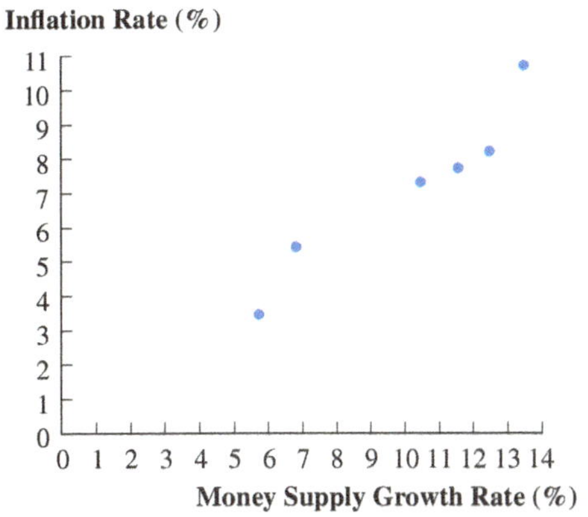

Note that each observation in the scatter plot is represented as a point, and the points are not connected. The scatter plot does not show which point relates to which country; it just plots the observations of both data series as pairs. The data plotted in Figure 1-1 suggests a fairly strong linear relationship with a positive slope for the countries in our sample over the sample period.

Correlation Analysis

Correlation analysis expresses the relationship between two data series in a single number. The correlation coefficient measures how closely two data series are related. More formally, it measures the strength and direction of the linear relationship between two random variables. The correlation coefficient can have a maximum value of +1 and a minimum value of –1.

- A correlation coefficient greater than 0 means that when one variable increases (decreases) the other tends to increase (decrease) as well.
- A correlation coefficient less than 0 means that when one variable increases (decreases) the other tends to decrease (increase).
- A correlation coefficient of 0 indicates that no linear relation exists between the two variables.

Figures 1-2, 1-3, and 1-4 illustrate the scatter plots for data sets with different correlations.

Figure 1-2: Scatter Plot of Variables with Correlation of +1

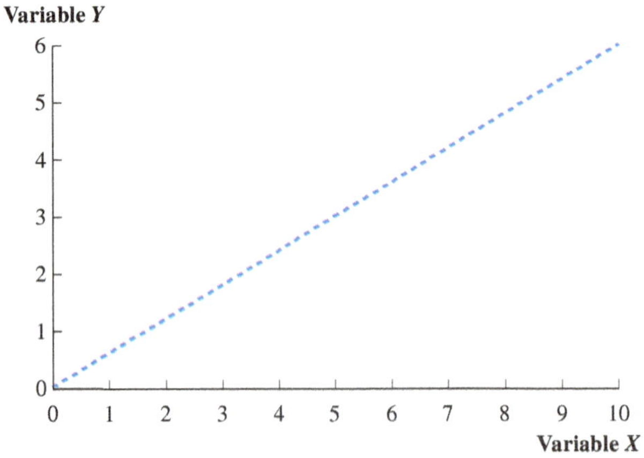

Analysis:

- Note that all the points on the scatter plot illustrating the relationship between the two variables lie along a straight line.
- The slope (gradient) of the line equals +0.6, which means that whenever the independent variable (X) increases by 1 unit, the dependent variable (Y) *increases* by 0.6 units.
- If the slope of the line (on which all the data points lie) were different (from +0.6), but positive, the correlation between the two variables would equal +1 as long as the points lie on a straight line.

Figure 1-3: Scatter Plot of Variables with Correlation of –1

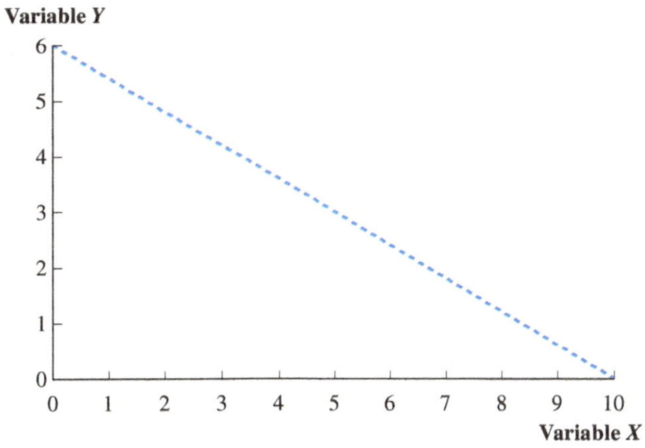

Analysis:

- Note that all the points on the scatter plot illustrating the relationship between the two variables lie along a straight line.
- The slope (gradient) of the line equals –0.6, which means that whenever the independent variable (*X*) increases by 1 unit, the dependent variable (*Y*) *decreases* by 0.6 units.
- If the slope of the line (on which all the data points lie) were different (from –0.6) but negative, the correlation between the two variables would equal –1 as long as all the points lie on a straight line.

Figure 1-4: Scatter Plot of Variables with Correlation of 0

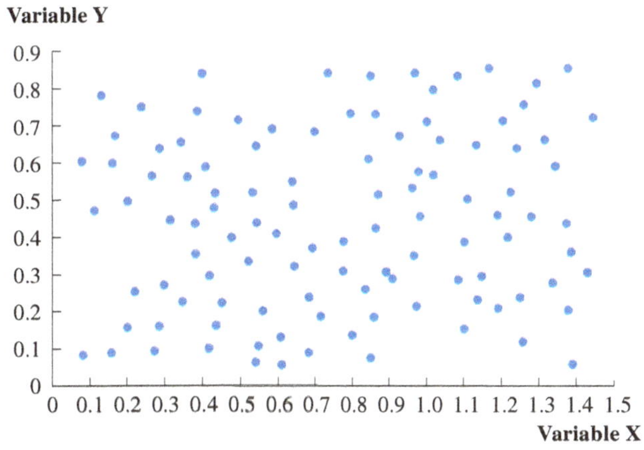

Analysis:

- Note that the two variables exhibit no linear relation.
- The value of the independent variable (*X*) tells us nothing about the value of the dependent variable (*Y*).

Calculating and Interpreting the Correlation Coefficient

In order to calculate the correlation coefficient, we first need to calculate covariance. Covariance is a similar concept to variance. The difference lies in the fact that variance measures how a random variable varies with itself, while covariance measures how a random variable varies with another random variable.

Properties of Covariance

- Covariance is symmetric, that is, $\text{Cov}(X, Y) = \text{Cov}(Y, X)$.
- The covariance of X with itself, $\text{Cov}(X, X)$, equals the variance of X, $\text{Var}(X)$.

Interpreting the Covariance

- Basically, covariance measures the nature of the relationship between two variables.
- When the covariance between two variables is *negative,* it means that they tend to move in opposite directions.
- When the covariance between two variables is *positive,* it means that they tend to move in the same direction.
- The covariance between two variables equals zero if they are not related.

Sample covariance is calculated as:

$$\text{Sample covariance} = \text{Cov}(X,Y) = \sum_{i=1}^{n}(X_i - \overline{X})(Y_i - \overline{Y})/(n-1)$$

where:
n = sample size
X_i = ith observation of Variable X
$\overline{X}$ = mean observation of Variable X
Y_i = ith observation of Variable Y
$\overline{Y}$ = mean observation of Variable Y

The numerical value of sample covariance is not very meaningful as it is presented in terms of units squared, and can range from negative infinity to positive infinity. To circumvent these problems, the covariance is standardized by dividing it by the product of the standard deviations of the two variables. This standardized measure is known as the sample correlation coefficient (denoted by r) and is easy to interpret as it always lies between −1 and +1, and has no unit of measurement attached. See Example 1-2.

$$\text{Sample correlation coefficient} = r = \frac{\text{Cov}(X,Y)}{s_X s_Y}$$

$$\text{Sample variance} = s_X^2 = \sum_{i=1}^{n}(X_i - \bar{X})^2/(n-1)$$

$$\text{Sample standard deviation} = s_X = \sqrt{s_X^2}$$

Example 1-2: Calculating the Correlation Coefficient

Using the money supply growth and inflation data from 1990 to 2010 for the 6 countries in Example 1-1, calculate the covariance and the correlation coefficient.

Solution:

Country	Money Supply Growth Rate (X_i)	Inflation Rate (Y_i)	Cross Product $(X_i - \bar{X})(Y_i - \bar{Y})$	Squared Deviations $(X_i - \bar{X})^2$	Squared Deviations $(Y_i - \bar{Y})^2$
A	0.0685	0.0545	0.000564	0.001067	0.000298
B	0.116	0.0776	0.000087	0.00022	0.000034
C	0.0575	0.0349	0.00161	0.001907	0.001359
D	0.105	0.0735	0.000007	0.000015	0.000003
E	0.125	0.0825	0.000256	0.000568	0.000115
F	0.135	0.1076	0.001212	0.001145	0.001284
Sum	0.607	0.4306	0.003735	0.004921	0.003094
Average	0.1012	0.0718			
Covariance			0.000747		
Variance				0.000984	0.000619
Std. Dev (s)				0.031373	0.024874

Illustrations of Calculations

Covariance = Sum of cross products / n – 1 = 0.003735/5 = 0.000747

Var (X) = Sum of squared deviations from the sample mean / n – 1 = 0.004921/5 = 0.000984

Var (Y) = Sum of squared deviations from the sample mean / n – 1 = 0.003094/5 = 0.000619

$$\textbf{Correlation coefficient} = r = \frac{\text{Cov}(X,Y)}{s_X s_Y} = \frac{0.000747}{(0.031373)(0.024874)} = 0.9573 \text{ or } 95.73\%$$

The correlation coefficient of 0.9573 suggests that over the period, a strong linear relationship exists between the money supply growth rate and the inflation rate for the countries in the sample.

r valid only if Var X, Y and μ is constant

Note that computed correlation coefficients are only valid if the means and variances of X and Y, as well as the covariance of X and Y, are finite and constant.

LOS 9b: Describe limitations to correlation analysis. Vol 1, pp 262–265

Limitations of Correlation Analysis

- It is important to remember that the correlation is a measure of linear association. Two variables can be connected through a very strong nonlinear relation and still exhibit low correlation. For example, the equation $Y = 10 + 3X$ represents a linear relationship. However, two variables may be perfectly linked by a nonlinear equation, for example, $Y = (5 + X)^2$ but their correlation coefficient may still be close to 0.
- Correlation may be an unreliable measure when there are outliers in one or both of the series. Outliers are a small number of observations that are markedly numerically different from the rest of the observations in the sample. Analysts must evaluate whether outliers represent relevant information about the association between the variables (news) and therefore, should be included in the analysis, or whether they do not contain information relevant to the analysis (noise) and should be excluded.
- Correlation does not imply causation. Even if two variables exhibit high correlation, it does not mean that certain values of one variable bring about the occurrence of certain values of the other.
- Correlations may be spurious in that they may highlight relationships that are misleading. For example, a study may highlight a statistically significant relationship between the number of snowy days in December and stock market performance. This relationship obviously has no economic explanation. The term spurious correlation is used to refer to relationships where:
  - Correlation reflects chance relationships in a data set.
  - Correlation is induced by a calculation that mixes the two variables with a third.
  - Correlation between two variables arises from both the variables being directly related to a third variable.

LOS 9c: Formulate a test of the hypothesis that the population correlation coefficient equals zero and determine whether the hypothesis is rejected at a given level of significance. Vol 1, pp 273–276

Testing the Significance of the Correlation Coefficient

Hypothesis tests allow us to evaluate whether apparent relationships between variables are caused by chance. If the relationship is not the result of chance, the parameters of the relationship can be used to make predictions about one variable based on the other. Let's go back to Example 1-2, where we calculated that the correlation coefficient between the money supply growth rate and inflation rate was 0.9573. This number seems pretty high, but is it statistically different from zero?

> In order to use the *t*-test, we assume that the two populations are normally distributed.
>
> ρ represents the population correlation.

To test whether the correlation between two variables is significantly different from zero the hypotheses are structured as follows:

$$H_0: \rho = 0$$
$$H_a: \rho \neq 0$$

Note: This would be a two-tailed *t*-test with $n - 2$ degrees of freedom.

The test statistic is calculated as:

$$\text{Test-stat} = t = \frac{r\sqrt{n-2}}{\sqrt{1-r^2}}$$

where:
n = Number of observations
r = Sample correlation

The decision rule for the test is that we reject H_0 if t-stat > $+t_{crit}$ or if t-stat < $-t_{crit}$

From the expression for the test-statistic above, notice that the value of sample correlation, r, required to reject the null hypothesis, decreases as sample size, n, increases:

- As n increases, the degrees of freedom also increase, which results in the absolute critical value for the test (t_{crit}) falling and the rejection region for the hypothesis test increasing in size.
- The absolute value of the numerator (in calculating the test statistic) increases with higher values of n, which results in higher t-values. This increases the likelihood of the test statistic exceeding the absolute value of t_{crit} and therefore, increases the chances of rejecting the null hypothesis.

See Example 1-3.

Example 1-3: Testing the Correlation between Money Supply Growth and Inflation

Based on the data provided in Example 1-1, we determined that the correlation coefficient between money supply growth and inflation during the period 1990 to 2010 for the six countries studied was 0.9573. Test the null hypothesis that the true population correlation coefficient equals 0 at the 5% significant level.

Solution:

$$\text{Test statistic} = \frac{0.9573 \times \sqrt{6-2}}{\sqrt{1-0.9573^2}} = 6.623$$

Degrees of freedom = 6 − 2 = 4

The critical t-values for a two-tailed test at the 5% significance level (2.5% in each tail) and 4 degrees of freedom are −2.776 and +2.776.

Since the test statistic (6.623) is greater than the upper critical value (+2.776) we can reject the null hypothesis of no correlation at the 5% significance level.

From the additional examples in the CFA Program Curriculum (Examples 3-4 and 4-1) you should understand the takeaways listed below. If you understand the math behind the computation of the test statistic, and the determination of the rejection region for hypothesis tests, you should be able to digest the following points quite comfortably:

- All other factors constant, a false null hypothesis (H_0: $\rho = 0$) is more likely to be rejected as we increase the sample size due to (1) lower and lower absolute values of t_{crit} and (2) higher absolute values of *t* test-stats.
- The smaller the size of the sample, the greater the value of sample correlation required to reject the null hypothesis of zero correlation (in order to make the value of the test statistic sufficiently large so that it exceeds the absolute value of t_{crit} at the given level of significance).
- When the relation between two variables is very strong, a false null hypothesis (H_0: $\rho = 0$) may be rejected with a relatively small sample size (as *r* would be sufficiently large to push the test-statistic beyond the absolute value of t_{crit}). Note that this is the case in Example 1-3.
- With large sample sizes, even relatively small correlation coefficients can be significantly different from zero (as a high value of *n* increases the absolute value of the test statistic and reduces the absolute value of the critical value for the hypothesis test).

Uses of Correlation Analysis

Correlation analysis is used for:

- Investment analysis (e.g., evaluating the accuracy of inflation forecasts in order to apply the forecasts in predicting asset prices).
- Identifying appropriate benchmarks in the evaluation of portfolio manager performance.
- Identifying appropriate avenues for effective diversification of investment portfolios.
- Evaluating the appropriateness of using other measures (e.g., net income) as proxies for cash flow in financial statement analysis.

LESSON 2: LINEAR REGRESSION

LOS 9d: Distinguish between the dependent and independent variables in a linear regression. **Vol 1, pp 276–280**

Linear Regression with One Independent Variable

> Another way to look at simple linear regression is that it aims to explain the variation in the dependent variable in terms of the variation in the independent variable. Note that variation refers to the extent that a variable deviates from its mean value. Do not confuse variation with variance.

Linear regression is used to summarize the relationship between two variables that are linearly related. It is used to make predictions about a dependent variable, *Y* (also known as the explained variable, endogenous variable, and predicted variable) using an independent variable, *X* (also known as the explanatory variable, exogenous variable, and predicting variable), to test hypotheses regarding the relation between the two variables, and to evaluate the strength of the relationship between them. The dependent variable is the variable whose variation we are seeking to explain, while the independent variable is the variable that is used to explain the variation in the dependent variable.

difference between y_i to $\bar{y}$

The following linear regression model describes the relation between the dependent and the independent variables.

$$\text{Regression model equation} = Y_i = b_0 + b_1 X_i + \varepsilon_i,\ i = 1, \ldots, n$$

where:

- b_1 and b_0 are the regression coefficients.
- b_1 is the slope coefficient.
- b_0 is the intercept term.
- ε is the error term that represents the variation in the dependent variable that is not explained by the independent variable.

Based on this model, the regression process estimates the line of best fit for the data in the sample. The regression line takes the following form:

$$\text{Regression line equation} = \hat{Y}_i = \hat{b}_0 + \hat{b}_1 X_i,\ i = 1, \ldots, n$$

Linear regression computes the line of best fit that minimizes the sum of the squared regression residuals (the squared vertical distances between actual observations of the dependent variable and the regression line). What this means is that it looks to obtain estimates, $\hat{b}_0$ and $\hat{b}_1$, for b_0 and b_1 respectively, that minimize the sum of the squared differences between the actual values of Y, Y_i, and the predicted values of Y, $\hat{Y}_i$, according to the regression equation ($\hat{Y}_i = \hat{b}_0 + \hat{b}_1 X_i$). Therefore, linear regression looks to minimize the expression:

Hats over the symbols for regression coefficients indicate estimated values. Note that it is these estimates that are used to conduct hypothesis tests and to make predictions about the dependent variable.

regression wants to minimize SSE

$$\sum_{i=1}^{n} [Y_i - (\hat{b}_0 + \hat{b}_1 X_i)]^2$$

→ SSE

where:
Y_i = Actual value of the dependent variable
$\hat{b}_0 + \hat{b}_1 X_i$ = Predicted value of dependent variable

The sum of the squared differences between actual and predicted values of Y is known as the sum of squared errors, or SSE.

LOS 9e: Describe the assumptions underlying linear regression and interpret regression coefficients. Vol 1, pp 280–281

Assumptions of the Linear Regression Model

The following six assumptions are known as the classic normal linear regression assumptions (see Example 2-1):

1. The relationship between the dependent variable (Y) and the independent variable (X) is linear in the parameters, b_1 and b_0. This means that b_1 and b_0 are raised to the first power only and neither of them is multiplied or divided by another regression parameter.
2. The independent variable, X, is not random.
3. The expected value of the error term is zero: $E(\varepsilon) = 0$.
4. The variance of the error term is constant for all observations ($E(\varepsilon_i^2) = \sigma_\varepsilon^2, i = 1, \ldots, n$). This is known as the homoskedasticity assumption.
5. The error term is uncorrelated across observations.
6. The error term is normally distributed.

Example 2-1: Linear Regression

For the money supply growth and inflation rate data that we have been working with in this reading, determine the slope coefficient and the intercept term of a simple linear regression using money supply growth as the independent variable and the inflation rate as the dependent variable. The data provided below is excerpted from Example 1-2:

Country	Money Supply Growth Rate (X_i)	Inflation Rate (Y_i)	Cross Product $(X_i - \bar{X})(Y_i - \bar{Y})$	Squared Deviations $(X_i - \bar{X})^2$	Squared Deviations $(Y_i - \bar{Y})^2$
Sum	0.607	0.4306	0.003735	0.004921	0.003094
Average	0.1012	0.0718			
Covariance			0.000747		
Variance				0.000984	0.000619
Std. Dev (s)				0.031373	0.024874

Inflation = $b_0 + b_1 \times$ money supply growth $+ \varepsilon$.

Solution:

The regression equation can be stated as:

Inflation rate $= b_0 + b_1$ (Money supply growth rate) $+ \varepsilon$

Typically, regression software is used to determine the regression coefficients. However, for illustrative purposes we perform the calculations to make the source of the numbers clear.

Slope coefficient $= \hat{b}_1 = \text{Cov}(X, Y) / \text{Var}(X) = 0.000747/0.000984 = 0.7591$

Note that the slope coefficient can be computed in this manner **only** when there is one independent variable.

In a linear regression, the regression line passes through the coordinates corresponding to the mean values of the independent and dependent variables. Using the mean values for money supply growth ($\bar{X} = 0.1012$) and the inflation rate ($\bar{Y} = 0.0718$) we can compute the intercept term as:

$$\bar{Y} = \hat{b}_0 + \hat{b}_1 \bar{X}$$

$$\hat{b}_0 = 0.0718 - (0.7591)(0.1012) = -0.005$$

Therefore, the relationship between the money supply growth rate and the inflation rate for our sample data can be expressed as:

Inflation rate = −0.005 + 0.7591(Money supply growth rate)

The regression equation implies that:

- For every 1-percentage-point increase in the money supply growth rate, the inflation rate is predicted to increase by 0.7591 percentage points. The slope coefficient ($\hat{b}_1$) is interpreted as the estimated change in the dependent variable for a 1-unit change in the independent variable.
- If the money supply growth rate in a country equals 0, the inflation rate in the country will be −0.5%. The intercept ($\hat{b}_0$) is an estimate of the dependent variable when the independent variable equals 0.

Figure 2-1 illustrates the regression line (blue line) along with the scatter plot of the actual sample data (blue dots). Using Country F as an example, we also illustrate the difference between the actual observation of the inflation rate in Country F, and the predicted value of inflation (according to the regression model) in Country F.

Figure 2-1: Regression Line and Scatter Plot

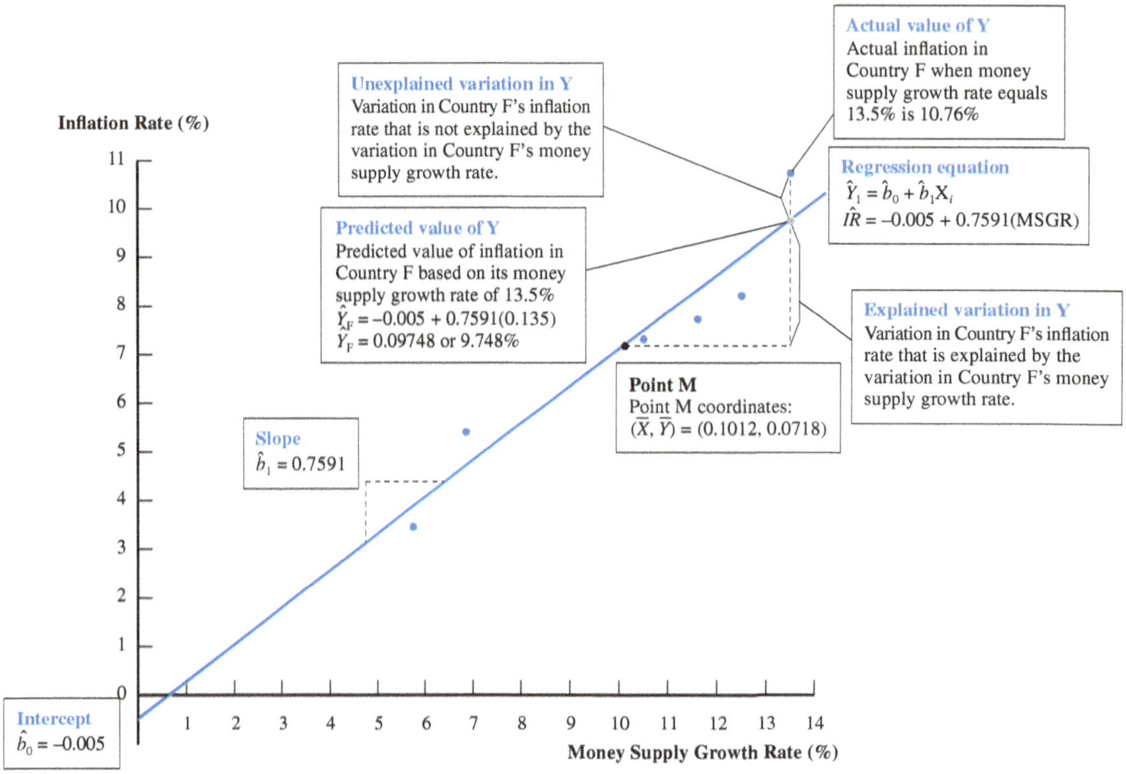

To determine the importance of the independent variable in the regression in explaining the variation in the dependent variable, we need to perform hypothesis tests or create confidence intervals to evaluate the statistical significance of the slope coefficient. Just looking at the magnitude of the slope coefficient does not tell us anything about the importance of the independent variable in explaining the variation in the dependent variable.

LESSON 3: THE STANDARD ERROR OF ESTIMATE, COEFFICIENT OF DETERMINATION, HYPOTHESIS TESTING, AND ANOVA

LOS 9f: Calculate and interpret the standard error of estimate, the coefficient of determination, and a confidence interval for a regression coefficient.

Vol 1, pp 282–287

LOS 9g: Formulate a null and alternative hypothesis about a population value of a regression coefficient and determine the appropriate test statistic and whether the null hypothesis is rejected at a given level of significance. Vol 1, pp 287–295

The Standard Error of Estimate

The standard error of estimate (SEE), also known as the standard error of the regression, is used to measure how well a regression model captures the relationship between the two variables. It indicates how well the regression line "fits" the sample data and is used to determine how certain we can be about a particular prediction of the dependent variable ($\hat{Y}_i$) based on a regression equation. A good way to look at the SEE is that it basically measures the standard deviation of the residual term ($\hat{\varepsilon}_i$) in the regression. At the risk of stating the obvious, the smaller the standard deviation of the residual term (the smaller the standard error of estimate), the more accurate the predictions based on the model. See Figure 2-1.

The formula for the SEE for a linear regression with one independent variable is:

$$\text{SEE} = \left(\frac{\sum_{i=1}^{n} (Y_i - \hat{b}_0 - \hat{b}_1 X_i)^2}{n-2} \right)^{1/2} = \left(\frac{\sum_{i=1}^{n} (\hat{\varepsilon}_i)^2}{n-2} \right)^{1/2} = \left(\frac{\text{SSE}}{n-2} \right)^{1/2}$$

Note:

- In the numerator of the SEE equation we are essentially calculating the sum of the squared differences between actual and predicted (based on the regression equation) values of the dependent variable.
- We divide the numerator by $n - 2$ (degrees of freedom) to ensure that the estimate of SEE is unbiased.

The squared residuals in the last column can also be denoted by $(\hat{\varepsilon}_i)^2$.

The sum of the squared residuals (0.000259) is known as sum of squared errors (SSE) or sum of squared residuals.

Example 3-1: Computing the Standard Error of Estimate

Based on the regression equation: Inflation rate = –0.005 + 0.7591(Money supply growth rate) compute the standard error of estimate (SEE) for the regression.

Country	Money Supply Growth Rate (X_i)	Inflation Rate (Y_i)	Predicted Inflation Rate $(\hat{Y}_i)$	Regression Residual $(Y_i - \hat{Y}_i)$	Squared Residual $(Y_i - \hat{Y}_i)^2$
A	0.0685	0.0545	0.0470	0.0075	0.000057
B	0.1160	0.0776	0.0830	–0.0054	0.000029
C	0.0575	0.0349	0.0386	–0.0037	0.000014
D	0.1050	0.0735	0.0747	–0.0012	0.000001
E	0.1250	0.0825	0.0899	–0.0074	0.000054
F	0.1350	0.1076	0.0974	0.0102	0.000103
Sum					0.000259

Candidates get VERY confused between SEE and SSE so we have introduced both of them here. SEE is the standard deviation of the error term in the regression while SSE equals the sum of the squared residuals in the regression. SSE (as you will see later in the reading) is used to calculate R^2 and the *F*-stat for the regression. Also note that the two are related by the following equation: $SEE = (SSE/n - 2)^{0.5}$

Just to illustrate how we obtained the values in this table, let's perform the calculations for Country A:

Predicted inflation rate = –0.005 + 0.7591(0.0685) = 0.046998
Regression residual = 0.0545 – 0.046998 = 0.0075
Squared residual = 0.0075^2 = 0.000057

From the table (by aggregating the values in the last column) we obtain a figure of 0.000259 as the sum of the squared residuals (SSE). This figure is then plugged into the SEE formula to determine the standard error of estimate.

$$SEE = \left(\frac{0.000259}{6-2}\right)^{1/2} = 0.00805 \text{ or } 0.8\%$$

The Coefficient of Determination

The coefficient of determination (R^2) tells us how well the independent variable explains the variation in the dependent variable. It measures the fraction of the total variation in the dependent variable that is explained by the independent variable. The coefficient of determination can be calculated in two ways:

> Note that the square root of the coefficient of determination in a one-independent variable linear regression, after attaching the sign of the estimated slope coefficient, gives the correlation coefficient for the regression.

1. $R^2 = (r)^2$
   For a linear regression with only one independent variable, the coefficient of determination (R^2) can be calculated by squaring the correlation coefficient (r). In Example 1-2, we calculated the correlation coefficient between inflation rates and money supply growth from 1990 to 2010 to be 0.9573. Thus, the coefficient of determination for the regression equals 0.9573^2 or 0.9164. What this means is that variation in money supply growth rate explains about 91.64% of the variation in inflation rates across the six countries from 1990–2010.
2. The following method can be used to calculate the coefficient of determination for regressions with one or more independent variables.
   - The total variation in the dependent variable (sum of squared deviations of observed values of Y from the average value of Y) denoted by $\sum_{i=1}^{n}(Y_i - \bar{Y})^2$ can be broken down into the variation explained by the independent variable(s) and the variation that remains unexplained by the independent variable(s).
   - The variation in the dependent variable that cannot be explained by the independent variable(s) (sum of squared deviations of actual values of Y from the values predicted by the regression equation) denoted by $\sum_{i=1}^{n}(Y_i - \hat{Y}_i)^2$ is known as unexplained variation.
   - The variation in the dependent variable that can be explained by the independent variable(s) (sum of squared deviations of predicted values of Y from the average value of Y) denoted by $\sum_{i=1}^{n}(\hat{Y}_i - \bar{Y})^2$ is known as explained variation.

The important thing to note is that R^2 measures the percentage of the total variation in the dependent variable that can be explained by the variation in the independent variable. See Example 3-2.

$$\text{Total variation} = \text{Unexplained variation} + \text{Explained variation}$$

$$R^2 = \frac{\text{Explained variation}}{\text{Total variation}} = \frac{\text{Total variation} - \text{Unexplained variation}}{\text{Total variation}}$$

$$= 1 - \frac{\text{Unexplained variation}}{\text{Total variation}}$$

Example 3-2: Calculating the Coefficient of Determination

From Example 3-1 we know that the unexplained variation (sum of squared differences between observed and predicted values of the dependent variable) for our regression involving money supply growth rates and inflation rates equals 0.000259 (SSE). Calculate the total variation in inflation rates and then compute the coefficient of determination for the regression.

Solution:

The computation of the total variation in the dependent variable (inflation rates) is illustrated in the table below:

Country	Money Supply Growth Rate (X_i)	Inflation Rate (Y_i)	Deviation from Mean ($Y_i - \bar{Y}$)	Squared Deviation $(Y_i - \bar{Y})^2$
A	0.0685	0.0545	–0.0173	0.000298
B	0.1160	0.0776	0.0058	0.000034
C	0.0575	0.0349	–0.0369	0.001359
D	0.1050	0.0735	0.0017	0.000003
E	0.1250	0.0825	0.0107	0.000115
F	0.1350	0.1076	0.0358	0.001284
	Average	$(\bar{Y}) = 0.0718$	Sum	0.003094

Just to illustrate how we obtained the values in this table, let's perform the calculations for Country A:

Deviation from mean = 0.0545 – 0.0718 = –0.0173
Squared deviation = -0.0173^2 = 0.000298

From the table (by aggregating the values in the last column) we obtain a figure of 0.003094 as the sum of the squared deviations of observed values of the dependent variable from their average value. This figure represents the total variation in the dependent variable, and given the unexplained variation in the dependent variable (SSE = 0.000259) can be used to calculate the coefficient of determination for the regression as follows:

$$R^2 = \frac{\text{Total variation} - \text{Unexplained variation}}{\text{Total variation}} = \frac{0.003094 - 0.000259}{0.003094} = 0.9162 \text{ or } 91.62\%$$

Hypothesis Tests on Regression Coefficients

Hypothesis tests on the population values of the slope coefficient and the intercept have important practical applications. For example, when using the capital asset pricing model (CAPM) to price a risky asset, ABC Stock, a hypothesis test may be used to test the belief that ABC Stock has a market-average level of systematic risk (beta = 1).

CAPM: $R_{ABC} = R_F + \beta_{ABC}(R_M - R_F)$

If we hypothesize that ABC Stock has a beta of 1, and therefore its required return in excess of the risk-free rate is the same as the market's required excess return (equity market risk premium), the regression may be structured as follows (see Example 3-3):

$$R_{ABC} - R_F = \alpha + \beta_{ABC}(R_M - R_F) + \varepsilon$$

- The intercept term for the regression, b_0, is α.
- The slope coefficient for the regression, b_1, is β_{ABC}.

Example 3-3: Hypothesis Tests on Regression Coefficients

Suppose we perform a regression on monthly returns data from January 2006 until December 2010 (60 months) for ABC Stock and the market index. We want to test the null hypothesis that the beta for ABC Stock equals 1 to determine whether the stock has the same required return premium as the market as a whole. The results of the regression are provided below:

Regression Statistics

Multiple R	0.5864
R-squared	0.3439
Standard error of estimate	0.0404
Observations	60

	Coefficients	**Standard Error**	***t*-Statistic**
Alpha	0.0041	0.0135	0.3037
Beta	1.1558	0.2096	5.5135

The null and alternative hypotheses for this test are structured as follows:

H_0: $\beta_{ABC} = 1$
H_a: $\beta_{ABC} \neq 1$

Note that this is a two-tailed test as the null hypothesis has the "=" sign.

The overall market has a Beta of 1.

The test statistic for hypothesis tests on the slope coefficient is calculated as:

$$\text{Test statistic} = t = \frac{\hat{b}_1 - b_1}{s_{\hat{b}_1}}$$

From the regression results, the estimate of the slope coefficient $\hat{\beta}_{ABC}$ equals 1.1558, while the estimated standard error of the slope coefficient, $s_{\hat{\beta}_{ABC}}$ equals 0.2096. Therefore, the test statistic equals (1.1558 – 1)/0.2096 = 0.7433.

To determine the critical *t*-values for the hypothesis test we need to ascertain the degrees of freedom and specify a level of significance for the test. The degrees of freedom are calculated as the number of observations (*n*) in the sample minus the number of parameters being estimated in the regression. In this example, we are estimating two parameters (coefficient on the independent variable and the intercept term). Therefore, the degrees of freedom equal 60 – 2 = 58. We shall assume a 5% significance level for this hypothesis test.

With 58 degrees of freedom, and a 5% level of significance, the critical *t*-values for this two-tailed hypothesis test are –2.00 and +2.00.

Comparing the test statistic (0.7433) to the upper critical value (2.00) we fail to reject the null hypothesis that ABC Stock has the same level of systematic risk (beta) as the overall market.

It is important to note that the *t*-statistic associated with the slope coefficient, beta, in the regression results is 5.5135. This *t*-value is computed as the slope coefficient divided by its standard error. It basically represents the test statistic were the null hypothesis structured to test whether β_{ABC} equals 0 (not 1 as is the case in our example). Based on this number (t = 5.5135) we would be able to reject the null hypothesis that $\beta_{ABC} = 0$ as it exceeds the critical *t*-value (2.00).

Notice that the coefficient of determination (R^2) in this regression is only 0.3439. This suggests that only 34.39% of the variation in the excess returns on ABC Stock can be explained by excess returns on the overall market. The remaining 65% of ABC's excess returns can be attributed to firm-specific factors.

We can also use the results of the regression to conduct hypothesis tests on the intercept term of the regression. In this example, the intercept term represents ABC Stock's excess return (alpha). Based on the test statistic provided in the regression results (0.3037) we fail to reject the null hypothesis and conclude that the excess return on ABC Stock was not significantly different from zero over the sample period.

Confidence Intervals for Regression Coefficients

A confidence interval is a range of values within which we believe the true population parameter (e.g., b_1) lies, with a certain degree of confidence (1 – α). Let's work with the same example that we just used to perform the hypothesis test on ABC Stock's beta to illustrate how confidence intervals are computed and interpreted.

According to the results of the regression in Example 3-3, the estimate of the slope coefficient ($\hat{b}_1$) is 1.1558 with a standard error ($s_{\hat{b}_1}$) of 0.2096. The hypothesized value of the population parameter (b_1) is 1 (the market's average slope coefficient or beta). Once again, we use a 5% significance level, or a 95% level of confidence to evaluate our hypothesis.

A confidence interval spans the range from $\hat{b}_1 - t_c\ s_{\hat{b}_1}$ to $\hat{b}_1 + t_c\ s_{\hat{b}_1}$

The critical value depends on the degrees of freedom for the test. The degrees of freedom when there are 60 observations equal 58 (calculated as n – 2). Given a significance level of 0.05, we determine that the critical t-value is 2.00. Therefore, our 95% confidence interval is calculated as:

$$\hat{b}_1 \pm t_c s_{\hat{b}_1} = 1.1558 \pm (2.00)(0.2096) = 0.7366 \text{ to } 1.575$$

Since we are testing whether b_1 equals 1, and this hypothesized value does lie within the computed interval, we fail to reject the null hypothesis. We can be 95% confident that ABC Stock's beta equals 1.

As you can see, we reach the same conclusion regarding our hypothesis using a hypothesis test and using confidence intervals. Confidence intervals and hypothesis test are linked by critical values.

- In a confidence interval, we aim to determine whether the hypothesized value of the population parameter, slope coefficient ($\beta_{ABC} = 1$) lies within a computed interval with a particular degree of confidence ($1-\alpha$). Here the interval represents the "fail-to-reject-the-null region" and is based around, or centered on, the estimated parameter value from sample data ($\hat{\beta}_{ABC} = 1.1558$).
- In a hypothesis test, we examine whether the estimated value of the parameter from sample data ($\hat{\beta}_{ABC} = 1.1558$) lies in the rejection region (i.e., outside an interval) or in the fail-to-reject-the-null region (i.e., within the interval) at a particular level of significance (α). Here the interval is based around, or centered on the hypothesized value of the population parameter ($\beta_{ABC} = 1$).

Some Important Points Relating to Hypothesis Tests on Regression Coefficients

- The choice of significance level is a matter of judgment. A lower level of significance increases the absolute value of t_{crit} resulting in a wider confidence interval and a lower likelihood of rejecting the null hypothesis.
- Increasing the significance level increases the probability of a Type I error, but decreases the probability of a Type II error.
- The p-value is the lowest level of significance at which the null hypothesis can be rejected. Note that the p-value that is generally reported by statistical software packages as part of the regression results applies to a null hypothesis that the true population parameter equals zero, versus an alternative hypothesis that the true population parameter does not equal zero (given the estimated coefficient and standard error of the coefficient). For example, a p-value of 0.007 tells us that we can reject the null hypothesis that the true population parameter equals zero at the 0.7% level of significance (or with a 99.3% level of confidence).
- The smaller the standard error of an estimated parameter, the stronger the results of the regression and the narrower the resulting confidence intervals.

LOS 9j: Describe the use of analysis of variance (ANOVA) in regression analysis, interpret ANOVA results, and calculate and interpret the *F*-statistic.

Vol 1, pp 295–298

Analysis of variance (ANOVA) is a statistical procedure that is used to determine the usefulness of the independent variable(s) in explaining the variation in the dependent variable. An important part of ANOVA is the *F*-test, which tests whether all the slope coefficients in the regression are equal to zero. Since we are working with linear regression with one independent variable in this reading, the *F*-test basically tests a null hypothesis of $b_1 = 0$ versus an alternate of $b_1 \neq 0$.

In order to calculate the *F*-stat (to perform the *F*-test) we need the following information:

- The total number of observations (*n*).
- The total number of parameters to be estimated. In a one-independent variable regression, there are two parameters that are estimated: the intercept term and the slope coefficient.
- The regression sum of squares (RSS)—the amount of variation in the dependent variable that is explained by the independent variable. It equals the sum of the squared deviations of predicted values of the dependent variable (based on the regression equation) from the mean value of the dependent variable.

$$RSS = \sum_{i=1}^{n} (\hat{Y}_i - \bar{Y})^2 \rightarrow \text{Explained variation}$$

Note that total variation in the dependent variable is the sum of SSE and RSS. It is calculated as the sum of the squared deviations of the actual values of the dependent variable from the mean value of the dependent variable.

$$\sum_{i=1}^{n} (Y_i - \bar{Y})^2$$

- The sum of squared errors or residuals (SSE)—the amount of variation in the dependent variable that cannot be explained by the independent variable. It equals the sum of the squared deviations of actual values of the dependent variable from their predicted values (based on the regression equation).

$$SSE = \sum_{i=1}^{n} (Y_i - \hat{Y}_i)^2 \rightarrow \text{Unexplained variation}$$

A typical ANOVA table for a simple linear regression is presented in Figure 3-1.

Figure 3-1: ANOVA Table

Source of Variation	Degrees of Freedom	Sum of Squares	Mean Sum of Squares
Regression (explained)	k	RSS	$MSR = \frac{RSS}{k} = \frac{RSS}{1} = RSS$
Error (unexplained)	$n - (k + 1)$	SSE	$MSE = \frac{SSE}{n-2}$
Total	$\mathbf{n - 1}$	**SST**	

k = the number of slope coefficients in the regression.

Figure 3-2 illustrates the components of total variation in the dependent variable.

Figure 3-2: Components of Total Variation

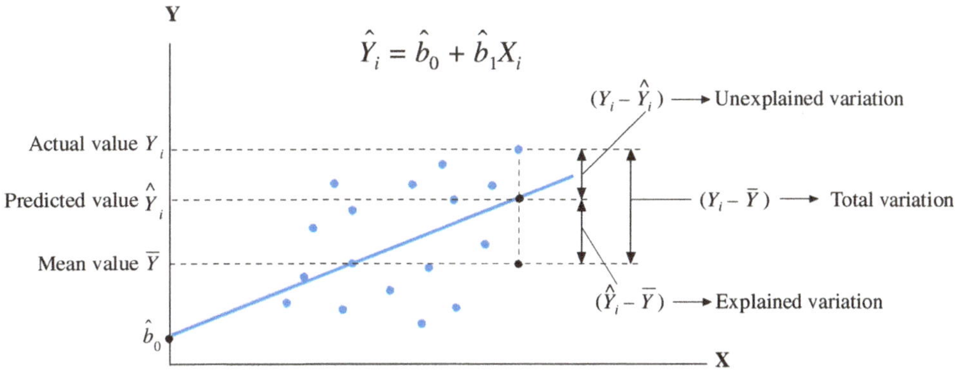

Given all the pieces of information mentioned on the previous page, the F-stat is calculated as follows:

$$F\text{-stat} = \frac{\text{MSR}}{\text{MSE}}$$

where:

$$\text{MSR} = \frac{\text{RSS}}{\text{k}}$$

$$\text{MSE} = \frac{\text{SSE}}{(n-2)}$$

k = Number of slope parameters estimated in the regression. In a one-independent variable regression, this number equals 1.
Degrees of freedom for F-test = k for numerator, $n - 2$ for denominator.

The F-test is a one-tailed test. The decision rule for the test is that we reject H_0 if F-stat > F_{crit}

If the regression model does a good job of explaining the variation in the dependent variable, explained variation should be relatively high, so MSR should be high relative to MSE, and the value of the F-stat should be higher.

For a one-independent variable regression, the F-stat is basically the same as the square of the t-stat for the slope coefficient. Since it duplicates the t-test for the significance of the slope coefficient for a one-independent variable regression, analysts only use the F-stat for multiple-independent variable regressions. However, we have introduced it in this reading so that you build a solid foundation before moving on to multiple regression in the next reading.

The ANOVA output can also be used to calculate the standard error of estimate (SEE) for the regression (see Example 3-4). SEE can be calculated as:

$$SEE = \sqrt{MSE} = \sqrt{\frac{SSE}{n-2}}$$

Example 3-4: ANOVA

The results of the regression of monthly returns data from January 2006 until December 2010 (60 months) for ABC Stock on the market index, along with the ANOVA table for the regression are provided below. Use the *F*-stat to determine whether the slope coefficient in the regression equals 0.

Multiple R	0.5864
R-squared	0.3439
Standard error of estimate	0.0404
Observations	60

ANOVA	Degrees of Freedom (df)	Sum of Squares (SS)	Mean Sum of Squares (MSS)	F
Regression	1	0.04953	0.04953	30.39937
Residual	58	0.0945	0.00162931	
Total	59	0.14403		

	Coefficients	Standard Error	*t*-Statistic
Alpha	0.0041	0.0135	0.3037
Beta	1.1558	0.2096	5.51356

Solution:

H_0: $\beta_{ABC} = 0$
H_a: $\beta_{ABC} \neq 0$

The *F*-stat is calculated as:

$$F = \frac{RSS/1}{SSE/(n-2)} = \frac{MSR}{MSE} = \frac{0.04953/1}{0.0945/(60-2)} = 30.399$$

The F-critical value at the 5% level of significance, $F_{1,58} = 4.00$

Since the *F*-stat for the test (30.399) exceeds the *F*-critical value (4.00), we reject the null hypothesis and conclude that the slope coefficient for the regression (ABC Stock beta) is significantly different from zero.

Note that the t-test we performed earlier on ABC Stock beta (in Example 3-3) was different because the null hypothesis then was that the slope coefficient was equal to 1. In this example, using the F-test, we are testing a null hypothesis that the slope coefficient equals 0.

Also notice that the t-stat in the regression results in Example 3-3 (5.51356), which as we mentioned earlier, is calculated based on a null hypothesis that the slope coefficient equals zero, equals the square root of our computed F-stat (30.399). Based on this t-stat, which assumes a hypothesized population parameter value of 0, we would reject the null hypothesis that ABC Stock beta equals 0.

Finally, notice the value of the standard error of estimate (SEE) that can be calculated as:

$$\text{SEE} = \sqrt{\text{MSE}} = \sqrt{0.00162931} = 0.0404$$

LESSON 4: PREDICTION INTERVALS AND LIMITATIONS OF REGRESSION ANALYSIS

LOS 9h: Calculate the predicted value for the dependent variable, given an estimated regression model and a value for the independent variable.
Vol 1, pp 298–301

LOS 9i: Calculate and interpret a confidence interval for the predicted value of the dependent variable. Vol 1, pp 298–301

Prediction Intervals

Regression analysis is often used to make predictions or forecasts of the dependent variable based on the regression equation. Typically, analysts construct confidence intervals around the regression forecasts. Note that when we illustrated confidence intervals earlier in the reading, we constructed a confidence interval for the slope coefficient of the independent variable in the regression. Now we shall attempt to create a confidence interval for the dependent variable.

There are two sources of uncertainty when we use a regression model to make a prediction regarding the value of the dependent variable.

- The uncertainty inherent in the error term, ε.
- The uncertainty in the estimated parameters, b_0 and b_1. If there was no uncertainty regarding the estimates of the regression parameters (i.e., the true population values of the parameters were known with certainty) the variance of any forecast (given an assumed value of X) would simply be s^2, the squared standard error of estimate, as the error term would be the only source of uncertainty.

Given that the parameters of the regression must be estimated and that their true population values are not known, the estimated variance of the prediction error, s_f^2, of Y is calculated as:

$$s_f^2 = s^2\left[1 + \frac{1}{n} + \frac{(X - \bar{X})^2}{(n-1)s_x^2}\right]$$

Once we have computed the estimate of the variance of the prediction error (s_f^2), the prediction interval is constructed using a similar procedure to that of constructing confidence intervals for the slope coefficient (see Example 4-1). The $(1 - \alpha)$ percent prediction interval is constructed as:

$$\hat{Y} \pm t_c s_f$$

Example 4-1: Computing the Prediction Interval

Go back to the inflation rate and money supply growth rate example that we were working with earlier in the reading. Determine the 95% prediction interval for the inflation rate given that the money supply growth rate is 9%.

Solution:

First, based on the estimate regression equation determine the predicted value of the dependent variable (inflation rate) given the value for the independent variable (money supply growth rate = 0.09).

$\hat{Y}$ = Inflation rate = −0.005 + 0.7591(Money supply growth rate)
$\hat{Y}$ = Inflation rate = −0.005 + (0.7591)(0.09) = 0.0633

To compute the variance of the prediction error we need to calculate (1) the standard error of estimate for the equation, (2) the mean money supply growth rate ($\bar{X}$), and (3) the variance of the money supply growth rate (Var X).

SEE = 0.0080 (Computed in Example 3-1)
$\bar{X}$ = 0.1012 (Computed in Example 1-2)
Var (X) = 0.000984 (Computed in Example 1-2)

$$s_f^2 = s^2\left[1 + \frac{1}{n} + \frac{(\mathrm{X} - \bar{\mathrm{X}})^2}{(n-1)s_x^2}\right]$$

$$s_f^2 = 0.008^2\left[1 + \frac{1}{6} + \frac{(0.09 - 0.1012)^2}{(6-1)(0.000984)}\right] = 0.0000763$$

$$s_f = 0.0087$$

The critical t-value for a 95% confidence interval with 4 degrees of freedom is 2.7764. Therefore, the confidence interval extends from 0.0633 − (2.7764)(0.0087) = 0.039 to 0.0633 + (2.7764)(0.0087) = 0.087.

Interpretation: If the money supply growth rate is 9%, the 95% prediction interval for the inflation rate will extend from 3.9% to 8.7%. Since the sample size is small, the prediction interval is relatively wide.

LOS 9k: Describe limitations of regression analysis.

Limitations of Regression Analysis

- Regression relations can change over time. For example, a time series regression estimating beta for a stock may come up with a different estimate of beta depending on the time period selected. This problem is referred to as parameter instability.
- Public knowledge of regression relationships (especially in the investment arena) may negate their usefulness going forward as more and more market participants make their investment decisions based on the perceived relationships.
- If the assumptions of regression analysis do not hold, the predictions based on the model will not be valid. These violations of regression assumptions and their repercussions on the analysis are discussed in the next reading.

READING 10: MULTIPLE REGRESSION AND ISSUES IN REGRESSION ANALYSIS

LESSON 1: MULTIPLE LINEAR REGRESSION

LOS 10a: Formulate a multiple regression equation to describe the relation between a dependent variable and several independent variables and determine the statistical significance of each independent variable. Vol 1, pp 326–332

LOS 10b: Interpret estimated regression coefficients and their *p*-values. Vol 1, pp 326–332

LOS 10c: Formulate a null and an alternative hypothesis about the population value of a regression coefficient, calculate the value of the test statistic, and determine whether to reject the null hypothesis at a given level of significance. Vol 1, pp 326–332

LOS 10d: Interpret the results of hypothesis tests of regression coefficients. Vol 1, pp 326–332

Multiple regression is a statistical procedure that allows us to evaluate the impact of more than one (multiple) independent variable on a dependent variable. A multiple linear regression model has the following general form:

$$\text{Multiple regression equation} = Y_i = b_0 + b_1X_{1i} + b_2X_{2i} + \ldots + b_kX_{ki} + \varepsilon_i, i = 1,2,\ldots, n$$

where:

Y_i = the *i*th observation of the dependent variable Y
X_{ji} = the *i*th observation of the independent variable X_j, $j = 1,2, \ldots, k$
b_0 = the intercept of the equation
$b_1, \ldots, b_k$ = the slope coefficients for each of the independent variables
ε_i = the error term for the *i*th observation
n = the number of observations

The slope coefficient, b_1, measures how much the dependent variable, Y, changes in response to a one-unit change in the independent variable, X_1, holding all other independent variables constant. For example, if b_1 equals −1, and all the other independent variables in the regression are held constant, a one unit increase in the independent variable, X_1, will result in a one-unit decrease in the dependent variable, Y. See Example 1-1.

Note:

- There are k slope coefficients in a multiple regression.
- The k slope coefficients and the intercept, b_0, are all known as regression coefficients. There are k+1 regression coefficients in a multiple regression.
- The residual term, ε_i, equals the difference between the actual value of Y (Y_i) and the predicted value of Y ($\hat{Y}_i$)

$$\hat{\varepsilon}_i = Y_i - \hat{Y}_i = Y_i - (\hat{b}_0 + \hat{b}_1X_{1i} + \hat{b}_2X_{2i} + \ldots + \hat{b}_kX_{ki})$$

The null hypothesis is the position the researcher is looking to reject. The alternative hypothesis is the condition whose existence the researcher is trying to validate.

For both tests we use a *t*-test, not the z-test, because we only know sample variances for b_1 and b_2; we do not know the population variances for b_1 and b_2.

Example 1-1: Determining the Significance of the Coefficients in a Multiple Regression

Amy is interested in predicting the GMAT scores of students looking to gain admission into MBA programs around the United States. She specifies a regression model with the GMAT score as the dependent variable and the number of hours spent studying for the test and the student's college GPA as the independent variables. The regression is estimated from using data from 50 students and is formulated as:

$$Y_i = b_0 + b_1X_{1i} + b_2X_{2i} + \varepsilon_i$$

where:

Y_i = A student's GMAT score
b_0 = Intercept term
X_{1i} = Independent Variable 1: The number of hours a student spends preparing for the test.
X_{2i} = Independent Variable 2: The student's undergraduate college GPA.

Amy believes that the higher the number of hours spent preparing for the test, the higher the score obtained on the test (i.e., a positive relationship exists between the two variables). Therefore, she sets up her null and alternative hypotheses for testing the significance of the slope coefficient of X_{1i} (the number of hours spent studying) as follows:

H_0: $b_1 \le 0$ looking to reject
H_a: $b_1 > 0$ looking to validate.

Amy also believes that the higher a student's college GPA, the higher the score obtained on the test (i.e., a positive relationship exists between the two variables). Therefore, she formulates the following hypotheses relating to the slope coefficient of X_{2i} (undergraduate GPA):

H_0: $b_2 \le 0$
H_a: $b_2 > 0$

Table 1-1 shows the results of the regression.

Table 1-1: Results from Regressing GMAT Scores on Hours of Prep and College GPA

	Coefficient	Standard Error	*t*-Statistic
Intercept	231.3476	47.3286	4.8881 → 231.3476 ÷ 47.3286
Number of hours of study	1.103	0.0939	11.7465
College GPA	68.3342	16.5938	4.1181

ANOVA	df	SS	MS	F	Significance F
Regression	2	444,866.09	222,433.04	73.12	0
Residual	47	142,983.91	3,042.21		
Total	49	587,850			

Standard Error	55.1562
R Square	0.7568
Observations	50
Adjusted R Square	0.7464

As the first step in multiple regression analysis, an analyst should evaluate the overall significance of the regression. The ANOVA section of the regression results provides us with the data that is used to evaluate the overall explanatory power and significance of the regression. We will get into this in detail in LOS 10e. For now, we will move directly into tests relating to the significance of the individual regression coefficients and assume that overall, the regression is significant.

If the regression is not significant overall, there is no point in proceeding to interpret the individual regression coefficients.

Just like in simple linear regression, the magnitude of the regression coefficients in a multiple regression does not tell us anything about their significance in explaining the variation in the dependent variable. Hypothesis tests must be performed on these coefficients to evaluate their importance in explaining the variation in the dependent variable.

First we evaluate the belief that the higher the number of hours spent studying for the test, the higher the score obtained.

$$H_0: b_1 \leq 0$$
$$H_a: b_1 > 0$$

$$t\text{-stat} = \frac{\hat{b}_1 - b_1}{s_{\hat{b}_1}}$$
$$= (1.103 - 0) / 0.0939 = 11.7465$$

Notice that the t-stat used in the hypothesis test is the same as the number listed in the regression results. This is because (as mentioned in Reading 9) the t-stats presented in the regression results are computed on the basis of a hypothesized parameter value of 0.

The critical t-value at the 5% level of significance for this one-tailed test with 47 (calculated as $n - (k + 1) = 50 - 3$) degrees of freedom is 1.678.

k represents the number of independent variables in the regression, and 1 is added to account for the intercept term. Therefore, the degrees of freedom equal $n - (k + 1)$.

The t-stat (11.7465) is greater than the critical t-value (1.678). Therefore, at the 5% level of significance, we can reject the null hypothesis and conclude that the higher the number of hours a student spends studying for the GMAT, the higher the score obtained.

Next, we evaluate the belief that the higher the student's college GPA, the higher the GMAT score obtained.

$$H_0: b_2 \leq 0$$
$$H_a: b_2 > 0$$

$$t\text{-stat} = \frac{\hat{b}_2 - b_2}{s_{\hat{b}_2}} = (68.3342 - 0)/16.5938 = 4.1181$$

The critical t-value at the 5% level of significance for this one-tailed test with 47 degrees of freedom is 1.678.

The t-stat (4.1181) is greater than the critical t-value (1.678). Therefore, at the 5% level of significance we can reject the null hypothesis and conclude that the higher the student's undergraduate GPA, the higher the GMAT score obtained.

Most software programs also report a p-value for each regression coefficient. The p-value represents the lowest level of significance at which a null hypothesis that the population value of the regression coefficient equals 0 can be rejected in a two-tailed test. For example, if the p-value for a regression coefficient equals 0.03, the null hypothesis that the coefficient equals

0 can be rejected at the 5% level of significance, but not at the 2% significance level. The lower the p-value, the stronger the case for rejecting the null hypothesis.

Based on the results of the regression, our estimated regression equation is:

$$\hat{Y}_i = \hat{b}_0 + \hat{b}_1 X_{1i} + \hat{b}_2 X_{2i} = 231.35 + 1.103 X_{1i} + 68.3342 X_{2i}$$

$$\hat{Y}_i = \hat{b}_0 + \hat{b}_1 X_{1i} + \hat{b}_2 X_{2i} = 231.35 + 1.103(\text{no. of hours}) + 68.3342(\text{college GPA})$$

Note that $\hat{Y}_i$ stands for the predicted value of Y_i, and $\hat{b}_0$, $\hat{b}_1$, and $\hat{b}_2$ are estimates of the values of b_0, b_1, and b_2 respectively.

Before moving into interpreting the results of a multiple regression, let's take a step back. Suppose Amy were to start off the process of explaining an individual's GMAT score with a one-independent variable regression model with the number of hours spent studying (X_{1i}) as the only independent variable. The regression equation for her one-independent variable regression is given as:

$$\hat{Y}_i = 260.54 + 2.134 X_{1i}$$

The appropriate interpretation of the slope coefficient for this regression equation is that if an individual studies for 1 additional hour, we would expect her GMAT score to increase by 2.134 points.

Then Amy decides to add a second independent variable, a student's college GPA, to her regression model. The equation for her two-independent variable regression model (obtained through the regression data in Table 1-1) is given as:

$$\hat{Y}_i = 231.35 + 1.103 X_{1i} + 68.3342 X_{2i}$$

Notice that the estimated slope coefficient for X_1 has changed from 2.134 (in the one-independent variable regression equation) to 1.103 (in the two-independent variable regression equation) when we add X_2 to the regression. This is a fairly typical outcome when another variable is added to a regression (unless X_1 is uncorrelated with X_2) because when X_1 changes by 1 unit, we would expect X_2 to be different as well. The results of the multiple regression capture this relationship between X_1 and X_2 in predicting $\hat{Y}$.

- In interpreting the slope coefficient for X_1 for the one-independent variable regression model, we state that if an individual studies for 1 additional hour, we would expect her GMAT score to increase by 2.134 points when X_2 is not held constant.
- In interpreting the slope coefficient for X_1 for the two-independent variable regression model, we state that if an individual studies for 1 more hour, we would expect her GMAT score to increase by 1.103 points, *holding her college GPA constant.* This is why the slope coefficients of a multiple regression model are also known as partial regression coefficients or partial slope coefficients.

Based on the results of her two-independent variable regression, Amy must be careful not to expect the difference in the expected GMAT scores of two individuals whose total number of hours of prep differed by one hour to be 1.103 points. This is because in all likelihood, the college GPAs of the two individuals would differ as well, which would have an impact on their GMAT scores. Therefore, 1.103 points is the expected net effect of each additional hour spent studying for the test (net of the impact of the student's GPA) on her expected GMAT score.

Interpreting the intercept term of the multiple regression equation is fairly straightforward. It represents the expected value of the dependent variable if all the independent variables in the regression equal 0.

LOS 10e: Calculate and interpret 1) a confidence interval for the population value of a regression coefficient and 2) a predicted value for the dependent variable, given an estimated regression model and assumed values for the independent variables. Vol 1, pp 336–337

Confidence Intervals

A confidence interval for a regression coefficient in a multiple regression is constructed in the same manner as we demonstrated in the previous reading, when we constructed a confidence interval for a regression coefficient in a simple linear regression. The confidence interval is constructed as follows:

$$\hat{b}_j \pm (t_c \times s_{\hat{b}_j})$$

estimated regression coefficient ± (critical t-value)(coefficient standard error)

The critical t-value is a two-tailed value computed based on the significance level (1 – confidence level) and $n - (k + 1)$ degrees of freedom. See Example 1-2.

Example 1-2: Confidence Interval for a Regression Coefficient in a Multiple Regression

Calculate the 95% confidence interval for the estimated coefficient of number of hours spent studying in our GMAT score example.

Solution:

The critical t-value for a two-tailed test at the 5% level of significance with 47 degrees of freedom is 2.012 Therefore, the confidence interval for the slope coefficient b_1 is:

$$1.103 \pm (2.012)(0.0939) = 0.914 \text{ to } 1.291$$

Since the hypothesized value (0) of the slope coefficient (b_1) of the independent variable, number of hours spent studying (X_1), does not lie within the computed 95% confidence interval, we reject the null hypothesis that the slope coefficient, b_1, equals 0 at the 5% level of significance.

Note that in the t-test pertaining to b_1 in Example 1-1, we were testing whether the slope coefficient was greater than zero. In Example 1-2, when working with a confidence interval, we are testing the hypothesis that the slope coefficient, b_1, is simply different from zero.

A t-test with a null hypothesis of "equal to zero" at a significance level of α, and a confidence interval with a $(1-\alpha)$ level of confidence will always give the same result.

Predicting the Dependent Variable

Predicting the value of the dependent variable from the multiple regression equation given forecasted or assumed values of the independent variables in the regression is quite straightforward. We simply follow the steps listed below:

- Obtain estimates for $\hat{b}_0, \hat{b}_1, \hat{b}_2, \ldots, \hat{b}_k$ of regression parameters $b_0, b_1, b_2, \ldots, b_k$.
- Determine the assumed values for independent variables $\hat{X}_1, \hat{X}_2, \ldots, \hat{X}_k$.
- Compute the value of the dependent variable, $\hat{Y}_1$, using the equation

$$\hat{Y}_i = \hat{b}_0 + \hat{b}_1\hat{X}_{1i} + \hat{b}_2\hat{X}_{2i} + \ldots + \hat{b}_k\hat{X}_{ki}$$

Do keep in mind that all the independent variables in the regression equation (regardless of whether or not their estimated slope coefficients are significantly different from 0), must be used in predicting the value of the dependent variable. See Example 1-3.

Example 1-3: Predicting the Dependent Variable

Amy has put in 270 hours of study for her upcoming GMAT test. Her undergraduate college GPA was 3.64. Based on her regression model, what score should she expect to obtain on her test?

Solution:

$$\begin{aligned}\text{GMAT score} &= 231.35 + 1.103(\text{no. of hours}) + 68.3342(\text{college GPA}) \\ &= 231.35 + 1.103(270) + 68.3342(3.64) \\ &= 777.90 \text{ or approximately } 778\end{aligned}$$

Amy's regression model predicts a score of approximately 778 for her on the GMAT based on 270 hours of prep and a 3.64 college GPA.

Note that when using the estimated regression equation to make predictions of the dependent variable:

- We should be confident that the assumptions of the regression model are met.
- We should be cautious about predictions based on out-of-sample values of the independent variables (values that are outside the range of data on which the model was estimated) as these predictions can be unreliable.

LOS 10f: Explain the assumptions of a multiple regression model.
Vol 1, pp 332–336

Assumptions of the Multiple Linear Regression Model

The classical normal multiple linear regression model makes the following six assumptions:

- The relationship between the dependent variable (Y) and the independent variables ($X_1, X_2, \ldots, X_k$) is linear.
- The independent variables ($X_1, X_2, \ldots, X_k$) are not random and no exact linear relationship exists between two or more independent variables.
- The expected value of the error term, conditioned on the independent variables, is zero: $E(\varepsilon | X_1, X_2, \ldots, X_k) = 0$.
- The variance of the error term is the same for all observations. $E(\varepsilon_i^2) = \sigma_\varepsilon^2$.
- The error term is uncorrelated across observations. $E(\varepsilon_i \varepsilon_j) = 0, j \neq i$.
- The error term is normally distributed.

LESSON 2: THE *F*-STAT, R2, ANOVA, AND DUMMY VARIABLES

LOS 10g: Calculate and interpret the *F*-statistic, and describe how it is used in regression analysis. Vol 1, pp 338–340

Testing Whether All the Population Regression Coefficients Equal Zero

In Example 1-1, we illustrated how to conduct hypothesis tests on the individual regression coefficients. We deferred the discussion relating to evaluation of the significance of the estimated regression model as a whole. To address the question, "How well do the independent variables as a group explain the variation in the dependent variable?", we perform an F-test with a null hypothesis that all the slope coefficients in the regression simultaneously equal zero versus an alternative hypothesis that at least one of the slope coefficients in the regression does not equal zero.

$H_0: b_1 = b_2 = \ldots = b_k = 0$

H_a: At least one of the slope coefficients $\neq 0$

If none of the independent variables significantly explain the variation in the dependent variable, none of the slope coefficients should be significantly different from zero. However, in a multiple regression, we cannot test the hypothesis that all the slope coefficients equal zero based on t-tests on the individual slope coefficients. This is because the individual t-tests do not account for the effects of the correlation or interaction between the independent variables. The F-test and individual t-tests on the slope coefficients may offer conflicting conclusions in the following scenarios:

1. We may be able to reject the null hypothesis that all the slope coefficients equal zero based on the F-test (and conclude that the regression model significantly explains the variation in the dependent variable) even though none of the individual slope coefficients appear significant based on the individual t-tests. (This is a classic symptom of multicollinearity, which we discuss in detail later in the reading).

2. We may fail to reject the null hypothesis that all the slope coefficients equal zero based on the *F*-test (and conclude that the regression model does not significantly explain the variation in the dependent variable) even though the individual slope coefficients appear to be statistically different from zero based on the individual *t*-tests.

Details for the ANOVA table for multiple regression are discussed in LOS 10g.

To calculate the *F*-stat (test statistic when testing the hypothesis that all the slope coefficients in a multiple regression are jointly equal to zero) we need the following inputs, which are typically included in the ANOVA section of the regression results.

- Total number of observations, *n*.
- Total number of regression coefficients that must be estimated $(k + 1)$ where k equals the number of slope coefficients.
- The sum of squared errors or residuals (SSE) which represents unexplained variation.

$$\sum_{i=1}^{n}(Y_i - \hat{Y}_i)^2 = \sum_{i=1}^{n}\hat{\varepsilon}_i^{\,2}$$

- The regression sum of squares (RSS) which represents explained variation.

$$\sum_{i=1}^{n}(\hat{Y}_i - \bar{Y})^2$$

The *F*-stat measures how well the regression model explains the variation in the dependent variable. The greater the *F*-stat, the better the performance of the regression model in explaining the variation in the dependent variable. From Reading 9, recall that the *F*-stat measures the ratio of the mean regression sum of squares (MSR) to the mean squared error (MSE). It is calculated as follows:

$$F\text{-stat} = \frac{\text{MSR}}{\text{MSE}} = \frac{\text{RSS}/k}{\text{SSE}/[n-(k+1)]}$$

Note that the *F*-test is a one-tailed test (even though the null hypothesis contains the "=" sign) with the critical *F*-value computed at the desired level of significance with k and $n - (k + 1)$ degrees of freedom for the numerator and denominator respectively. See Example 2-1.

Example 2-1: Testing Whether All the Population Regression Coefficients Equal Zero

Evaluate the significance of Amy's two-independent variable regression in explaining students' GMAT scores at the 5% level of significance. An excerpt from the regression results is reproduced in Table 2-1:

Table 2-1: Excerpt

ANOVA	df	SS	MS	F	Significance F
Regression	2	444,866.09	222,433.04	73.12	0.00
Residual	47	142,983.91	3,042.21		
Total	49	587,850			

Solution:

$H_0: b_1 = b_2 = 0$
H_a: At least one of the slope coefficients $\neq 0$

$$F\text{-stat} = \frac{444{,}866.09/2}{142{,}983.91/47} = 73.12$$

At the 5% significance level, the critical F-value with 2 and 47 degrees of freedom for the numerator and denominator respectively is between 3.15 and 3.23.

Since the F-stat (73.12) is greater than the critical F-value, we reject the null hypothesis that the slope coefficients on both the independent variables equal zero. We conclude that at least one of the slope coefficients in the regression is significantly different from 0, which basically implies that at least one of the independent variables in the regression explains the variation in the dependent variable to a significant extent. The p-value of the F-stat (0) means that the smallest level of significance at which the null hypothesis can be rejected is practically 0. The p-value also (as we might expect) suggests that there is a strong case for rejecting the null hypothesis.

LOS 10h: Distinguish between and interpret the R^2 and adjusted R^2 in multiple regression. Vol 1, pp 340–341

R^2 and Adjusted R^2

From Reading 9, recall that the coefficient of determination (R^2) measures how much of the variation in the dependent variable is captured by the independent variables in the regression collectively. It is calculated as:

$$R^2 = \frac{\text{Total variation} - \text{Unexplained variation}}{\text{Total variation}} = \frac{\text{SST} - \text{SSE}}{\text{SST}} = \frac{\text{RSS}}{\text{SST}}$$

In multiple regression analysis, as more and more independent variables are added to the mix, the total amount of unexplained variation will decrease (as the amount of explained variation increases) and the R^2 measure will reflect an improvement on the previous model in terms of the variation explained by the group of independent variables as a proportion of total variation in the dependent variable. This will be the case as long as each newly added independent variable is even slightly correlated with the dependent variable and is not a linear combination of the other independent variables already in the regression model.

Therefore, when evaluating a multiple regression model, analysts typically use adjusted R^2. Adjusted R^2 does not automatically increase when another variable is added to the regression as it is adjusted for degrees of freedom.

It is calculated as:

$$\text{Adjusted } R^2 = \bar{R}^2 = 1 - \left(\frac{n-1}{n-k-1}\right)(1-R^2)$$

Note:

- If $k = 1$, R^2 will be greater than adjusted R^2.
- Adjusted R^2 will decrease if the inclusion of another independent variable in the regression model results in a nominal increase in explained variation (RSS) and R^2.
- Adjusted R^2 can be negative (in which case we consider its value to equal 0) while R^2 can never be negative.
- If we use adjusted R^2 to compare two regression models, we must ensure that the dependent variable is defined in the same manner in the two models and that the sample sizes used to estimate the models are the same. See Example 2-2.

Example 2-2: R^2 versus Adjusted R^2

Amy now decides to add a third independent variable (X_{3i}) to her regression model. Upon adding the variable "number of practice tests taken" to the regression, the regression sum of squares (RSS) in the ANOVA increases to 487,342.64, while the sum of squared errors (SSE) falls to 100,507.36. Calculate the R^2 and adjusted R^2 for the new (three-independent variable) regression model and comment on the values.

Solution:

Note that total variation in the independent variable SST is the same in both (two-independent variable and three-independent variable) regression models. This should make sense because the total variation in the dependent variable remains the same regardless of the number of independent variables employed in the regression.

The R^2 and adjusted R^2 for the two-independent variable regression are provided in Table 2-1 (Example 2-1).

$R^2 = 0.7568$ or 75.68%
Adjusted $R^2 = 0.7464$ or 74.64%

For the new (three-independent variable) regression, R^2 and adjusted R^2 are calculated as:

$$R^2 = \text{RSS}/\text{SST} = 487{,}342.64/587{,}850 = 0.8290 \text{ or } 82.90\%$$

$$\text{Adjusted } R^2 = 1 - \left(\frac{n-1}{n-k-1}\right)(1-R^2) = 0.8179 \text{ or } 81.79\%$$

The R^2 of the three-independent variable regression is higher (82.9% versus 75.68% earlier), but more importantly, the adjusted R^2 of the three-independent variable regression is also higher (81.79% versus 74.64% earlier), which suggests that the new model should be preferred. The addition of the third independent variable has improved the model.

LOS 10i: Evaluate how well a regression model explains the dependent variable by analyzing the output of the regression equation and an ANOVA table.

Vol 1, pp 338–340

This LOS basically covers all the LOSs that we have already covered in this reading. Below we summarize the process of analyzing the output of a regression.

Regression Equation

- Shows the relationship between the dependent variable and the independent variables.
- Can be used to predict the value of the dependent variable given specific values for the independent variables.
- The significance of the individual regression coefficients is evaluated using *t*-tests or *p*-values.
- The *t*-stat for each regression coefficient is calculated by dividing the value of the coefficient by its standard error.

Table 2-2: ANOVA Table

Source of Variation	Degrees of Freedom (*df*)	Sum of Squares (*SS*)	Mean Sum of Squares (*SS/df*)
Regression	k	RSS	MSR
Error	$n - (k + 1)$	SSE	MSE
Total	$n - 1$	**SST**	

ANOVA Table (see Table 2-2.)

- Lists the regression sum of squares (RSS), sum of squared errors (SSE), and total sum of squares (SST) along with associated degrees of freedom.
- Also includes calculated values for mean regression sum of squares (MSR) and mean squared error (MSE).
- The *F*-stat can be calculated by dividing MSR by MSE. The *F*-test is used to test whether at least one of the slope coefficients on the independent variables in the regression is significantly different from 0.
- R^2 (and adjusted R^2) can be calculated from the data in the ANOVA table by dividing RSS by SST. R^2 is used to determine the goodness of fit of the regression equation to the data.
- The standard error of estimate (SEE) can also be computed from the information in the ANOVA table. SEE = $\sqrt{\text{MSE}}$

LOS 10j: Formulate a multiple regression equation by using dummy variables to represent qualitative factors and interpret the coefficients and regression results.

Vol 1, pp 341–345

Using Dummy Variables in a Regression

Dummy variables in regression models help analysts determine whether a particular qualitative variable explains the variation in the model's dependent variable to a significant extent. See Example 2-3.

- A dummy variable must be binary in nature (i.e., it may take on a value of either 0 or 1).
- If the model aims to distinguish between n categories, it must employ n–1 dummy variables. The category that is omitted is used as a reference point for the other categories.
- The intercept term in the regression indicates the average value of the dependent variable for the omitted category.
- The slope coefficient of each dummy variable estimates the difference (compared to the omitted category) a particular dummy variable makes to the dependent variable.

If we use n dummy variables (instead of $n - 1$) we would be violating the regression assumption of no linear relationship between the independent variables.

Example 2-3: Hypothesis Testing with Dummy Variables

Let's suppose we are trying to evaluate the seasonality of a company's annual sales. Management believes that sales are significantly different in the fourth quarter compared to the other three quarters. Therefore, we use the fourth quarter as the reference point (i.e., the fourth quarter represents the omitted category) in our regression. The results of the regression based on quarterly sales data for the last 15 years are presented in Table 2-3:

Table 2-3: Results from Regressing Sales on Quarterly Dummy Variables

	Coefficient	Standard Error	*t*-Statistic	
Intercept	4.27	0.97	4.4021	
$Sales_{Q1}$	−2.735	0.83	−3.295	
$Sales_{Q2}$	−2.415	0.83	−2.91	
$Sales_{Q3}$	−2.69	0.83	−3.241	
ANOVA	**df**	**SS**	**MS**	**F**
Regression	3	37.328	12.443	26.174
Residual	56	26.623	0.4754	
Total	59	63.951		
Standard Error	0.6763			
R Square	0.5837			
Observations	60 =15×4 quarters			

Let's first state the regression equation to understand what the variables actually represent

$Y_t = b_0 + b_1(\text{Sales}_{Q1}) + b_2(\text{Sales}_{Q2}) + b_3(\text{Sales}_{Q3}) + \varepsilon$

Quarterly sales $= 4.27 - 2.735\ (\text{Sales}_{Q1}) - 2.415\ (\text{Sales}_{Q2}) - 2.690\ (\text{Sales}_{Q3}) + \varepsilon$

- b_0 (4.27) is the intercept term. It represents average sales in the fourth quarter (the omitted category).
- b_1 is the slope coefficient for sales in the first quarter (Sales_{Q1}). It represents the average difference in sales between the first quarter and the fourth quarter (the omitted category). According to the regression results, sales in Q1 are on average 2.735m less than sales in the fourth quarter. Sales in Q1 equal 4.27m – 2.735m = 1.535m on average.
- Similarly, sales in Q2 are on average 2.415m less than sales in the fourth quarter, while sales in Q3 are on average 2.69m less than sales in the fourth quarter. Average sales in Q2 and Q3 are 1.855m and 1.58m respectively.

The *F*-test is used to evaluate the null hypothesis that jointly, the slope coefficients all equal 0.

H_0: $b_1 = b_2 = b_3 = 0$
H_a: At least one of the slope coefficients $\neq 0$

The *F*-stat is given in the regression results (26.174). The critical *F*-value at the 5% significance level with 3 and 56 degrees of freedom for the numerator and denominator respectively lies between 2.76 and 2.84. Given that the *F*-stat for the regression is higher, we can reject the null hypothesis that all the slope coefficients in the regression jointly equal 0.

When working with dummy variables, *t*-stats are used to test whether the value of the dependent variable in each category is different from the value of the dependent variable in the omitted category. In our example, the *t*-stats can be used to test whether sales in each of the first three quarters of the year are different from sales in the fourth quarter on average.

H_0: $b_1 = 0$ versus H_a: $b_1 \neq 0$ tests whether Q1 sales are significantly different from Q4 sales.
H_0: $b_2 = 0$ versus H_a: $b_2 \neq 0$ tests whether Q2 sales are significantly different from Q4 sales.
H_0: $b_3 = 0$ versus H_a: $b_3 \neq 0$ tests whether Q3 sales are significantly different from Q4 sales.

The critical *t*-values for a two-tailed test with 56 (calculated as $n - (k + 1)$) degrees of freedom are –2.0 and +2.0. Since the absolute values of *t*-stats for the coefficients on each of the three quarters are higher than +2.0, we reject all three null hypotheses (that Q1 sales equal Q4 sales, that Q2 sales equal Q4 sales, and that Q3 sales equal Q4 sales) and conclude that sales in each of the first 3 quarters of the year are significantly different from sales in the fourth quarter on average.

LESSON 3: VIOLATIONS OF REGRESSION ASSUMPTIONS

LOS 10k: Explain the types of heteroskedasticity and how heteroskedasticity and serial correlation affect statistical inference. Vol 1, pp 345–356

Violations of Regression Assumptions

Heteroskedasticity

Heteroskedasticity occurs when the variance of the error term in the regression is not constant across observations. Figure 3-1 shows the scatter plot and regression line for a model with homoskedastic errors. There seems to be no systematic relationship between the regression residuals (vertical distances between the data points and the regression line) and the independent variable. Figure 3-2 shows the scatter plot and regression line for a model with heteroskedastic errors. Notice that the regression residuals appear to increase in size as the value of the independent variable increases.

Figure 3-1: Regression with Homoskedasticity

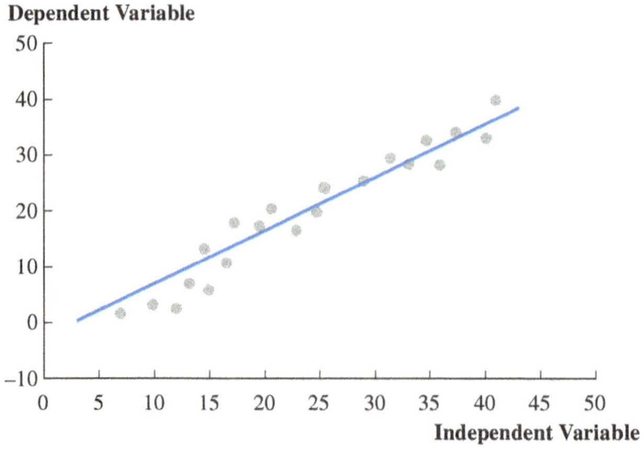

Figure 3-2: Regression with Heteroskedasticity

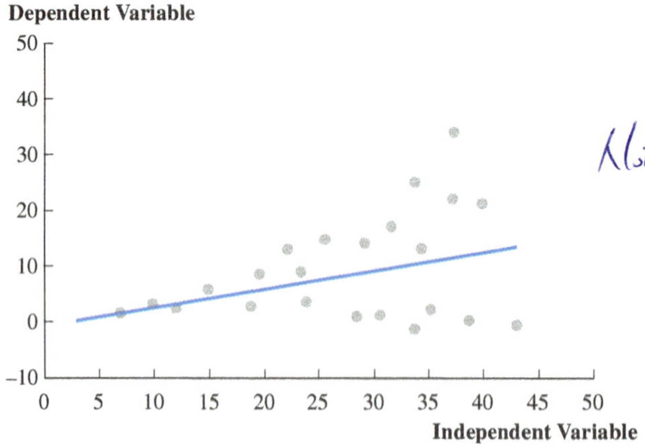

Not Constant

Effects of Heteroskedasticity

- Heteroskedasticity does not affect the consistency of estimators of regression parameters.
- However, it can lead to mistakes in inferences made from parameter estimates.
  - The *F*-test for the overall significance of the regression becomes unreliable as the MSE becomes a biased estimator of the true population variance.
  - The *t*-tests for the significance of each regression coefficient become unreliable as the estimates of the standard errors of regression coefficients become biased.
    - Typically, in regressions with financial data, standard errors of regression coefficients are underestimated and *t*-stats are inflated due to heteroskedasticity. Therefore, ignoring heteroskedasticity results in significant relationships being found when none actually exist. (Null hypotheses are rejected too often.)
    - Sometimes however, heteroskedasticity leads to standard errors that are too large, which makes *t*-stats too small.

Note that heteroskedasticity does not affect estimates of the regression coefficients.

Types of Heteroskedasticity

- Unconditional heteroskedasticity occurs when the heteroskedasticity of the variance in the error term is not related to the independent variables in the regression. Unconditional heteroskedasticity does not create major problems for regression analysis.
- Conditional heteroskedasticity occurs when the heteroskedasticity in the error variance is correlated with the independent variables in the regression. While conditional heteroskedasticity does create problems for statistical inference, it can be easily identified and corrected.

Testing for Heteroskedasticity—The Breusch-Pagan (BP) Test

The BP test requires a regression of **the squared residuals from the original estimated regression equation** (in which the dependent variable is regressed on the independent variables) on the independent variables in the regression.

- If conditional heteroskedasticity does not exist, the independent variables will not explain much of the variation in the squared residuals from the original regression.
- If conditional heteroskedasticity is present, the independent variables will explain the variation in the squared residuals to a significant extent.

The test statistic for the BP test is a Chi-squared (χ^2) random variable that is calculated as:

$\chi^2 = nR^2$ with k degrees of freedom

n = Number of observations
R^2 = Coefficient of determination of the **second regression** (the regression when the squared residuals of the original regression are regressed on the independent variables).
k = Number of independent variables

H_0: The original regression's squared error term is uncorrelated with the independent variables.
H_a: The original regression's squared error term is correlated with the independent variables.

Note: The BP test is a one-tailed Chi-squared test because conditional heteroskedasticity is only a problem if it is too large. See Example 3-1.

Example 3-1: Testing for Heteroskedasticity

An analyst wants to test a hypothesis suggested by Irving Fisher that nominal interest rates increase by 1% for every 1% increase in expected inflation. The Fisher effect assumes the following relationship:

$$i = r + \pi^e$$

where:
i = Nominal interest rate
r = Real interest rate (assumed constant)
π^e = Expected inflation

The analyst specifies the regression model as: $i_i = b_0 + b_1\pi^e + \varepsilon_i$

Since the Fisher effect basically asserts that the coefficient on the expected inflation (b_1) variable equals 1, the hypotheses are structured as:

H_0: $b_1 = 1$
H_a: $b_1 \neq 1$

Quarterly data for 3-month T-bill returns (nominal interest rate) are regressed on inflation rate expectations over the last 25 years. The results of the regression are presented in Table 3-1:

Table 3-1: Results from Regressing T-Bill Returns on Expected Inflation

	Coefficient	Standard Error	*t*-Statistic
Intercept	0.04	0.0051	7.843
Expected inflation	1.153	0.065	17.738
Residual standard error	0.029		
Multiple R-squared	0.45		
Observations	100		
Durbin-Watson statistic	0.547		

To determine whether the data support the assertions of the Fisher relation, we compute the *t*-stat for the slope coefficient on expected inflation as:

$$\text{Test statistic} = t = \frac{\hat{b}_1 - b_1}{s_{\hat{b}_1}} = \frac{1.153 - 1}{0.065} = 2.35$$

The critical *t*-values with 98 degrees of freedom at the 5% significance level are approximately −1.98 and +1.98. Comparing the test statistic (+2.35) to the upper critical *t*-value (+1.98) we reject the null hypothesis and lean towards concluding that the Fisher Effect does not hold because the coefficient on expected inflation appears to be significantly different from 1.

However, before accepting the validity of the results of this test, we should test the null hypothesis that the regression errors do not suffer from conditional heteroskedasticity. A regression of the squared residuals from the original regression on expected inflation rates yields an R^2 of 0.193.

The test statistic for the BP test is calculated as:

$$\chi^2 = nR^2 = (100)(0.193) = 19.3$$

The critical χ^2 value at the 5% significance level for a one-tailed test with 1 degree of freedom is 3.84. Since the test-statistic (19.3) is higher, we reject the null hypothesis of no conditional heteroskedasticity in the error terms. Since conditional heteroskedasticity is present in the residuals (of the original regression) the standard errors computed in the original regression are incorrect and we cannot accept the result of the *t*-test above (which provides evidence against the Fisher relation) as valid.

Correcting Heteroskedasticity

There are two ways to correct for conditional heteroskedasticity in linear regression models:

- Use robust standard errors (White-corrected standard errors or heteroskedasticity-consistent standard errors) to recalculate the *t*-statistics for the original regression coefficients based on corrected-for-heteroskedasticity standard errors.
- Use generalized least squares, where the original regression equation is modified to eliminate heteroskedasticity. See Example 3-2.

Example 3-2: Using Robust Standard Errors to Adjust for Conditional Heteroskedasticity

The analyst corrects the standard errors obtained in the initial regression of 3-month T-bill returns (nominal interest rates) on expected inflation rates for heteroskedasticity and obtains the results presented in Table 3-2:

Table 3-2: Results from Regressing T-Bill Returns on Expected Inflation (Standard Errors Corrected for Conditional Heteroskedasticity)

	Coefficient	Standard Error	*t*-Statistic
Intercept	0.04	0.0048	8.333
Expected inflation	1.153	0.085	13.565
Residual standard error	0.029		
Multiple R-squared	0.45		
Observations	100		

Compared to the regression results in Table 3-1 (Example 3-1) notice that the standard error for the intercept does not change significantly, but the standard error for the coefficient on expected inflation increases by about 30% (from 0.065 to 0.085). Further, the regression coefficients remain the same (0.04 for the intercept and 1.153 for expected inflation).

Using the adjusted standard error for the slope coefficient, the test-statistic for our hypothesis test is calculated as:

$$\text{Test statistic} = t = \frac{\hat{b}_1 - b_1}{s_{\hat{b}_1}} = \frac{1.153 - 1}{0.085} = 1.8$$

> Comparing this test statistic to the upper critical t-value (1.98) leads us to fail to reject the null hypothesis. The conditional heteroskedasticity in the data was so significant that the result of our hypothesis test changed (compared to Example 3-1) once the standard errors were corrected for heteroskedasticity (in Example 3-2). We now conclude that the Fisher Effect does hold as the slope coefficient on the expected inflation independent variable does not significantly differ from 1.

Serial Correlation

Serial correlation (autocorrelation) occurs when regression errors are correlated across observations. It typically arises in time-series regressions.

- Positive serial correlation occurs when a positive (negative) error for one observation increases the chances of a positive (negative) error for another.
- Negative serial correlation occurs when a positive (negative) error for one observation increases the chances of a negative (positive) error for another.

Effects of Serial Correlation

> In this reading we also make the common assumption that serial correlation takes the form of first-order serial correlation (i.e., serial correlation only exists between adjacent observations).

- Serial correlation does not affect the consistency of the estimated regression coefficients unless one of the independent variables in the regression is a lagged value of the dependent variable. For example, when examining the Fisher relation, if we were to use the T-bill return for the previous month as an independent variable (even though the T-bill return that represents the nominal interest rate is actually the dependent variable in our regression model) serial correlation would cause the parameter estimates from the regression to be inconsistent. In this reading, we assume that none of the independent variables is a lagged value of the dependent variable.
- When a lagged value of the dependent variable is not an independent variable in the regression, positive (negative) serial correlation:
  - Does not affect the consistency of the estimated regression coefficients.
  - Causes the F-stat (which is used to test the overall significance of the regression) to be inflated (deflated) because MSE will tend to underestimate (overestimate) the population error variance.
  - Causes the standard errors for the regression coefficients to be underestimated (overestimated), which results in larger (smaller) t-values. Consequently, analysts may reject (fail to reject) null hypotheses incorrectly, make Type I errors (Type II errors) and attach (fail to attach) significance to relationships that are in fact not significant (significant).

Testing for Serial Correlation—The Durbin-Watson (DW) Test

The DW test-statistic is approximated as:

$DW \approx 2(1 - r)$; where r is the sample correlation between squared residuals from one period and those from the previous period. See Example 3-3.

- The DW-stat can range from 0 (when serial correlation equals +1) to 4 (when serial correlation equals −1)
- If the regression has no serial correlation, the DW stat equals 2.
- If the regression residuals are positively serially correlated, the DW stat will be less than 2.

- If the regression residuals are negatively serially correlated, the DW stat will be greater than 2.
- For a given sample, the critical DW value (d*) is not known with certainty. We only know that it lies between two values (d_l and d_u). Figure 3-3 depicts the lower and upper values for d* as they relate to the results of the DW test.

Figure 3-3: Value of Durbin-Watson Statistic

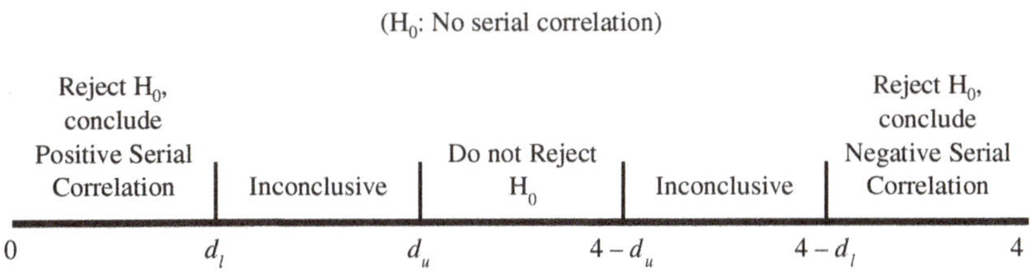

Decision rules for Durbin-Watson tests:

When testing for positive serial correlation:

- Reject H_0 of no positive serial correlation if the DW stat is lower than d_l. Conclude that there is positive serial correlation.
- The test is inconclusive if the DW stat lies between d_l and d_u.
- Fail to reject H_0 of no positive serial correlation when DW stat is greater than d_u.

When testing for negative serial correlation:

- Reject H_0 of no negative serial correlation if the DW stat is higher than $4 - d_l$. Conclude that there is negative serial correlation.
- The test is inconclusive if the DW stat lies between $4 - d_u$ and $4 - d_l$.
- Fail to reject H_0 of no negative serial correlation when DW stat is less than $4 - d_u$.

Example 3-3: Testing for Serial Correlation

Let's go back to the regression in Table 3-1 (Example 3-1) where we were examining the Fisher relation. We are given a Durbin-Watson statistic of 0.547 for the regression. Based on the DW stat formula on the previous page, we use this value to first determine whether the regression residuals are positively or negatively serially correlated.

$$\text{DW} \approx 2(1-r) = 0.547$$
$$r = 1 - \text{DW}/2$$
$$r = 0.7265$$

This positive value of r raises a concern that the standard errors of the regression may suffer from positive serial correlation, which may cause the OLS regression standard errors to be underestimated. Therefore, we must determine whether the observed value of the DW stat provides enough evidence to reject the null hypothesis of no positive serial correlation.

Given that the Fisher relation regression has one independent variable and 100 observations, the critical DW value lies between 1.65 (d_l) and 1.69 (d_u). Since the DW test stat (0.547) lies below d_l, we reject the null hypothesis of no positive serial correlation. The results of the test suggest that the standard errors of the original regression are positively serially correlated and are therefore too small.

Correcting Serial Correlation

There are two ways to correct for serial correlation in the regression residuals (see Example 3-4):

- Adjust the coefficient standard errors to account for serial correlation using Hansen's method (which incidentally also corrects for heteroskedasticity). The regression coefficients remain the same but the standard errors change. After correcting for positive serial correlation, the robust standard errors are larger than they were originally. Note that the DW stat still remains the same.
- Modify the regression equation to eliminate the serial correlation.

Example 3-4: Correcting for Serial Correlation

Table 3-3 shows the results of correcting the standard errors of the original regression for serial correlation and heteroskedasticity using Hansen's method.

Table 3-3: Results from Regressing T-Bill Returns on Expected Inflation (Standard Errors Corrected for Conditional Heteroskedasticity and Serial Correlation)

	Coefficient	Standard Error	*t*-Statistic
Intercept	0.04	0.0088	4.545
Expected inflation	1.153	0.155	7.439
Residual standard error	0.029		
Multiple R-squared	0.45		
Observations	100		
Durbin-Watson statistic	0.547		

Note that the coefficients for the intercept and slope are exactly the same (0.04 for the intercept and 1.153 for expected inflation) as in the original regression (Example 3-1). Further, note that the DW stat is the same (0.547), but the standard errors have been corrected (they are now much larger) to account for the positive serial correlation.

Given these new and more accurate coefficient standard errors let's once again test the null hypothesis that the coefficient on the expected inflation independent variable equals 1. The test statistic for the hypothesis test is computed as:

$$\text{Test statistic} = t = \frac{\hat{b}_1 - b_1}{s_{\hat{b}_1}} = \frac{1.153 - 1}{0.155} = 0.987$$

The critical *t*-values with 98 degrees of freedom at the 5% significance level are approximately −1.98 and +1.98. Comparing the test statistic (0.987) to the upper critical *t*-value (+1.98) we fail to reject the null hypothesis and conclude that the Fisher Effect does hold as the slope coefficient on the expected inflation independent variable does not significantly differ from 1. Note that the result of this hypothesis test is different from the test we conducted using the standard errors of the original regression (which were affected by serial correlation and heteroskedasticity) in Example 3-1. Further, the result is the same as the test conducted on White-corrected standard errors (which were corrected for heteroskedasticity) in Example 3-2.

LOS 10l: Describe multicollinearity and explain its causes and effects in regression analysis. Vol 1, pp 356–360

Multicollinearity

Multicollinearity occurs when two or more independent variables (or combinations of independent variables) in a regression model are highly (but not perfectly) correlated with each other.

Perfect collinearity is much less of a practical concern than multicollinearity.

Effects of Multicollinearity

- Multicollinearity does not affect the consistency of OLS estimates and regression coefficients, but makes them inaccurate and unreliable.
- It becomes difficult to isolate the impact of each independent variable on the dependent variable.
- The standard errors for the regression coefficients are inflated, which results in *t*-stats becoming too small and less powerful (in terms of their ability to reject null hypotheses).

Detecting Multicollinearity

It has been suggested that high pair-wise correlations between the independent variables may indicate the existence of multicollinearity. However, this is not always the case. Only when there are exactly two independent variables in the regression is the magnitude of the correlation between the independent variables a reasonable indicator of multicollinearity (especially when the correlation between them is greater than 0.7). Otherwise, low pair-wise correlations between the independent variables in the regression do not mean that multicollinearity is not present, and high pair-wise correlations between the independent variables in the regression are not necessary for multicollinearity to exist.

A high R^2 and a significant *F*-stat (both of which indicate that the regression model overall does a good job of explaining the dependent variable) coupled with insignificant *t*-stats of slope coefficients (which indicate that the independent variables individually do not significantly explain the variation in the dependent variable) provide the classic case of multicollinearity. The low *t*-stats on the slope coefficients increase the chances of Type II errors: failure to reject the null hypothesis when it is false.

Bear in mind that multicollinearity may be present even when we do not observe insignificant *t*-stats and a highly significant *F*-stat for the regression model. See Example 3-5.

Example 3-5: Multicollinearity

An individual is trying to determine how closely associated the investment strategy followed by her portfolio manager is with the returns of a value index and the returns of a growth index over the last 60 years. She regresses the historical annual returns of her portfolio on the historical returns of the S&P 500/BARRA Growth Index, S&P 500/BARRA Value Index, and the S&P 500. Results of her regression are given in Table 3-4:

Table 3-4: Results from Regressing Portfolio Returns against S&P 500/BARRA Growth and Value Indexes and the S&P 500

Regression Coefficient	*t*-Stat
Intercept	1.250
S&P 500/BARRA Growth Index	–0.825
S&P 500/BARRA Value Index	–0.756
S&P 500 Index	1.520

F-Stat	35.17
R^2	82.34%
Observations	60

Evaluate the results of the regression.

Solution:

The absolute values of the *t*-stats for all the regression coefficients—the intercept (1.25), slope coefficient on the growth index (0.825), slope coefficient on the value index (0.756) and the slope coefficient on the S&P 500 (1.52)—are lower than the absolute value of t_{crit} (2.00) at the 5% level of significance (df = 56). This suggests that none of the coefficients on the independent variables in the regression are significantly different from 0.

However, the *F*-stat (35.17) is greater than the *F* critical value of 2.76 ($\alpha = 0.05$, df = 3, 56), which suggests that the slope coefficients on the independent variables do not jointly equal zero (at least one of them is significantly different from 0). Further, the R^2 (82.34%) is quite high, which means that the model as a whole does a good job of explaining the variation in the portfolio's returns.

This regression, therefore, clearly suffers from the classic case of multicollinearity as described earlier.

Correcting for Multicollinearity

Analysts may correct for multicollinearity by excluding one or more of the independent variables from the regression model. Stepwise regression is a technique that systematically removes variables from the regression until multicollinearity is eliminated. See Example 3-6.

Example 3-6: Correcting for Multicollinearity

Given that the regression in Example 3-4 suffers from multicollinearity, the independent variable-return on the S&P 500 is removed from the regression. Results of the regression with only the return on the S&P 500/BARRA Growth Index and the return on the S&P 500/BARRA Value Index as independent variables are given in Table 3-5:

Table 3-5: Results from Regressing Portfolio Returns against S&P 500/BARRA Growth and Value Indexes

Regression Coefficient	***t*-Stat**
Intercept	1.35
S&P 500/BARRA Growth Index	6.53
S&P 500/BARRA Value Index	−1.16

F-Stat	57.62
R^2	82.12%
Observations	60

Evaluate the results of this regression.

Solution:

The *t*-stat of the slope coefficient on the growth index (6.53) is greater than the *t*-critical value (2.00) indicating that the slope coefficient on the growth index is significantly different from 0 at the 5% significance level. However, the *t*-stat of the value index (−1.16) is not different from 0 at the 5% significance level. This suggests that returns on the portfolio are linked to the returns on the growth index, but not closely related to the returns on the value index.

The *F*-stat (57.62) is greater than the *F* critical value of 3.15 ($\alpha = 0.05$, df = 2, 57), which suggests that the slope coefficients on the independent variables do not jointly equal zero. Further, the R^2 (82.12%) is quite high, which means that the model as a whole does a good job of explaining the variation in the portfolio's returns.

Removing the return on the S&P 500 as an independent variable in the regression corrected the multicollinearity problem in the initial regression. The significant relationship between the portfolio's returns and the return on the growth index was uncovered as a result.

Table 3-6: Problems in Linear Regression and Solutions[1]

Problem	Effect	Solution
Heteroskedasticity	Incorrect standard errors Does not affect consistency	Use robust standard errors (corrected for conditional heteroskedasticity)
Serial correlation	Incorrect standard errors (additional problems if a lagged value of the dependent variable is used as an independent variable) Does not affect consistency	Use robust standard errors (corrected for serial correlation)
Multicollinearity	High R^2 and low t-statistics Does Not Affect Consistency	Remove one or more independent variables; often no solution based in theory

LESSON 4: ERRORS IN SPECIFICATION AND QUALITATIVE DEPENDENT VARIABLES

LOS 10m: Describe how model misspecification affects the results of a regression analysis, and describe how to avoid common forms of misspecification.

Vol 1, pp 360–373

Model Specification

Principles of Model Specification

- The model should be backed by solid economic reasoning. Data mining (where the model is based on the characteristics of the data) should be avoided.
- The functional form for the variables in the regression should be in line with the nature of the variables.
- Each variable in the model should be relevant, making the model "parsimonious."
- The model should be tested for violations of regression assumptions before being accepted.
- The model should be found useful out of sample.

Model Specification Errors

In describing different model specification errors, we shall work with the following regression equation, which represents the "true regression model" for explaining the variation in a particular dependent variable.

$$Y_i = b_0 + b_1 lnX_{1i} + b_2 X_{2i} + \varepsilon$$

1 - Table 11, Volume 1, Level II CFA Program Curriculum 2015

Misspecified Functional Form

1. One or more important variables may have been omitted from the regression (e.g., if we were to leave out X_2 from our model altogether and estimate the following regression equation: $Y_i = a_0 + a_1 lnX_{1i} + \varepsilon$. If the omitted variable (X_2) is correlated with the included variable (lnX_1), the error term in the model would be correlated with lnX_1, the estimates of the regression coefficients (a_0 and a_1) would be biased and inconsistent, while their estimated standard errors would also be inconsistent. As a result, neither the coefficients nor their standard errors would be useful for statistical analysis.
2. A wrong form of the data may be used in the regression. One or more of the variables may need to be transformed before estimating the regression.
   - If the relationship between the dependent and independent variables is nonlinear, but becomes linear when one or more of the variables is presented as a proportional change in the variable, the misspecification may be corrected by using the natural logarithm of the variable(s). For example, in our true regression equation, Variable X_1 has been transformed to lnX_1.
   - Sometimes it is more appropriate to use a scaled version of the data as opposed to unscaled data. When comparing financial statements of companies, analysts often use common size statements to ensure that the results of the regression are based on companies' underlying economics, not on differences in their respective sizes. For example, a regression seeking to identify a relationship between cash flow from operations and free cash flow for different companies should scale the data by dividing both (the dependent and independent) variables by sales so that differences in company size are accounted for, and the regression is correctly specified.
3. The model may pool data from different sources that should not have been pooled. Figure 4-1 illustrates this type of misspecification. In each cluster of data, there seems to be no clear relationship between X and Y. However, if both these clusters are treated as one sample when estimating the regression, the analyst may find a "statistical" relationship (spurious correlation) when no economic relationship actually exists.

> Note that when X_2 is omitted from the regression, the values of the intercept and slope coefficient on lnX_i are different than in our true regression. Hence we represent the regression coefficients as a_0 and a_1 instead of b_0 and b_1.

Figure 4-1: Regression Line Based on Two Different Sources of Data

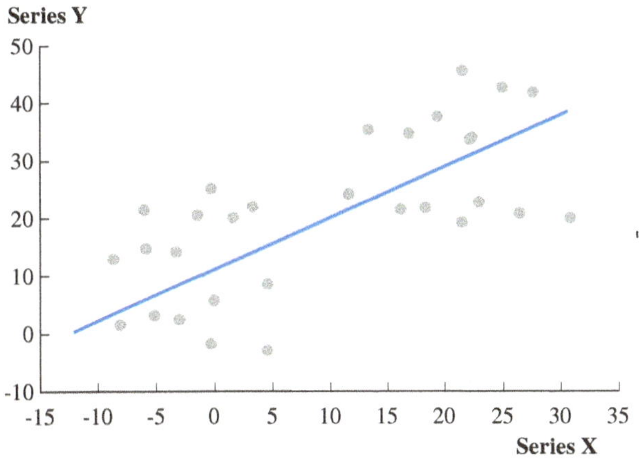

Time-Series Misspecification

Time-series misspecification results from the kinds of independent variables included in the regression. It causes a violation of the regression assumption that the expected value of the error term equals zero. Time-series misspecification can result from:

1. Including lagged dependent variables as independent variables in regressions with serially correlated errors. The lagged dependent variable (which serves as an independent variable in the regression) will be correlated with the error term (violating the regression assumption that independent variables must be uncorrelated with the error term). When such a misspecification occurs, estimates of regression coefficients will be biased and inconsistent. An example of this type of misspecification was mentioned earlier in the reading (in our discussion regarding the effects of serial correlation), when we proposed adding the previous month's T-Bill rate (lagged version of the dependent variable, nominal interest rates) as an independent variable to predict the 3-month T-Bill rate. In our true regression model, adding Y_{t-1} as a third independent variable in the regression would create a similar problem.
2. Using the regression to forecast the dependent variable at time, t+1 based on independent variables that are a function of the dependent variable at time, t+1. When this occurs, the independent variable is correlated with the error term, so the model is misspecified. For example, suppose an analyst builds a model to predict the returns of various stocks over 2010 based on their P/BV ratios at the end of 2010. In this case, a high return (the dependent variable) for 2010 actually causes the high P/BV ratio (independent variable) at the end of 2010 rather than the other way round. The same variable (price return) effectively appears on both sides of the regression equation so it would be incorrect to assert (based on this model) that returns can be predicted based on P/BV ratios.
3. Independent variables are measured with error. For example, in the Fisher relation equation, if we were to use actual inflation instead of expected inflation as the independent variable in the regression, the independent variable (actual inflation rates) would be correlated with the error term and the regression coefficients would be biased and inconsistent.
4. Another source of misspecification in time-series models is nonstationarity (which is discussed in detail in the next reading) which occurs when a variable's properties (e.g., mean and variance) are not constant over time.

LOS 10n: Describe models with qualitative dependent variables. Vol 1, pp 373–375

Qualitative Dependent Variables

A qualitative dependent variable is basically a dummy variable used as a dependent variable instead of as an independent variable (as we discussed earlier in the reading) in the regression. For example, whether or not a company will go bankrupt can be modeled as a qualitative dependent variable (1 = Will go bankrupt; 0 = Will not go bankrupt) based on various independent variables like its return on equity, leverage ratios, interest coverage ratios, etc. A linear regression model cannot be used to capture the relationship between the variables because the value that the dependent variable can take under such a model could be less than 0 or even greater than 1 (which is not empirically possible as the probability of going bankrupt cannot possibly be less than 0% or greater than 100%). Therefore, probit, logit, or discriminant models are used to model such regressions.

The probit model is based on the normal distribution. It estimates the probability that a qualitative condition is fulfilled (Y = 1) given the value of the independent variable (X). The logit model is similar except that it is based on the logistic distribution. Both models use maximum likelihood methodologies.

Discriminant analysis offers a linear function (similar to a regression equation) that is used to create an overall score on the basis of which an observation can be classified qualitatively (e.g., into a bankrupt or not bankrupt category).

The analysis of these models is very similar to the analysis of linear regression models as illustrated in this reading. The significance of the individual coefficients is evaluated using *t*-tests, while the strength of the overall model is judged on the basis of the *F*-test and R^2. Analysts must also watch out for heteroskedasticity, serial correlation, and multicollinearity in the regression.

LOS 10o: Evaluate and interpret a multiple regression model and its results.

This LOS basically covers everything we have covered in this reading. Just to help you review, we list the steps in assessing a multiple regression model in the flowchart in Figure 4-2:

Figure 4-2: Steps in Assessing a Multiple Regression Model

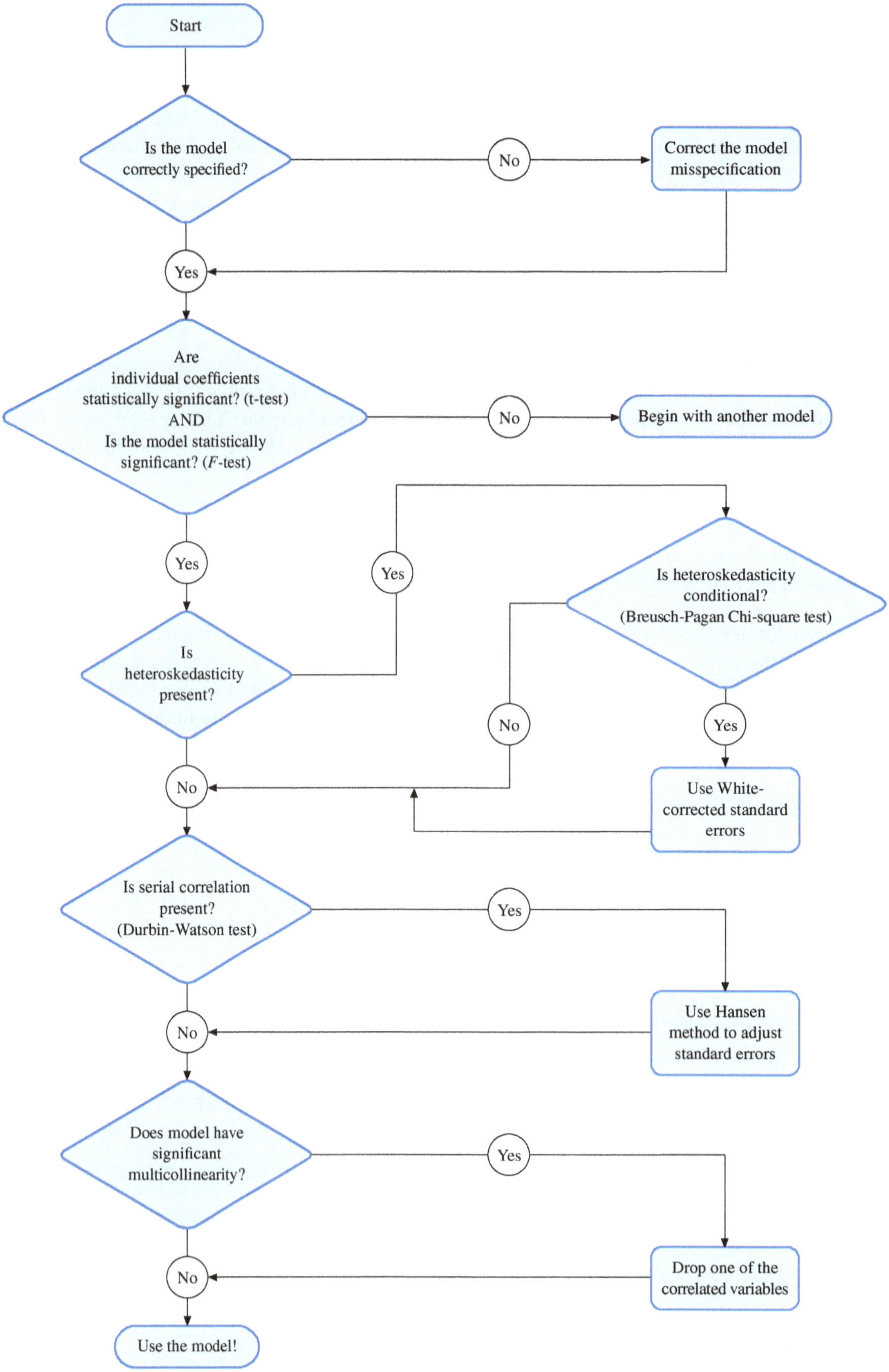

READING 11: TIME-SERIES ANALYSIS

LESSON 1: TREND MODELS

A **time series** is a set of observations of the outcomes for a particular variable over a period of time (e.g., the quarterly sales of a company over the last 10 years). Time-series analysis is undertaken (1) to explain the past and (2) to predict the future.

LOS 11a: Calculate and evaluate the predicted trend value for a time series, modeled as either a linear trend or a log-linear trend, given the estimated trend coefficients. Vol 1, pp 411–421

LOS 11b: Describe factors that determine whether a linear or a log-linear trend should be used with a particular time series, and evaluate limitations of trend models. Vol 1, pp 411–421

Trend Models

Linear Trend Models

A **linear trend model** is one in which the dependent variable changes by a constant amount in each period. On a graph, a linear trend is presented as a straight line, with a positively sloped line indicating an upward trend, and a negatively sloped line indicating a downward trend. Linear trends can be modeled with the following regression equation:

$$y_t = b_0 + b_1 t + \varepsilon_t, \qquad t = 1, 2, \ldots, T$$

where:
y_t = the value of the time series at time t (value of the dependent variable)
b_0 = the y-intercept term
b_1 = the slope coefficient/trend coefficient
t = time, the independent or explanatory variable
ε_t = a random-error term

Ordinary least squares (OLS) regression is used to estimate the regression coefficients ($\hat{b}_0$ and $\hat{b}_1$) and the resulting regression equation is used to predict the value of the time series (y_t) for any period (t). Notice that this model is very similar to the simple linear regression model that we studied earlier. In a linear trend model, the independent variable is the time period.

Another thing to note is that in a linear trend model, the value of the dependent variable changes by b_1 (the trend coefficient) in each successive time period (as t increases by 1 unit) irrespective of the level of the series in the previous period. See Example 1-1.

Example 1-1: Linear Trend Models

Keiron Gibbs wants to estimate the linear trend in inflation in Gunnerland over time. He uses monthly observations of the inflation rate (expressed as annual percentage rates) over the 30-year period from January 1981 to December 2010 and obtains the regression results shown in Table 1-1:

Table 1-1: Estimating a Linear Trend for Monthly Inflation Data

Regression Statistics	
R-squared	0.0537
Standard error	2.3541
Observations	360
Durbin-Watson	1.27

	Coefficient	Standard Error	*t*-Stat
Intercept	4.2587	0.4132	10.3066
Trend	–0.0087	0.0029	–3

Evaluating the Significance of Regression Coefficients

At the 5% significance level with 358 [calculated as 360 – (1 + 1)] degrees of freedom, the critical *t*-value for a two-tailed test is 1.972. Since the absolute values of the *t*-statistics for both the intercept (10.3066) and the trend coefficient (–3.00) are greater than the absolute value of the critical *t*-value, we conclude that both the regression coefficients ($\hat{b}_0 = 4.2587$, $\hat{b}_1 = -0.0087$) are statistically significant.

Estimating the Regression Equation

Based on these results, the estimated regression equation would be written as:

$$y_t = 4.2587 - 0.0087t$$

Using the Regression Results to Make Forecasts

The regression equation can be used to make in-sample forecasts (e.g., inflation for t =12, December 1981 is estimated at 4.2587 – 0.0087(12) = 4.1543%) and out-of-sample forecasts (e.g., inflation for t =384, December 2012 is estimated at 4.2587 – 0.0087(384) = 0.9179%). The regression equation also tells us that the inflation rate decreased by approximately 0.0087% (the trend coefficient) each month during the sample period.

Figure 1-1 shows a plot of the actual time series (monthly observations of the inflation rate during the sample period) along with the estimated regression line. Notice that the residuals appear to be uncorrelated and unpredictable over time and are not as persistent. Therefore, use of the linear trend to model the time series seems appropriate. However, the low R^2 of the model (5.37%) suggests that inflation forecasts from the model are quite uncertain, and that a better model may be available.

Figure 1-1: Monthly CPI Inflation with Trend

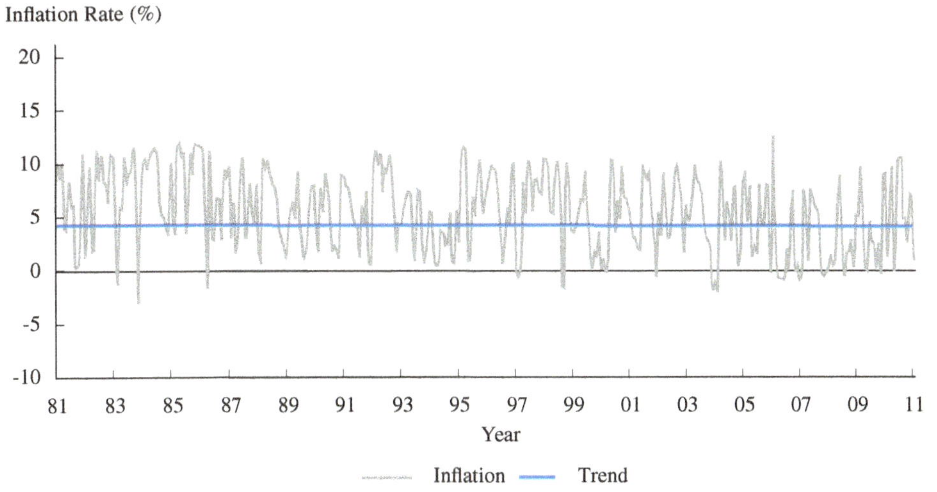

Log-Linear Trend Models

> Exponential growth is growth at a constant rate ($e^{b_1} - 1$) with continuous compounding.

A linear trend would not be appropriate to model a time series that exhibits exponential growth (i.e., constant growth at a particular rate) because the regression residuals would be persistent. Use of a log-linear trend may be more appropriate as such a model typically fits a time series that exhibits exponential growth quite well. A series that grows exponentially can be described using the following equation:

$$y_t = e^{b_0 + b_1 t}$$

where:
y_t = the value of the time series at time t (value of the dependent variable)
b_0 = the y-intercept term
b_1 = the slope coefficient
t = time = 1, 2, 3 … T

In this equation, the dependent variable (y_t) is an exponential function of the independent variable, time (t). We take the natural logarithm of both sides of the equation to arrive at the equation for the log-linear model:

$$\ln y_t = b_0 + b_1 t + \varepsilon_t, \qquad t = 1, 2, \ldots, T$$

> No time series grows at an exact exponential rate so we add the error term to the log-linear model equation.

The equation linking the variables, y_t and t, has been transformed from an exponential function to a linear function (the equation is linear in the coefficients, b_0 and b_1) so we can now use linear regression to model the series. See Example 1-2.

If we plot the data from a time series with positive exponential growth, the observations will form a convex curve like in Figure 1-2. Negative exponential growth means that the observed values of the series decrease at a constant rate, so the time series forms a concave curve.

Example 1-2: Linear versus Log-Linear Trend Model

Samir Nasri wants to model the quarterly sales made by ABC Company over the 15-year period from 1991 to 2005. Quarterly sales data over the period is illustrated in Figure 1-2 below:

Figure 1-2: ABC Company Quarterly Sales

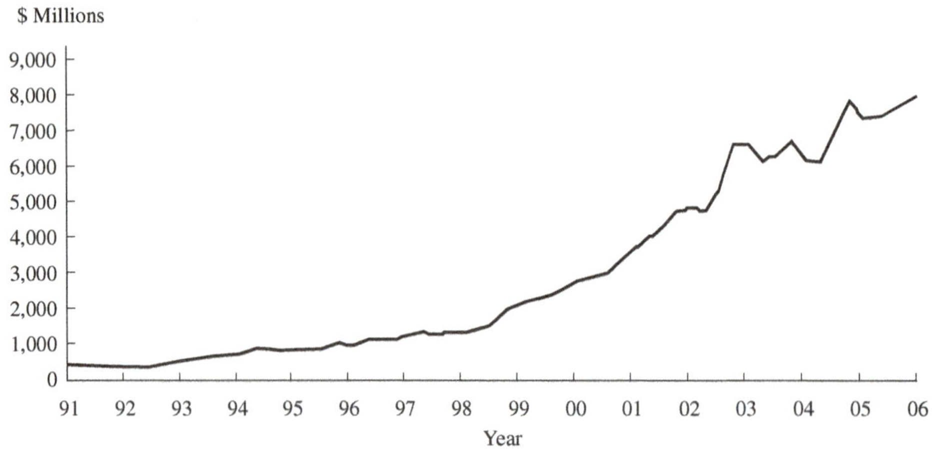

Initially, Nasri uses a linear trend model to capture the data. The results from the regression are presented in Table 1-2:

Table 1-2: Estimating a Linear Trend for ABC Company Sales

Regression Statistics	
R-squared	0.8443
Standard error	786.32
Observations	60
Durbin-Watson	0.15

	Coefficient	**Standard Error**	***t*-Stat**
Intercept	−1,212.46	335.8417	−3.6102
Trend	125.3872	6.3542	19.733

The results of the regression seem to support the use of a linear trend model to fit the data. The absolute values of the *t*-stats of both the intercept and the trend coefficient (−3.61 and 19.73 respectively) appear statistically significant as they exceed the critical *t*-value of 2.0 ($\alpha = 0.05$, df = 58). However, when quarterly sales are plotted along with the trend line (Figure 1-3), the errors seem to be persistent (the residuals remain above or below the trend line for an extended period of time), which suggests that they are positively serially correlated. The persistent serial correlation in the residuals makes the linear regression model inappropriate (even though the R^2 is quite high at 84.43%) to fit ABC's sales as it violates the regression assumption of uncorrelated residual errors.

Figure 1-3: ABC Company Quarterly Sales with Trend

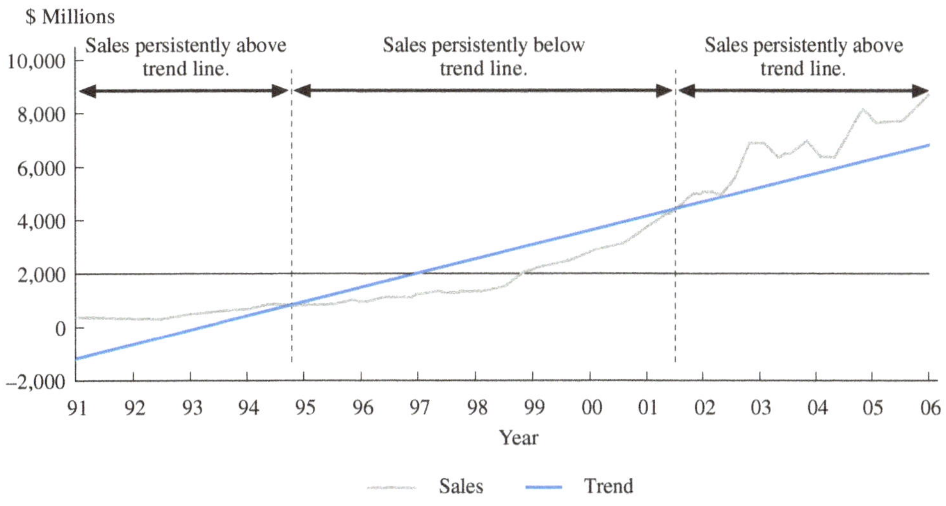

Since the sales data plot (Figure 1-2) is curved upward, Nasri's supervisor suggests that he use the log-linear model. Nasri then estimates the following log-linear regression equation:

$$\ln y_t = b_0 + b_1 t + \varepsilon_t, \qquad t = 1, 2, \ldots, 60$$

Table 1-3 presents the log-linear regression results.

Table 1-3: Estimating a Linear Trend in Lognormal ABC Company Sales

Regression Statistics	
R-squared	0.9524
Standard error	0.1235
Observations	60
Durbin-Watson	0.37

	Coefficient	Standard Error	*t*-Stat
Intercept	4.6842	0.0453	103.404
Trend	0.0686	0.0008	85.75

An R^2 of 0.9524 means that 95.24% of the variation in the natural log of ABC's sales is explained solely by a linear trend.

The high *t*-stats for the intercept and trend coefficient suggest that the regression parameters are significantly different from zero so the log-linear model (like the linear model described on the previous page) does hold explanatory power. Further, notice that the R^2 (95.24%) is now much higher than in Table 1-2 (linear trend model regression results where the R^2 was 84.43%). This suggests that the log-linear model fits the sales data much better than the linear trend model. Figure 1-4 plots the linear trend line suggested by the log-linear regression along with the natural logs of the sales data. Notice that the vertical distances between the lines are quite small, and that the residuals are not persistent (log actual sales are not above or below the trend line for an extended period of time). Consequently, Nasri concludes that the log-linear trend model is more suitable for modeling ABC's sales compared to the linear trend model.

Figure 1-4: Natural Log of ABC Company Quarterly Sales

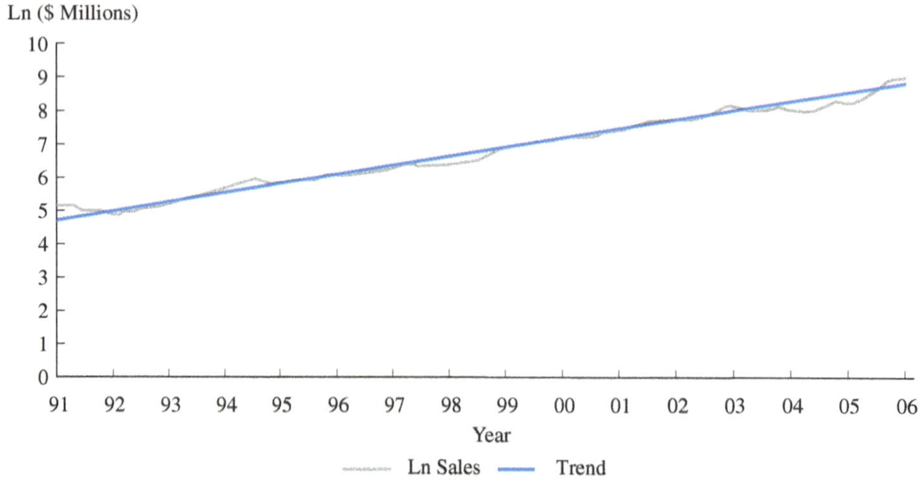

To illustrate how log-linear trend models are used in making forecasts, let's calculate ABC's expected sales for Q3 2006, or Quarter 63 (an out-of-sample forecast).

$$\ln \hat{y} = 4.6842 + 0.0686(63)$$
$$\hat{y}_{63} = \$8{,}151.849 \text{ million}$$

Compared to the forecast for Quarter 63 sales based on the linear trend model (–1,212.46 + 125.3872(63) = \$6,686.93 million) the log-linear regression model offers a much higher forecast.

An important difference between the linear and log-linear trend models lies in the interpretation of the slope coefficient, b_1.

- A linear trend model predicts that y_t will grow by a **constant amount** (b_1) each period. For example, if b_1 equals 0.1%, y_t will grow by 0.1% in each period.
- A log-linear trend model predicts that **ln y_t** will grow by a constant amount (b_1) in each period. This means that y_t itself will witness a **constant growth rate** of $e^{b_1} - 1$ in each period. For example, if b_1 equals 0.1% then the predicted growth rate of y_t in each period equals $e^{0.001} - 1 = 0.0010005$ or 0.10005%.

Also, in a linear trend model the predicted value of y_t is $\hat{b}_0 + \hat{b}_1 t$, but in a log-linear trend model the predicted value of y_t is $e^{\hat{b}_0 + \hat{b}_1 t}$ because $e^{\ln y_t} = y_t$.

Testing for Correlated Errors in Trend Models

If a regression model is correctly specified, the regression error for one time period will be uncorrelated with the regression errors for other time periods. One way to determine whether the error terms are correlated across time periods is to inspect the plot of residuals. Figure 1-5 plots the residuals when a **linear trend** is used to model ABC Company's sales. The figure clearly indicates that there is persistent serial correlation in the residuals of the model.

Figure 1-5: Residual from Predicting ABC Company Sales with a Linear Trend

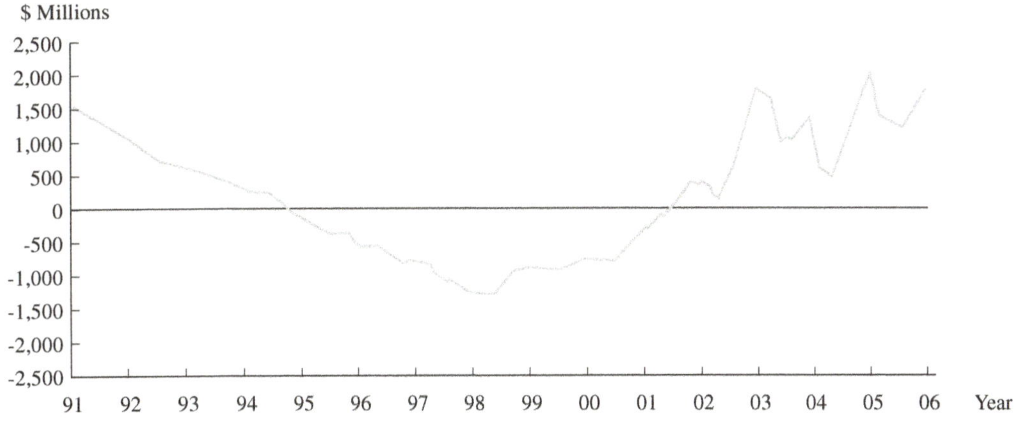

Figure 1-5 shows us that the errors of the **linear trend model** are serially correlated.

The Durbin-Watson test shows us that the errors of the **log-linear trend** are also serially correlated.

However, a more formal test to determine whether the regression errors are serially correlated is the Durbin-Watson (DW) test.

The DW stat for the **log-linear trend model** (Table 1-3 in Example 1-2) equals 0.37. To test the null hypothesis of no positive serial correlation in the residuals at the 5% level of significance, the critical value (d_l) equals 1.55 (k = 1, n = 60). Since the value of the DW stat is less than d_l, we reject the null hypothesis and conclude that the log-linear model does suffer from positive serial correlation. Consequently, we need to build a different kind of model to represent the relation between time and ABC Company's sales.

Existence of serial correlation suggests that we can build better forecasting models than trend models to fit the series.

LESSON 2: AUTOREGRESSIVE (AR) TIME SERIES MODELS

LOS 11c: Explain the requirement for a time series to be covariance stationary and describe the significance of a series that is not stationary. Vol 1, pp 422–423

LOS 11d: Describe the structure of an autoregressive (AR) model of order *p* and calculate one- and two-period-ahead forecasts, given the estimated coefficients. Vol 1, pp 421–434

LOS 11e: Explain how autocorrelations of the residuals can be used to test whether the autoregressive model fits the time series. Vol 1, pp 421–434

LOS 11f: Explain mean reversion, and calculate a mean-reverting level. Vol 1, pp 426–430

Autoregressive (AR) Time-Series Models

An autoregressive (AR) model is a time series that is regressed on its own past values. Since the same variable essentially shows up on both sides of the equation (as a dependent and an independent variable), we drop the normal notation of y_t as the dependent variable and only use x_t. For example, an AR(1) model (first-order autoregressive model) is represented as:

$$x_t = b_0 + b_1 x_{t-1} + \varepsilon_t$$

Note: In an AR(1) model, only the single most-recent past value of x_t is used to predict the current value of x_t.

A *p*th order autoregressive model is represented as:

$$x_t = b_0 + b_1 x_{t-1} + b_2 x_{t-2} + \ldots + b_p x_{t-p} + \varepsilon_t$$

Note: An AR(*p*) model uses *p* past values of x_t to predict the current value of x_t.

Covariance Stationary Series

When an independent variable in the regression equation is a lagged value of the dependent variable (as is the case in autoregressive time-series models) statistical inferences based on OLS regression are not always valid. In order to conduct statistical inference based on these models, we must assume that the time series is **covariance stationary** or **weakly stationary**. There are three basic requirements for a time series to be covariance stationary:

1. The expected value or mean of the time series must be constant and finite in all periods.
2. The variance of the time series must be constant and finite in all periods.
3. The covariance of the time series with itself for a fixed number of periods in the past or future must be constant and finite in all periods.

If an AR model is used to model a time series that is not covariance stationary, the analyst would obtain biased estimates of the slope coefficient(s), which would render the results of any hypothesis tests invalid. Such a model would only yield spurious results.

One way to determine whether a time series is covariance stationary is by looking at a graphical plot of the data. The inflation data in Example 1-1 appears to be covariance stationary (see Figure 1-1). The data seem to have the same mean and variance over the sample period. On the other hand, ABC Company's quarterly sales appear to grow steadily over time, which implies that the mean is not constant and therefore, the series is not covariance stationary (see Figure 1-2).

Other (more sophisticated) ways to determine whether a time series is covariance stationary are presented under LOS 11j. If a time series is not covariance stationary, there is a way to convert it into a stationary time series. This method (first differencing) is also demonstrated later in the reading.

> Aside from being covariance stationary and having uncorrelated residuals, an appropriately specified AR model should have homoskedastic (not heteroskedastic) errors. We learn to test the residuals of an AR model for heteroskedasticity in LOS 11m.

Detecting Serially Correlated Errors in an AR Model

An AR model can be estimated using ordinary least squares if (1) the time series is covariance stationary and (2) the errors are uncorrelated. Tests for stationarity are discussed later in the reading (examining the time-series autocorrelations at various lags and the unit-root test), but first let's discuss how we can test whether the residuals are serially correlated. The Durbin-Watson test cannot be used to test for serial correlation in an AR model because the independent variables include past values of the dependent variable. However, another test based on the **autocorrelations of the error term** can be used to determine if the errors in the AR time series model are serially correlated.

> Note that this test for serial correlation focuses on the **autocorrelations of the error term**, which are different from the autocorrelations of the time series itself.

We determine whether the residuals of the time-series model are serially correlated by testing whether the autocorrelations of the error terms (error autocorrelations or residual autocorrelations) are significantly different from 0.

- If any of the error autocorrelations are significantly different from 0, the errors are serially correlated and the model is not specified correctly.
- If all the error autocorrelations are not significantly different from 0, the errors are not serially correlated and the model is specified correctly.

To determine whether an error autocorrelation for a particular lag is significantly different from 0, we perform a *t*-test, where the *t*-stat is calculated as the error autocorrelation for that particular lag divided by the standard error of the residual autocorrelation (which equals $1/\sqrt{T}$).

$$t\text{-stat} = \frac{\text{Residual autocorrelation for lag}}{\text{Standard error of residual autocorrelation}}$$

where:
Standard error of residual autocorrelation = $1/\sqrt{T}$
T = Number of observations in the time series

There are three basic steps (illustrated in Example 2-1) for detecting serially correlated errors in an AR time-series model:

1. Estimate a particular AR model.
2. Compute the autocorrelations of the residuals from the model.
3. Determine whether the residual autocorrelations significantly differ from 0.

Example 2-1: Testing whether an AR Time-Series Model Has Serially Correlated Errors

Jack Wilshire uses a time-series model to predict ABC Company's gross margins. He uses quarterly data from Q1 1981 to Q4 1995. Since he believes that the gross margin in the current period is dependent on the gross margin in the previous period, he starts with an AR(1) model:

$$\text{Gross margin}_t = b_0 + b_1(\text{Gross margin}_{t-1}) + \varepsilon_t$$

Table 2-1 presents the results from estimating the AR(1) model while Table 2-2 presents the autocorrelations of the residuals from the model.

Table 2-1: AR(1) Model Regression Results

Regression Statistics	
R-squared	0.7521
Standard error	0.0387
Observations	60
Durbin-Watson	1.9132

	Coefficient	**Standard Error**	***t*-Stat**
Intercept	0.0795	0.0352	2.259
Lag 1	0.8524	0.0602	14.159

Table 2-2: Autocorrelations of the Residuals from the AR(1) Model

Lag	Autocorrelation	Standard Error	*t*-Stat
1	0.0583	0.1291	0.4516
2	0.0796	0.1291	0.6166
3	–0.1921	0.1291	–1.4880
4	–0.1285	0.1291	–0.9954

The first lag of a time series is the value of the time series in the previous period.

From Table 2-1 notice that the intercept ($\hat{b}_0 = 0.0795$) and the coefficient on the first lag ($\hat{b}_1 = 0.8524$) are highly significant in this regression. The *t*-stat of the intercept (2.259) and that of the coefficient on the first lag of the gross margin (14.159) are both greater than the critical *t*-value for a 2-tail test at the 5% significance level with 58 degrees of freedom ($t_c = 2.0$).

Even though Wilshire concludes that both the regression coefficients individually do not equal 0 (or are statistically significant), he must still evaluate the validity of the model by ensuring that the residuals from his model are not serially correlated. Since this is an AR model (the independent variables include past values of the dependent variable) the Durbin-Watson test for serial correlation cannot be used.

Table 2-2 lists the first four autocorrelations of the residual along with their standard errors and *t*-statistics. Since there are 60 observations, the standard error for each of the residual autocorrelations equals 0.1291 (calculated as $1/\sqrt{60}$). None of the *t*-stats in Table 2-2 is greater than 2.0 (critical *t*-value) in absolute value, which indicates that none of the residual autocorrelations significantly differs from 0. Wilshire concludes that the regression residuals are not serially correlated and that his AR(1) model is correctly specified. Therefore, he can use ordinary least squares to estimate the parameters and the standard errors of the parameters in his model.

Note that if any of the lag autocorrelations were significantly different from zero (if they had *t*-stats that were greater than the critical *t*-value in absolute value) the model would be misspecified due to serial correlation between the residuals. If the residuals of an AR model are serially correlated, the model can be improved by adding more lags of the dependent variable as explanatory (independent) variables. More and more lags of the dependent variable must be added as independent variables in the model until all the residual autocorrelations are insignificant.

Once it has been established that the residuals are not serially correlated and that the model is correctly specified, it can be used to make forecasts. The estimated regression equation in this example is given as:

$$\text{Gross margin}_t = 0.0795 + 0.8524(\text{Gross margin}_{t-1})$$

From the regression equation, note that:

- If the gross margin is currently 50%, the model predicts that next quarter's gross margin will *increase* to 0.5057 or 50.57%.
- If the gross margin is currently 60%, the model predicts that next quarter's gross margin will *decrease* to 0.5909 or 59.09%.

As we will learn in the next section, the model predicts an increase in the gross margin during a particular quarter if the gross margin in the previous quarter was less than 53.86%, and a decrease in the gross margin during a particular quarter if the gross margin in the previous quarter was greater than 53.86%.

Mean Reversion

A time series is said to exhibit mean reversion if it tends to fall when its current level is above the mean and tends to rise when its current level is below the mean. The mean-reverting level, x_t, for a time series is given as:

$$x_t = \frac{b_0}{1-b_1}$$

- If a time series is currently at its mean-reverting level, the model predicts that its value will remain unchanged in the next period.
- If a time series is currently above its mean-reverting level, the model predicts that its value will decrease in the next period.
- If a time series is currently below its mean-reverting level, the model predicts that its value will increase in the next period.

In the case of gross margins for ABC Company (Example 2-1), the mean-reverting level is calculated as 0.0795/(1 – 0.8524) = 0.5386 or 53.86%.

Important: All covariance stationary time series have a finite mean-reverting level. An AR(1) time series will have a finite mean-reverting level if the absolute value of the lag coefficient, b_1, is less than 1.

An AR(1) time series is said to have a unit root if b_1 equals 1, and is said to have an explosive root if b_1 is greater than 1. Only if the time series has a finite mean-reverting level ($b_1 < 1$) can standard regression analysis be applied to estimate an AR(1) model to fit the series. More on this in LOS 11 i, j, and k.

Multiperiod Forecasts and the Chain Rule of Forecasting

The chain rule of forecasting is used to make multiperiod forecasts based on an autoregressive time-series model. For example, a one-period forecast ($\hat{x}_{t+1}$) based on an AR(1) model is calculated as:

$$\hat{x}_{t+1} = \hat{b}_0 + \hat{b}_1 x_t$$

Using this one-period forecast ($\hat{x}_{t+1}$), the two-period forecast is calculated as:

$$\hat{x}_{t+2} = \hat{b}_0 + \hat{b}_1 x_{t+1}$$

Since we do not know x_{t+1} in period t, we must start by forecasting x_{t+1} using x_t as an input and then forecast x_{t+2} using our forecast of x_{t+1} as an input. See Example 2-2.

Note that multiperiod forecasts entail more uncertainty than single-period forecasts because each period's forecast (used as an input to eventually arrive at the multiperiod forecast) entails uncertainty. Generally speaking, the more periods a forecast has, the greater the uncertainty.

Notice that since x_t and x_{t+1} are greater than the mean-reverting level (0.5386), the value of the series falls in subsequent periods.

Example 2-2: Chain Rule of Forecasting

Assume that ABC Company's gross margin for the current quarter is 65%. Using the AR(1) model in Example 2-1, forecast ABC's gross margin in two quarters.

Solution:

First we forecast next quarter's gross margin based on the current quarter's gross margin:

Gross $\text{margin}_{t+1} = 0.0795 + 0.8524(\text{Gross margin}_t) = 0.0795 + 0.8524(0.65) = 0.6336$ or 63.36%

Then we forecast the gross margin in two quarters based on next period's gross margin forecast:

Gross $\text{margin}_{t+2} = 0.0795 + 0.8524(\text{Gross margin}_{t+1}) = 0.0795 + 0.8524(0.6336) = 0.6196$ or 61.96%

LOS 11g: Contrast in-sample and out-of-sample forecasts and compare the forecasting accuracy of different time-series models based on the root mean squared error criterion. Vol 1, pp 430–432

Comparing Forecast Model Performance

One way to evaluate the forecasting performance of two models is by comparing their standard errors. The standard error for the time-series regression is typically reported in the statistical output for the regression. The model with the smaller standard error will be more accurate as it will have a smaller forecast error variance (s_f^2).

When comparing the forecasting performance of various models, analysts distinguish between in-sample forecast errors and out-of-sample forecast errors. In-sample forecast errors are differences between the actual values of the dependent variable and predicted values of the dependent variable (based on the estimated regression equation) **for data from within the sample period**. In essence, in-sample forecasts are the residuals from a fitted time-series model. For instance, in Example 1-1, the residuals of the regression (differences between actual inflation and forecasted inflation for the months lying in the January 1981 to December 2010 sample period) represent in-sample forecast errors. If we were to predict inflation for a month **outside the sample period** (e.g., July 2012) based on this model, the difference between actual and predicted inflation would represent an out-of-sample forecast error. Out-of-sample forecasts are important in evaluating the model's contribution and applicability in the real world.

The out-of-sample forecasting performance of autoregressive models is evaluated on the basis of their root mean square error (RMSE). The RMSE for each model under consideration is calculated based on out-of-sample data. The model with the lowest RMSE has the lowest forecast error and hence carries the most predictive power.

For example, consider a data set that includes 35 observations of historical annual unemployment rates. Suppose we considered only the first 30 years as the sample period in developing our time-series models, and we came up with an AR(1) and an AR(2) model to fit the 30-year unemployment data. The remaining 5 years of data from Year 31 to Year 35 (the out-of-sample data) would be used to calculate the RMSE for the two models, and the model with the lower RMSE would be judged to have greater predictive power. Bear in mind that a model with the lower RMSE (more accuracy) for in-sample data will not necessarily have a lower RMSE for out-of-sample data.

In addition to the forecasting accuracy of a model, the stability of the regression coefficients (discussed in the next LOS) is an important consideration when evaluating a model.

LOS 11h: Explain the instability of coefficients of time-series models.

Vol 1, pp 432–434

Instability of Regression Coefficients

The choice of sample period is a very important consideration when constructing time-series models. This is because:

- Regression estimates from time-series models based on different sample periods can be quite different.
- Regression estimates obtained from models based on longer sample periods can be quite different from estimates from models based on shorter sample periods.

There are no clear-cut rules that define an ideal length for the sample period. Based on the fact that models are only valid if the time series is covariance stationary, analysts look to define sample periods as times during which important underlying economic conditions have remained unchanged. For example, data from a period when exchange rates were fixed should not be combined with data from a period when they were floating as the variance of the exchange rate would be different under the two regimes. Usually, analysts look at graphs of the data to see if the series looks stationary. If there has been a significant shift in governmental policy during the period, analysts use their experience and judgement to determine whether the time-series relation has remained the same before and after the shift. If the relation has changed and the series is not covariance stationary, models based on the data will not be valid.

The point here is that even if the autocorrelations of the residuals of a time-series model are statistically insignificant, analysts cannot conclude that the sample period used is appropriate (and hence deem the model valid) until they are, at the same time, confident that the series is covariance stationary and that important external factors have remained constant during the sample period used in the study.

LESSON 3: RANDOM WALKS AND UNIT ROOTS

LOS 11i: Describe characteristics of random walk processes and contrast them to covariance stationary processes. Vol 1, pp 435–438

Random Walks

A random walk, simple random walk, or random walk without a drift is a time series in which the value of the series in one period equals its value in the previous period plus an unpredictable random error, where the error has a constant variance and is uncorrelated with its value in previous periods.

$$x_t = x_{t-1} + \varepsilon_t, \ E(\varepsilon_t) = 0, \ E(\varepsilon_t^2) = \sigma^2, \ E(\varepsilon_t \varepsilon_s) = 0 \text{ if } t \neq s$$

It is important to note the following regarding random walks:

- The random walk equation is a special case of the AR(1) model where b_0 equals 0, and b_1 equals 1.
- The best forecast of x_t is essentially x_{t-1} as the expected value of the error term is 0.

Standard regression analysis cannot be applied to estimate an AR(1) model for a time series that follows a random walk. Statistical conclusions based on such a model would be incorrect because AR models cannot be used to model any time series that is not covariance stationary. Random walks are not covariance stationary as:

- They do not have a finite mean-reverting level. For a random walk, the mean-reverting level is undefined. $b_0/(1-b_1) = 0/(1-1) = 0/0$
- They do not have a finite variance. As t increases, the variance of x_t grows with no upper bound (it approaches infinity).

A random walk can be converted to a covariance stationary time series. This is done through first differencing, which subtracts the value of the time series in the previous period from its value in the current period. The new time series, y_t, is calculated as x_t minus x_{t-1}. The first difference of the random walk equation is given as:

$$y_t = x_t - x_{t-1} = x_{t-1} + \varepsilon_t - x_{t-1} = \varepsilon_t, \ E(\varepsilon_t) = 0, \ E(\varepsilon_t^2) = \sigma^2, \ E(\varepsilon_t \varepsilon_s) = 0 \text{ for } t \neq s$$

By using the first-differenced time series, we are essentially modeling the change in the value of the dependent variable ($\Delta x_t = x_t - x_{t-1}$) rather than the value of the variable itself (x_t). From the first differenced random walk equation, note that:

By definition, changes in a random walk (y_t or $x_t - x_{t-1}$) are unpredictable.

- Since the expected value of the error term is 0, the best forecast of y_t is 0, which implies that there will be no change in the value of the current time series, x_{t-1}.
- y_t, the first-differenced variable, is covariance stationary with a finite mean-reverting level of 0 [calculated as 0/(1 – 0)] as b_0 and b_1 both equal 0, and a finite variance [$\text{Var}(\varepsilon_t) = \sigma^2$].
- Therefore, we can use linear regression to model the first-differenced series.

Modeling the first-differenced time series with an AR(1) model does not hold predictive value (as b_0 and b_1 both equal 0). It only serves to confirm a suspicion that the original time series is indeed a random walk. See Example 3-1.

Example 3-1: Determining Whether a Time Series Is a Random Walk

Aaron Ramsey develops the following **AR(1) model** for the Japanese Yen/USD exchange rate (x_t) based on monthly observations over 30 years.

$$x_t = x_{t-1} + \varepsilon_t$$

Table 3-1 contains data relating to his AR(1) model.

Table 3-1: AR(1) Model for JPY/USD Exchange Rate

Regression Statistics	
R-squared	0.9852
Standard error	5.8623
Observations	360
Durbin-Watson	1.9512

	Coefficient	**Standard Error**	***t*-Stat**
Intercept	1.0175	0.9523	1.0685
Lag 1	0.9954	0.0052	191.42

Autocorrelations of the Residuals

Lag	**Autocorrelation**	**Standard Error**	***t*-Stat**
1	0.0745	0.0527	1.4137
2	0.0852	0.0527	1.6167
3	0.0321	0.0527	0.6091
4	0.0525	0.0527	0.9962

Notice the following:

- The intercept term is not significantly different from 0. The low *t*-stat of 1.06 does not allow you to reject the null hypothesis that the intercept term equals 0 as it is less than the critical *t*-value of 1.972 at the 5% significance level.
- The coefficient on the first lag of the exchange rate is significantly different from 0 (high *t*-stat of 191.42 allows you to reject the null hypothesis that it equals 0) and is actually very close to 1 (coefficient on the first lag of the time series equals 0.9954).

However, we cannot use the *t*-stats in Table 3-1 to determine whether the exchange rate is a random walk (by conducting a hypothesis test on H_0: $b_0 = 0$ and H_0: $b_1 = 1$) because the standard errors of this AR model would be invalid if the model is based on a time series that is not covariance stationary. Recall that a random walk is not covariance stationary.

In order to determine whether the time series is indeed a random walk, we must run a regression on the first-differenced time series. If the exchange rate is, in fact, a random walk then:

1. The first-differenced time series will be covariance stationary as b_0 and b_1 would equal 0; and
2. The error term will not be serially correlated.

Table 3-2 presents the regression results for the first-differenced AR(1) model for the JPY/USD exchange rate.

Table 3-2: First-Differenced AR(1) Model for JPY/USD Exchange Rate

Regression Statistics	
R-squared	0.0052
Standard error	5.8751
Observations	360
Durbin-Watson	1.9812

	Coefficient	**Standard Error**	***t*-Stat**
Intercept	–0.4855	0.3287	–1.477
Lag 1	0.0651	0.0525	1.240

Autocorrelations of the Residuals

Lag	**Autocorrelation**	**Standard Error**	***t*-Stat**
1	0.0695	0.0527	1.3188
2	–0.0523	0.0527	–0.9924
3	0.0231	0.0527	0.4383
4	0.0514	0.0527	0.9753

From Table 3-2, notice that:

- The intercept term (b_0) and the coefficient on the first lag of the first-differenced exchange rate (b_1) both individually do not significantly differ from 0. The absolute values of their t-stats (1.477 and 1.24 respectively) are lower than the absolute value of t_{crit} (1.972) at the 5% significance level.
- The t-stats for all the residual autocorrelations are lower than the critical t-value (1.972). None of the residual autocorrelations significantly differs from 0 which means that there is no serial correlation.

Since (1) b_0 and b_1 for the first-differenced AR(1) model both equal 0, and (2) there is no serial correlation in the error terms of the first-differenced time series, we can conclude that the JPY/USD exchange rate is a random walk.

Just one minor point before we move ahead. The R^2 in Table 3-1 for the AR(1) model on the original time series ($R^2 = 0.9852$) is much higher than the R^2 in Table 3-2 for the AR(1) model on the first-differenced time series ($R^2 = 0.0052$). If we were to base our choice of model on R^2 alone, we would make the incorrect choice and go with the AR(1) model on the original time series (which is not covariance stationary) instead of the AR(1) model on the first-differenced time series (which actually is covariance stationary). The interpretations of the R^2's of the two models are fundamentally different:

- The R^2 in Table 3-1 measures how well the exchange rate in one period predicts the exchange rate in the next period. If the exchange rate is a random walk, this number should be extremely high (which it is).

- The R^2 in Table 3-2 measures how well the **change** in the exchange rate in one period predicts the **change** in the exchange rate in the next period. If the exchange rate is a random walk, changes in the exchange rate should be completely unpredictable and this number should be relatively low (which it is).

Random Walk with a Drift

A random walk with a drift is a time series that increases or decreases by a constant amount in each period. The equation for a random walk with a drift is given as:

$$x_t = b_0 + b_1 x_{t-1} + \varepsilon_t$$
$$b_1 = 1, b_0 \neq 0, \text{ or}$$
$$x_t = b_0 + x_{t-1} + \varepsilon_t, \ E(\varepsilon_t) = 0$$

Unlike a simple random walk (which has $b_0 = 0$), a random walk with a drift has $b_0 \neq 0$. Similar to a simple random walk, a random walk with a drift also has an undefined mean-reverting level (because $b_1 = 1$) and is therefore, not covariance stationary. Consequently, an AR(1) model cannot be used to analyze a random walk with a drift without first-differencing it. The first-difference of the random walk with a drift equation is given as:

$$y_t = x_t - x_{t-1}, \ y_t = b_0 + \varepsilon_t, \ b_0 \neq 0$$

LOS 11j: Describe implications of unit roots for time-series analysis, explain when unit roots are likely to occur and how to test for them, and demonstrate how a time series with a unit root can be transformed so it can be analyzed with an AR model. Vol 1, pp 439–443

LOS 11k: Describe the steps of the unit root test for nonstationarity and explain the relation of the test to autoregressive time-series models. Vol 1, pp 439–443

The Unit Root Test of Nonstationarity

When we introduced covariance stationarity earlier in this reading (under LOS 11c), we stated that one way to determine whether a time series is covariance stationary is by examining a graph that plots the data. There are two (more sophisticated) ways to determine whether a time series is covariance stationary:

> Here we are not talking about the residual autocorrelations (which are used to test for serial correlation as in Example 2-1), but are referring to the autocorrelations of the **actual time series.**

1. Examine the autocorrelations of the time series at various lags. For a stationary time series, either the time series autocorrelations at all lags do not significantly differ from 0, or the autocorrelations drop off rapidly to 0 as the number of lags become large. For a nonstationary time series, the time series autocorrelations do not exhibit either of these characteristics.

2. Conduct the Dickey-Fuller test for unit root (preferred approach). A time series is said to have a unit root when the estimated value of the lag coefficient equals 1. A time series that has a unit root is a random walk, which is not covariance stationary. As we have mentioned before, for statistical reasons, simple t-tests cannot be used to test whether the coefficient on the first lag of the time series in an AR(1) model is significantly different from 1. However, the Dickey-Fuller test can be used to test for a unit root.

The Dickey-Fuller test starts by converting the lag coefficient, b_1, in a simple AR(1) model into g_1, which effectively represents $b_1 - 1$, by subtracting x_{t-1} from both sides of the AR(1) equation:

$$
\begin{aligned}
x_t &= b_0 + b_1 x_{t-1} + \varepsilon_t \\
x_t - x_{t-1} &= b_0 + b_1 x_{t-1} - x_{t-1} + \varepsilon_t \\
x_t - x_{t-1} &= b_0 + (b_1 - 1) x_{t-1} + \varepsilon_t \\
x_t - x_{t-1} &= b_0 + g_1 x_{t-1} + \varepsilon_t
\end{aligned}
$$

We have already introduced first-differencing in an earlier LOS.

Note that the dependent variable $(x_t - x_{t-1})$ is the first difference of the time series and the independent variable (x_{t-1}) is the first lag of the time series.

- The null hypothesis for the Dickey-Fuller test is that $g_1 = 0$ (effectively means that $b_1 = 1$) and that the time series has a unit root, which makes it nonstationary.
- The alternative hypothesis for the Dickey-Fuller test is that $g_1 < 0$, (effectively means that $b_1 < 1$) and that the time series is covariance stationary (i.e., it does not have a unit root).
- The t-stat for the Dickey-Fuller test is calculated in the same manner that we have been using in the reading so far, but the critical values used in the test are different. Dickey-Fuller critical values are larger in absolute value than conventional critical t-values. See Example 3-2.

Example 3-2: Using First Differenced Data to Make Forecasts

Samir Nasri (the analyst from Example 1-2) is convinced, after looking at Figures 1-2 and 1-4, that ABC's quarterly sales and the logs of ABC's quarterly sales do not represent covariance stationary time series. He therefore first-differences the log of ABC's quarterly sales (see Figure 3-1).

Figure 3-1: Log Difference of ABC Company Quarterly Sales

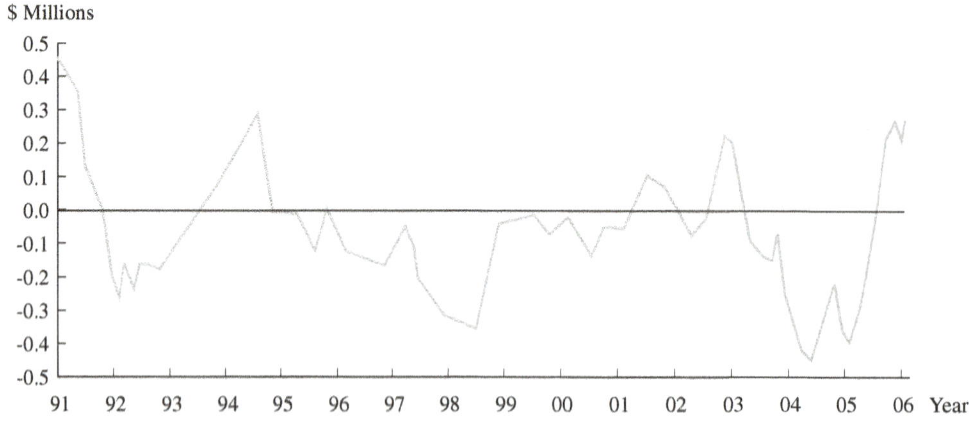

Figure 3-1 shows that the first-differenced series does not exhibit any strong trend and appears to be covariance stationary. He therefore decides to model the first-differenced time series as an AR(1) model:

$$\ln(\text{Sales}_t) - (\ln \text{Sales}_{t-1}) = b_0 + b_1[\ln(\text{Sales}_{t-1}) - (\ln \text{Sales}_{t-2})] + \varepsilon_t$$

Table 3-3 shows the results of the regression:

Table 3-3: Log Differenced Sales: AR(1) Model for ABC Company Quarterly Sales

Regression Statistics	
R-squared	0.1065
Standard error	0.0617
Observations	60
Durbin-Watson	1.9835

	Coefficient	Standard Error	*t*-Stat
Intercept	0.0485	0.0152	3.1908
Lag 1	0.3728	0.1324	2.8158

Autocorrelations of the Residuals from the AR(1) Model

Lag	Autocorrelation	Standard Error	*t*-Stat
1	−0.0185	0.1291	−0.1433
2	−0.0758	0.1291	−0.5871
3	−0.0496	0.1291	−0.3842
4	0.2026	0.1291	1.5693

From Table 3-3 notice the following:

- At the 5% significance level, both the regression coefficients ($\hat{b}_0 = 0.0485$, $\hat{b}_1 = 0.3728$) of the first-differenced series are statistically significant as their *t*-stats (3.19 and 2.82 respectively are greater than t_{crit} (2.00) with df = 58.
- The four autocorrelations of the residuals are statistically insignificant. Their *t*-stats are smaller in absolute value than t_{crit} so we fail to reject the null hypotheses that each of the residual autocorrelations equals 0. We therefore conclude that there is no serial correlation in the residuals of the regression.

These results suggest that the model is correctly specified and can be used to make predictions of ABC Company's quarterly sales. The value of the intercept ($\hat{b}_0 = 0.0485$) indicates that if sales have not changed in the current quarter ($\ln \text{Sales}_t - \ln \text{Sales}_{t-1} = 0$) sales will grow by 4.85% in the next quarter ($\ln \text{Sales}_{t+1} - \ln \text{Sales}_t$). If sales have changed in the current quarter, the slope coefficient ($\hat{b}_1 = 0.3728$) tells us that in the next quarter, sales will grow by 4.85% plus 0.3728 times sales growth in the current quarter.

Suppose we want to predict sales for the first quarter of 2006 based on the first-differenced model. We are given the following pieces of information:

Sales Q4 2005 = Sales_t = \$8,157m
Sales Q3 2005 = Sales_{t-1} = \$7,452m
Sales Q1 2006 = Sales_{t+1} = ?

Our regression equation is given as:

$$\ln \text{Sales}_t - \ln \text{Sales}_{t-1} = 0.0485 + 0.3728\ (\ln \text{Sales}_{t-1} - \ln \text{Sales}_{t-2})$$

Therefore:

$$\ln \text{Sales}_{t+1} - \ln \text{Sales}_t = 0.0485 + 0.3728\ (\ln \text{Sales}_t - \ln \text{Sales}_{t-1})$$
$$\ln \text{Sales}_{t+1} - \ln 8{,}157 = 0.0485 + 0.3728\ (\ln 8{,}157 - \ln 7{,}452)$$
$$\ln \text{Sales}_{t+1} = 0.0485 + (0.3728)(0.0904) + 9.0066$$
$$\ln \text{Sales}_{t+1} = 9.0888$$
$$\text{Sales}_{t+1} = \$8{,}855.56\text{m}$$

Therefore, based on Q4 2005 sales of \$8,157m the model predicts that ABC's sales in Q1 2006 would be \$8,855.56m.

Moving-Average Time-Series Models **Vol 1, pp 443–448**

Smoothing Past Values with Moving Averages

Moving averages are generally calculated to eliminate the "noise" from a time series in order to focus on the underlying trend. An *n*-period moving average is based on the current value and previous $n - 1$ values of a time series. It is calculated as:

$$\frac{x_t + x_{t-1} + \ldots + x_{t-(n-1)}}{n}$$

One of the weaknesses of the moving average is that it always lags large movements in the underlying data. Further, even though moving averages are useful in smoothing out a time series, they do not hold much predictive value (as they give equal weight to all observations). In order to enhance the forecasting performance of moving averages, analysts use moving-average time-series models.

Moving-Average Time-Series Models for Forecasting

A moving-average (MA) model of order 1 is given as:

$$x_t = \varepsilon_t + \theta\varepsilon_{t-1},\ E(\varepsilon_t) = 0,\ E(\varepsilon_t^2) = \sigma^2,\ E(\varepsilon_t\varepsilon_s) = 0 \text{ for } t \neq s$$

x_t is a moving average of ε_t and ε_{t-1}, and ε_t and ε_{t-1} are uncorrelated random variables that have an expected value of 0. Note that in contrast to the simple moving-average model equation (where all observations receive an equal weight) this moving-average model attaches a weight of 1 on ε_t and a weight of θ on ε_{t-1}.

An MA(q) moving-average model (a moving-average model of order q) is given as:

$$x_t = \varepsilon_t + \theta_1\varepsilon_{t-1} + \ldots \theta_q\varepsilon_{t-q},\ E(\varepsilon_t) = 0,\ E(\varepsilon_t^2) = \sigma^2,\ E(\varepsilon_t\varepsilon_s) = 0 \text{ for } t \neq s$$

To determine whether a time series follows an MA(q) model we examine the autocorrelations of the **original time series** (not the residual autocorrelations that we examine in AR models to determine whether serial correlation exists). For an MA(q) model, the first q autocorrelations will be significant, and all the autocorrelations beyond that will equal 0.

The **time-series autocorrelations** can also be used to determine whether an autoregressive or a moving-average model is more appropriate to fit the data.

- For most AR models, the time series autocorrelations start out large and then decline gradually.
- For MA models, the first q time series autocorrelations are significantly different from 0, and then suddenly drop to 0 beyond that.

Note that most time series are best modeled with AR models.

LESSON 4: SEASONALITY, ARCH MODELS, REGRESSIONS WITH MORE THAN ONE TIME SERIES

LOS 11l: Explain how to test and correct for seasonality in a time-series model and calculate and interpret a forecasted value using an AR model with a seasonal lag. Vol 1, pp 444–448

Seasonality in Time-Series Models

A common problem in time series is seasonality. Seasonality may cause us to incorrectly conclude that an autoregressive model is inappropriate to model a particular time series (as seasonality may cause one or more of the residual autocorrelations to be significantly different from 0). To detect seasonality in the time series, we examine the **autocorrelations of the residuals** to determine whether the seasonal autocorrelation of the error term is significantly different from 0. The seasonal error autocorrelation corresponds to the seasonal lag, which is the value of the time series one year before the current period. For example, if we are working with monthly data, the seasonal lag would be the twelfth lag of the series.

To correct for seasonality, we simply add a seasonal lag to the AR model. Example 4-1 illustrates the processes of detecting seasonality in a time series, correcting for it, and making forecasts once a seasonal lag has been added to the model.

This regression equation expresses the change in sales in the current quarter as a function of the change in sales in the last (previous) quarter.

Example 4-1: Seasonality in a Time Series

Robin Van Persie estimates an AR(1) model based on first-differenced sales data to model XYZ Company's quarterly sales for 10 years from Q1 1991 to Q4 2000. He comes up with the following regression equation:

$$\ln \text{Sales}_t - \ln \text{Sales}_{t-1} = b_0 + b_1(\ln \text{Sales}_{t-1} - \ln \text{Sales}_{t-2}) + \varepsilon_t$$

Table 4-1 presents the results of the regression.

Table 4-1: AR(1) Model on Log First-Differenced Quarterly Sales

Regression Statistics	
R-squared	0.1763
Standard error	0.0751
Observations	40
Durbin-Watson	2.056

	Coefficient	Standard Error	t-Stat
Intercept	0.0555	0.0087	6.3793
Lag 1	–0.3928	0.1052	–3.7338

Autocorrelations of the Residuals from the AR(1) Model

Lag	Autocorrelation	Standard Error	t-Stat
1	–0.0695	0.1581	–0.4396
2	–0.1523	0.1581	–0.9633
3	–0.1231	0.1581	–0.7786
4	0.4542	0.1581	2.8729

seasonal lag

seasonal autocorrelation of the error term

The intercept term and the coefficient on the first lag appear to be significantly different from 0, but the striking thing about the data in Table 4-1 is that the fourth error autocorrelation is significantly different from 0. The t-stat of 2.8729 is greater than the critical t-value of 2.024 (significance level = 5%, degrees of freedom = 38) so we reject the null hypothesis that the residual autocorrelation for the fourth lag equals 0. The model is therefore misspecified and cannot be used for forecasting.

This regression equation expresses the change in sales in the current quarter as a function of the change in sales in the last (previous) quarter and the change in sales four quarters ago.

The fourth autocorrelation is a seasonal autocorrelation as we are working with quarterly data. The model can be improved (adjusted for the seasonal autocorrelation) by introducing a seasonal lag as an independent variable in the model. The regression equation will then be structured as:

$$\ln \text{Sales}_t - \ln \text{Sales}_{t-1} = b_0 + b_1(\ln \text{Sales}_{t-1} - \ln \text{Sales}_{t-2}) + b_2(\ln \text{Sales}_{t-4} - \ln \text{Sales}_{t-5}) + \varepsilon_t$$

Table 4-2 presents the results of the regression after introducing the seasonal lag.

Table 4-2: AR(1) Model with Seasonal Lag on Log First-Differenced Quarterly Sales

Regression Statistics	
R-squared	0.3483 higher.
Standard error	0.0672
Observations	40
Durbin-Watson	2.031

	Coefficient	**Standard Error**	***t*-Stat**
Intercept	0.0386	0.0092	4.1957 ✓
Lag 1	–0.3725	0.0987	–3.7741 ✓
Lag 4	0.4284	0.1008	4.25 ✓

Autocorrelations of the Residuals from the AR(1) Model

Lag	**Autocorrelation**	**Standard Error**	***t*-Stat**
1	–0.0248	0.1581	–0.1569 ✓
2	0.0928	0.1581	0.587 ✓
3	–0.0318	0.1581	–0.2011 ✓
4	–0.0542	0.1581	–0.3428 ✓

From the data in Table 4-2, notice that the intercept, and the coefficients on the first and second lags of the time series, are all significantly different from 0. Further, none of the residual autocorrelations is significantly different from 0 so there is no serial correlation. The model is therefore correctly specified and can be used to make forecasts. Also notice that the R^2 in Table 4-2 (0.3483) is almost two times the R^2 in Table 4-1 (0.1763), which means that the model does a much better job in explaining ABC's quarterly sales once the seasonal lag is introduced.

In order to make predictions based on the model, we need to know sales growth in the previous quarter ($\ln \text{Sales}_{t-1} - \ln \text{Sales}_{t-2}$) and sales growth four quarters ago ($\ln \text{Sales}_{t-4} - \ln \text{Sales}_{t-5}$). For example, if the exponential growth rate in sales was 3% in the previous quarter and 5% four quarters ago, the model predicts that sales growth for the current quarter would equal 4.88%, calculated as:

$$\ln \text{Sales}_t - \ln \text{Sales}_{t-1} = 0.0386 - 0.3725(0.03) + 0.4284(0.05) = 0.48845 \text{ or } 4.88\%$$

The regression underlying Table 4-1 actually uses sales data for 41 quarters starting Q4 1990 so that we are able to have 40 observations of current quarter sales.

In the new model that includes the seasonal lag, we actually use sales data for 44 quarters starting Q1 1990 so that we have 40 observations of current quarter sales (which can be regressed on previous quarter sales and sales four quarters earlier).

If sales data prior to Q1 1991 is not available, then there would be 39 observations in Table 4-1 and 36 observations in Table 4-2.

Important: This example computes the predicted sales growth rate by using the presented exponential growth rates (0.03 and 0.05 respectively). The relevant BB example in the curriculum also calculates the predicted sales growth rate in this manner. However, EOC question 17B (pg 475, Vol 1) calculates the predicted growth rate by using 1 + the presented growth rates (1.01 and 1.02) respectively. Be aware of this important difference. Use the method employed in the example when presented with *b* growth rates; otherwise, use the method employed to solve the EOC question.

Just one more thing before we move ahead. It is not necessary for only the residual autocorrelation corresponding to the seasonal lag to appear significant in a time series suffering from seasonality. For example, in Table 4-1, it may have been the case that the residual autocorrelation for the second lag was significantly different from 0 along with the residual autocorrelation for the fourth lag (the seasonal lag). After incorporating the seasonal lag as an independent variable in the model, if seasonality is present in the time series, the residual autocorrelations for the seasonal lag, and for any other lags for whom the residual autocorrelations were significant previously (before the introduction of the seasonal lag as an independent variable in the model), will now equal 0.

Autoregressive Moving-Average (ARMA) Models

An ARMA model combines autoregressive lags of the dependent variable and moving-average errors in order to provide better forecasts than simple AR models. The equation for an ARMA model with p autoregressive terms and q moving-average terms, denoted ARMA (p,q) is:

$$x_t = b_0 + b_1 x_{t-1} + \ldots + b_p x_{t-p} + \varepsilon_t + \theta_1 \varepsilon_{t-1} + \ldots + \theta_q \varepsilon_{t-q}$$
$$\mathrm{E}(\varepsilon_t) = 0,\ \mathrm{E}(\varepsilon_t^2) = \sigma^2,\ \mathrm{E}(\varepsilon_t \varepsilon_s) = 0 \text{ for } t \neq s$$

ARMA models have the following limitations:

- The parameters of the model can be very unstable.
- There are no set criteria for determining p and q.
- Even after a model is selected, it may not do a good job of forecasting.

LOS 11m: Explain autoregressive conditional heteroskedasticity (ARCH) and describe how ARCH models can be applied to predict the variance of a time series. Vol 1, pp 455–457

Autoregressive Conditional Heteroskedasticity Models (ARCH Models)

Heteroskedasticity occurs when the variance of the error term varies with the independent variable. If heteroskedasticity is present in a time series, one or more of the independent variables in the model may appear statistically significant when they are actually not.

ARCH models are used to determine whether the variance of the error in one period depends on the variance of the error in previous periods. In an ARCH(l) model, the squared residuals from a particular time-series model (the model may be an AR, MA, or ARMA model) are regressed on a constant and on one lag of the squared residuals (see Example 4-2). The regression equation takes the following form:

$$\hat{\varepsilon}_t^2 = a_0 + a_1 \hat{\varepsilon}_{t-1}^2 + u_t$$

- If a_1 equals 0, the variance of the error term in each period is simply a_0. The variance is constant over time and does not depend on the error in the previous period. When this is the case, the regression coefficients of the time series model are correct and the model can be used for decision-making.
- If a_1 is statistically different from 0, the error in a particular period depends on the size of the error in the previous period. If a_1 is greater (less) than 0, the variance increases (decreases) over time. Such a time series is ARCH(1) and the time-series model cannot be used for decision-making. The error in period t+1 can then be predicted using the following formula:

$$\hat{\sigma}_{t+1}^2 = \hat{a}_0 + \hat{a}_1 \hat{\varepsilon}_t^2$$

Example 4-2: Testing for ARCH

Thomas Rosicky develops an AR(1) model for monthly inflation over the last 15 years. The regression results indicate that the intercept and lag coefficient are significantly different from 0. Also, none of the residual autocorrelations are significantly different from 0, so he concludes that serial correlation is not a problem. However, before using his AR(1) model to predict inflation, Rosicky wants to ensure that the time series does not suffer from heteroskedasticity. He therefore estimates an ARCH(1) model using the residuals from his AR(1) model. Table 4-3 contains the results of the regression.

Table 4-3: ARCH(1) Regression Results for AR(1) Model Residuals

Regression Statistics	
R-squared	0.0154
Standard error	12.65
Observations	180
Durbin-Watson	1.9855

	Coefficient	Standard Error	*t*-Stat
Intercept	4.6386	0.892	5.2
Lag 1	0.1782	0.0658	2.708

The regression results indicate that the coefficient on the previous period's squared residual (a_1) is significantly different from 0. The *t*-stat of 2.708 is high enough for us to be able to reject the null hypothesis that the errors have no autoregressive conditional heteroskedasticity (H_0: $a_1 = 0$). Since the model does contain ARCH(1) errors, the standard errors for the regression parameters estimated in Rosicky's AR(1) model are inaccurate and he cannot use the AR(1) model to forecast inflation even though (as mentioned in the question) the OLS regression coefficients are different from 0 and the residuals do not suffer from serial correlation.

Rosicky can use his estimated ARCH(1) model to predict the variance of the errors. For example, if the error in predicting inflation in one period is 1%, the predicted variance of the error in the next period is calculated as:

$$\hat{\varepsilon}_t^2 = 4.6386 + 0.1782\hat{\varepsilon}_{t-1}^2 = 4.6386 + 0.1782(1^2) = 4.8168\%$$

If ARCH errors are found to exist, generalized least squares may be used to correct for heteroskedasticity.

LOS 11n: Explain how time-series variables should be analyzed for nonstationarity and/or cointegration before use in a linear regression.

Regressions with More than One Time Series

So far we have only been working with time-series models for one time series. Now we discuss whether linear regression can be used to analyze the relationship between more than one time series. Let's assume we are presented with two time series, one corresponding to the dependent variable and the other corresponding to the independent variable. Whether we can use linear regression to model the two series depends on whether the series have a unit root. The Dickey-Fuller test is used to make this determination.

There are several possible scenarios regarding the outcome of the Dickey-Fuller tests on the two series:

- If neither of the time series has a unit root, linear regression can be used to test the relationship between the two series.
- If either of the series has a unit root, the error term in the regression would not be covariance stationary and therefore, linear regression cannot be used to analyze the relationship between the two time series.
- If both the series have unit roots, we must determine whether they are cointegrated. Two time series are cointegrated if a long-term economic relationship exists between them such that they do not diverge from each other significantly in the long run.
  - If they are not cointegrated, linear regression cannot be used as the error term in the regression will not be covariance stationary.
  - If they are cointegrated, linear regression can be used as the error term will be covariance stationary, the regression coefficients and standard errors will be consistent, and they can be used to conduct hypothesis tests. However, analysts should still be cautious in interpreting the results from the regression.

Testing for Cointegration

To test whether two time series that each have a unit root are cointegrated, we perform the following steps:

1. Estimate the regression:

$$y_t = b_0 + b_1 x_t + \varepsilon_t$$

> Engle-Granger critical values are adjusted for the effect of the uncertainty about the regression parameters on the distribution of the Dickey-Fuller test.

2. Test whether the error term (ε_t) has a unit root using the Dickey-Fuller test but with Engle-Granger critical values.
3. H_0: Error term has a unit root versus H_a: Error term does not have a unit root
4. If we fail to reject the null hypothesis, we conclude that the error term in the regression has a unit root, it is not covariance stationary, the time series are not cointegrated, and the regression relation is spurious.
5. If we reject the null hypothesis, we conclude that the error term does not have a unit root, it is covariance stationary, the time series are cointegrated, and therefore, the results of linear regression can be used to test hypotheses about the relation between the variables.

If there are more than two time series, the following rules apply:

- If at least one time series (the dependent variable or one of the independent variables) has a unit root and at least one time series (the dependent variable or one of the independent variables) does not, the error term cannot be covariance stationary so multiple linear regression cannot be used.
- If all of them have unit roots, the time series must be tested for cointegration using a similar process as outlined previously (except that the regression will have more than one independent variable).
    - If we fail to reject the null hypothesis of a unit root, the error term in the regression is not covariance stationary and we conclude that the time series are not cointegrated. Multiple regression cannot be used in this scenario.
    - If we reject the null hypothesis of a unit root, the error term in the regression is covariance stationary and we conclude that the time series are cointegrated. However, bear in mind that modeling three or more time series that are cointegrated is very complex.

Note that when making forecasts based on time-series analysis, we need to consider:

- The uncertainty associated with the error term; and
- The uncertainty about the estimates of the parameters in the model.

LOS 11o: Determine an appropriate time-series model to analyze a given investment problem and justify that choice. Vol 1, pp 458–460

Suggested Steps in Time-Series Forecasting

The following is a step-by-step guide to building a model to predict a time series.

1. Understand the investment problem you have, and make an initial choice of model. There are two options:
    - A regression model that predicts the future behavior of a variable based on hypothesized causal relationships with other variables. We studied these models in Readings 9 and 10.
    - A time-series model that attempts to predict the future behavior of a variable based on the past behavior of the same variable. We studied these models in this reading.
2. If you go with a time-series model, compile the data and plot it to see whether it looks covariance stationary. The plot might show deviations from covariance stationarity, such as:
    - A linear trend
    - An exponential trend
    - Seasonality
    - A change in mean or variance

3. If you find no significant seasonality or a change in mean or variance, then either a linear trend or an exponential trend may be appropriate to model the time series. In that case, take the following steps:
   - Determine whether a linear or exponential trend seems most reasonable (usually by plotting the series).
   - Estimate the trend.
   - Compute the residuals.
   - Use the Durbin-Watson statistic to determine whether the residuals have significant serial correlation. If you find no significant serial correlation in the residuals, then the trend model is specified correctly and you can use that model for forecasting.
4. If you find significant serial correlation in the residuals from the trend model, use a more complex model, such as an autoregressive model. First however, ensure that the time series is covariance stationary. Following is a list of violations of stationarity, along with potential methods to adjust the time series to make it covariance stationary:
   - If the time series has a linear trend, first-difference the time series.
   - If the time series has an exponential trend, take the natural log of the time series and then first-difference it.
   - If the time series shifts significantly during the sample period, estimate different time-series models before and after the shift.
   - If the time series has significant seasonality, include a seasonal lag (discussed in Step 7).
5. After you have successfully transformed a raw time series into a covariance-stationary time series, you can usually model the transformed series with an autoregressive model. To decide which autoregressive model to use, take the following steps:
   - Estimate an AR(1) model.
   - Test to see whether the residuals from this model have significant serial correlation.
   - If there is no significant serial correlation, you can use the AR(1) model to forecast.
6. If you find significant serial correlation in the residuals, use an AR(2) model and test for significant serial correlation of the residuals of the AR(2) model.
   - If you find no significant serial correlation, use the AR(2) model.
   - If you find significant serial correlation of the residuals, keep increasing the order of the AR model until the residual serial correlation is no longer significant.
7. Check for seasonality. You can use one of two approaches:
   - Graph the data and check for regular seasonal patterns.
   - Examine the data to see whether the seasonal autocorrelations of the residuals from an AR model are significant (for example, if you are using quarterly data, you should check the fourth residual autocorrelation for significance) and whether other autocorrelations are significant. To correct for seasonality, add a seasonal lag of the time series to the model.

8. Test whether the residuals have autoregressive conditional heteroskedasticity. To test for ARCH(1) errors:
   - Regress the squared residuals from your time-series model on a lagged value of the squared residual.
   - Test whether the coefficient on the squared lagged residual differs significantly from 0.
   - If the coefficient on the squared lagged residual does not differ significantly from 0, the residuals do not display ARCH and you can rely on the standard errors from your time-series estimates.
   - If the coefficient on the squared lagged residual does differ significantly from 0, use generalized least squares or other methods to correct for ARCH.
9. As a final step, you may also want to perform tests of the model's out-of-sample forecasting performance to see how the model's out-of-sample performance compares to its in-sample performance.

READING 12: PROBABILISTIC APPROACHES: SCENARIO ANALYSIS, DECISION TREES, AND SIMULATIONS

LESSON 1: SIMULATIONS

- Scenario analysis and decision trees are used to evaluate the impact of **discrete** risk.
- Simulations are used to evaluate the impact of **continuous** risk.

Practically speaking, there can be hundreds of outcomes for any investment decision, so simulations offer us a more complete picture of the risk inherent in an asset or investment.

LOS 12a: Describe steps in running a simulation. **Vol 1, pp 482–488**

LOS 12b: Explain three ways to define the probability distributions for a simulation's variables. **Vol 1, pp 482–484**

LOS 12c: Describe how to treat correlation across variables in a simulation. **Vol 1, p 484**

Steps in Simulation

In a classic simulation, distributions of values are estimated for each input parameter in the analysis (e.g., growth, market share, operating margin, etc.). Any simulation exercise is composed of many iterations or individual simulations. In each individual simulation, one possible value of each input parameter is drawn from its distribution and used to generate a unique value for the output (e.g., cash flow, value, etc.). Across a large number of simulations, we obtain a set of possible outcomes for the output variable, and the distribution of possible outcomes across these individual simulations reflects the underlying uncertainty we face in estimating the inputs to the valuation.

Running a simulation involves the following steps:

1. Determine probabilistic variables.
    - Simulations place no constraint on the number of input variables that can be incorporated into the analysis.
    - Input variables may or may not be predictable. Probability distributions are defined for each variable that is allowed to vary in the simulation.
    - Practically speaking, analysts should focus on defining probability distributions for those variables that have a significant impact on value.
2. Define probability distributions for these variables.
    - This is the most important and most difficult step in any simulation exercise.
    - Generally speaking, there are three ways in which we can go about defining probability distributions:
        - Historical data:
            - Historical data can be used to develop probability distributions for variables that have a long history and reliable data over that history.
            - For example, in trying to specify the distribution of expected changes in the long-term Treasury bond rate, we could use

historical annual changes in Treasury bond rates from 1928 to 2005 as the distribution for future changes.
        - Note that in this approach, the implicit assumption is that the market has not undergone any structural shifts that might make historical data unreliable as an indicator of the future distribution of the variable.
    - Cross-sectional data:
        - The cross-sectional data approach uses differences in a specific variable across existing investments that are similar to the investment being analyzed as observations of the variable.
        - For example, in order to address the uncertainty in the operating profit margin of a software company, we could use the operating margin for a particular year of firms in the same industry.
        - As another example, consider a large retailer with several stores across the country. We could use sales per square foot across the company's existing stores to run a simulation on expected sales at a new store.
    - Statistical distribution and parameters:
        - This approach involves choosing a statistical distribution that best captures the variability in the input variable and estimating the parameters for that distribution.
        - For example, one could conclude that operating margins for a software company will follow the continuous uniform distribution, with a minimum of 3% and a maximum of 8%, or that revenue growth will follow the normal distribution with an expected value of 5% and a standard deviation of 8%.
        - While computer software companies offer a wide variety of distributions to choose from, picking the right distribution and specifying the parameters for the distribution remain difficult because:
            - Practically speaking, only a few inputs that are commonly required in the analysis conform to the assumptions made by statistical distributions. For example, revenue growth cannot follow the normal distribution, because it has a defined lowest value of –100%, whereas the normal distribution has no lower bound.
            - Once the distribution has been selected, the parameters still need to be estimated. For this, we can draw on historical or cross-sectional data, but then we should be wary of (1) structural shifts making historical data unreliable, and (2) peer companies not being comparable.
        - Note that discrete probability distributions can be used for some variables, and continuous distributions for others.

3. Check for correlation across variables.
    - Correlations can be estimated by looking at historical data.
    - If it is found that there is strong (positive or negative) correlation between input variables, one can:
        - Retain the variable that has a more significant impact on value in the analysis, and discard the other.
        - Build the correlation explicitly into the simulation. Note that this requires more sophisticated simulation packages and adds more detail to the estimation process.

LOS 12C

    - For example, if interest rate and inflation are both employed as input variables in a simulation (because they both are critical in determining value) it is highly likely that they are (positively) correlated. Generally speaking, high inflation rates usually call for high interest rates, and low inflation rates usually call for low interest rates.

4. Run the simulation.
    - For each individual simulation/iteration, one outcome is drawn for each input variable (from its distribution), and the value of the output variable is computed.
    - This process is repeated several times, though the marginal contribution of each individual simulation drops off as the number of simulations increases.
    - The number of individual simulations run depends on:
        - Number of probabilistic inputs: The larger the number of probabilistic input variables, the greater the number of simulations required.
        - Characteristics of probability distributions: The wider the variety of distributions used in an analysis, the greater the number of simulations required.
        - Range of outcomes: The wider the range of potential outcomes for the input variable, the greater the number of simulations required.
    - Since most simulation packages allow users to run thousands of simulations, it is better to err on the side of too many simulations rather than two few.

Over the years, both informational impediments (in terms of estimating distribution types and parameters for input variables) and computational impediments (in terms of the time and resources required to run simulations) to running good simulations have eased, making their use in business and investment decision making more popular.

An Example of a Simulation

Let's talk about a large retailer running a simulation to determine expected annual sales revenue at a new store it is considering opening. The company can use the extensive data that it has gathered from hundreds of its other locations (each of a different age, and at a different state of its life cycle) to make its estimates more accurate in terms of how long it takes for a new store to become established, and how revenues change as the store ages and competitors open stores in the vicinity. Note that we are not asserting that the company's experience with opening stores in the past removes uncertainty about the project from the analysis. The company is still exposed to considerable risk from each new store that it considers opening, but its experience in the past does make the estimation process easier and more accurate than it would be for a new company entering the retail industry.

Once it has a sense of the distribution of annual revenue across its existing store locations, the company must employ some assumptions to run a simulation of expected store cash flows and value.

- Based on revenues from its existing store locations, the company comes up with a base-year revenue estimate of $24 million. It then assumes that revenues will follow the normal distribution with an expected value of $24 million and standard deviation of $5 million.
- The company then assumes that pre-tax operating margin is uniformly distributed with a minimum value of 4% and a maximum value of 10%, giving it an expected value of 7%. Non-operating expenses are anticipated to be $1.0 million a year.
- Since average historical real GDP growth is 3% and expected inflation is 2%, the company assumes that revenue will grow at 5% per annum.

- The store is expected to generate cash flows for 10 years, and there is no expected salvage value when the store closes.
- The company's cost of capital is 11%.
- The applicable tax rate is 35%.

The value of the new store based entirely on the expected value of each input variable can be computed as:

- Expected base-year revenue = $24 million
- Expected base-year after-tax cash flow can be calculated as:

$$(\text{Revenue} \times \text{Pre-tax margin} - \text{Non-operating expenses})(1 - \text{Tax rate})$$
$$= (24 \times 0.07 - 1.0)(1 - 0.35) = \$0.442 \text{ million}$$

- The value of the store can be calculated as:

$$\frac{CF(1+g)\left(1 - \frac{(1+g)^n}{(1+r)^n}\right)}{r-g}$$

$$= 0.442(1+0.05)\frac{1 - \frac{(1+0.05)^{10}}{(1+0.11)^{10}}}{0.11-0.05} = \$3.298 \text{ millon}$$

Now if we were to run a simulation with a large number of runs/iterations (let's say 10,000) based on the probability distribution defined for each input variable, the simulation may present us with results that are slightly different than those obtained in the previous valuation exercise. When we ran the simulation, we obtained the following:

- The average value across risk-adjusted simulations was $3.326 million, which is slightly higher than the risk-adjusted value we obtained ($3.298 million). The median was $3.127 million.
- There was substantial variation in output values, ranging from –$4.245 million to $26.814 million. The standard deviation was $4.923 million.

LOS 12d: Describe advantages of using simulations in decision making.
Vol 1, pp 488–489

Use in Decision Making

Aside from just providing an estimate for the expected value of an asset/investment, a good simulation:

- Offers insights to improve input estimation. Analysts can play with both cross-sectional and historical data for each input variable before deciding which distribution to use, and the parameters of the distribution.

- Yields a distribution for expected value rather than a point estimate. Consider the valuation exercise we performed earlier. We obtained an expected value of $3.298 million for the store, with a standard deviation of $4.923 million for that value, and we could also see (if we made the request in the simulation program) a graphical representation of the distribution of expected values along with a breakdown of values by percentile. The distribution of values reminds us as users that estimates of value obtained from the exercise are imprecise, and explains why there is variation of value estimates across analysts.

Note the following:

- We are *not* saying that simulations yield better estimates of expected value than conventional risk-adjusted value models. In fact, the expected values from simulations should be fairly close to the expected value that we would obtain using the expected values for each of the input variables (as is the case in our example).
- Nor are we saying that simulations, by providing estimates of expected value and the distribution in that value, lead to better decisions. While decision makers can benefit from getting a fuller picture of the uncertainty in value, there is a common tendency for risk to be double counted in simulations and for decisions to be based on the wrong type of risk (more on this later in the reading).

LOS 12e: Describe some common constraints introduced into simulations.

Vol 1, pp 489–490

Simulations with Constraints

Simulations are also used as tools in the analysis of risk. Constraints are introduced into the simulation with the idea being that if these constraints are violated, the firm may have to incur significant costs that can put its own sustainability in jeopardy. Simulations can help in evaluating the effectiveness of risk hedging strategies by examining the likelihood that the constraint will be violated under each strategy and weighing that likelihood against the cost of the strategy. Some common constraints that are introduced into simulations include book value constraints, earnings and cash flow constraints, and market value constraints.

Book Value Constraints

There are two types of restrictions on the book value of equity that may call for risk hedging.

- Regulatory capital restrictions: Financial services companies such as banks and insurance firms are required to maintain a certain minimum ratio of book value of equity to loans or other assets. If firms violate these minimum capital requirements, they can be taken over by the regulatory authorities, a scenario that can lead to equity holders losing their entire investment in the company. As a result, these companies not only keep a close eye on their book value of equity (and related ratios), but also remain wary of the possibility that a decline in the value of their investment portfolios can result in a drop in the book value of equity.

One risk measure that is commonly used by financial companies is value at risk, or VaR, which helps these companies (1) to quantify and understand the potential risks in their investments, and (2) to be prepared for the possibility of a catastrophic outcome, albeit a highly improbable one. By simulating the values of their investments under a variety of scenarios, risk analysts can (1) identify the possibility of falling below the regulatory ratios, and (2) identify ways of hedging against this event occurring. The simulation forces the company to think about ways to mitigate or even eliminate the risk of violating regulatory constraints.

- Negative book value for equity: In some countries, a negative book value of equity can give rise to substantial costs for the firm and its investors. In parts of Europe, for example, companies with negative book values of equity are required to raise fresh equity capital to bring their book values above zero, while in some Asian countries, companies that have negative book values of equity are barred from paying dividends. Companies therefore use simulations to assess the probability of a negative book value for equity and to evaluate the effectiveness of various options to protect themselves against it occurring.

Earnings and Cash Flow Constraints

Earnings and cash flow constraints can be internally or externally imposed.

- Management may place such a high priority on meeting earnings expectations (perhaps to safeguard their jobs) that it may be willing to use hedging products to reduce or eliminate the risk of that happening. Such activities have nothing to do with company value maximization, but are driven by self-interest.
- Loan covenants can be related to earnings outcomes or other financial ratios. For example, the interest rate on a loan can be tied to whether the company makes a profit. Companies with such covenants built into their bond indentures use simulations (1) to assess the probability that loan covenants will be violated, and (2) to examine the effectiveness of risk-hedging products in mitigating this risk.

Market Value Constraints

In discounted cash flow (DCF) valuation, the value of the firm is computed by discounting expected cash flows at a risk-adjusted discount rate. The value of equity is then computed by deducting the value of debt from the value of the firm. The problem in this approach is that the possibility and potential costs of not being able to meet debt payments are considered only peripherally in the discount rate. Practically speaking, the costs of default can be substantial, and include indirect bankruptcy costs such as loss of customers, tighter supplier credit, and higher employee turnover. Simulations enable us to:

- Compare the value of a business to its outstanding claims in all possible scenarios (rather than just the most likely one).
- Quantify the likelihood of distress.
- Build indirect bankruptcy costs into the valuation by explicitly modeling the effects of distress on expected cash flows and on discount rates.

LOS 12f: Describe issues in using simulations in risk assessment.

Vol 1, pp 490–492

Issues

In recent times, simulations have become a very popular tool in risk assessment, especially when it comes to using and valuing derivatives. However, it is very important to keep the following in mind when using simulations in risk assessment:

- Garbage in, garbage out: For a simulation to have value, the distributions chosen for the inputs should be based on analysis and data. Further, users must possess more than a passing knowledge of statistical distributions and their characteristics.
- Real data may not fit distributions: If probability distributions that are not very similar to the actual distributions of input variables are assigned to them, the simulation will yield misleading results.
- Non-stationary distributions: Even when the data fit a statistical distribution or where historical data distributions are available, shifts in the market structure can lead to (1) a change in the type of distribution, or (2) a change in the parameters of the distribution. Ideally, forward-looking probability distributions should be used.
- Changing correlation across inputs: Correlations across input variables can be modeled into simulations only if they remain stable and predictable. If correlations between input variables change over time, it becomes far more difficult to model them.

Risk-Adjusted Value and Simulations

A common misconception regarding simulations is that since probability distributions are used, cash flow outcomes from simulations are somehow risk adjusted, and therefore the risk-free rate should be used in discounting these cash flows. Generally speaking, cash flow outcomes obtained from simulations are expected cash flows that are **not** risk adjusted. Therefore, they should be discounted at a **risk-adjusted** rate.

There is, however, one exception. This exception occurs when we use the standard deviation of the output variable (obtained from the results of a simulation) as a measure of risk and use this measure to make decisions. If we were to use a risk-adjusted discount rate in this case, we would be double counting risk, as illustrated in Example 1-1.

Example 1-1: Analyzing Two Risky Investments

An investor is trying to choose between two assets, A and B. She values both the assets using simulations and risk-adjusted discount rates. Her findings are presented in Table 1-1.

Table 1-1: Results of Simulation

Asset	Risk-Adjusted Discount Rate	Simulation Expected Value	Simulation Standard Deviation
A	11%	$200	14%
B	14%	$200	20%

Evaluate the two investments based on their respective risks.

Solution:

Based on the risk-adjusted discount rate, Asset B is clearly more risky. However, when this higher discount rate is used to value it, the simulation concludes that Asset B has the same value as Asset A ($200). If we were now to reject Asset B based on its higher standard deviation across simulated values (20% versus 14%), we would effectively be penalizing it twice (as the higher risk has already been accounted for in the higher risk-adjusted discount rate used to discount its cash flows).

What we could do is run the simulation again using the risk-free rate as the discount rate for both assets, and then evaluate the trade-off between the higher expected value of Asset B (B's expected value would be higher than A's now since the difference between the risk-adjusted rate and risk-free rate is greater for B) and the lower risk of Asset A (as reflected in its lower standard deviation). There is one caveat, however, in using the standard deviation as a measure of risk. Standard deviation reflects both systematic and unsystematic risk. In evaluating whether to add a particular asset to a portfolio, we should consider only the risk that cannot be diversified away (i.e., systematic risk, not total risk).

Example 1-1 should not lead you to conclude that simulations are not useful in understanding risk. Looking at the variance of expected outcomes around expected value offers the following benefits:

- A visual reminder that our value estimates are uncertain.
- A tool in choosing between two stocks that are equally undervalued but have different distributions. In this case, we should choose the stock with lower expected volatility (i.e., lower standard deviation).

LOS 12g: Compare scenario analysis, decision trees, and simulations.

Vol 1, pp 492–494

LESSON 2: AN OVERALL ASSESSMENT OF PROBABILISTIC RISK ASSESSMENT APPROACHES

Comparing the Approaches

When choosing among scenario analysis, decision trees, and simulations to assess risk, we should consider (1) the types of risks we face and (2) how we plan to use the output.

Selective versus Full Risk Analysis

- In **scenario analysis**, we generally consider what we believe to be the most likely scenarios, and ignore all other scenarios.
    - Therefore, the sum of the probabilities of the scenarios considered can be less than 1.
- With **decision trees** and **simulations**, we attempt to consider **all** possible outcomes.
    - In decision trees, we try to accomplish this by converting continuous risk into a manageable set of possible outcomes.
    - In simulations, we use probability distributions to capture all possible outcomes.
    - Therefore, the sum of the probabilities of outcomes in decision trees and simulations equals 1.

As a result, when we employ decision trees or simulations, we can compute expected values across all outcomes, using the probabilities as weights. These expected values can be compared to the (single-estimate) risk-adjusted values obtained using discounted cash flow and relative valuation models.

Type of Risk

- **Scenario analysis** and **decision trees** are generally more suitable for discrete risks.
    - Decision trees are more useful in modeling **sequential** risks, where risks are considered in phases.
    - Scenario analysis is more useful when risks occur **concurrently**.
- **Simulations** are better suited for **continuous** risks.

Correlation across Risks

- If the various risks inherent in an investment are correlated, **simulations** are more appropriate because they allow for these correlations to be explicitly modeled into the analysis.
- In **scenario analysis**, these correlations can be incorporated into the analysis only to the extent that we can subjectively create scenarios that account for them. For example, higher interest rate scenarios will include slower economic growth, and lower interest rate scenarios will include higher economic growth.
- Correlated risks are difficult to model in **decision trees**.

We summarize the relationship between risk type and probabilistic approach used in Table 2-1.

Table 2-1: Risk Types and Probabilistic Approaches

Discrete/ Continuous	Correlated/ Independent	Sequential/ Concurrent	Risk Approach
Discrete	Independent	Sequential	Decision tree %
Discrete	Correlated	Concurrent	Scenario analysis
Continuous	Either	Either	Simulations

Note that the quality of information also affects the approach chosen:

- **Simulations** work best when there is substantial historical and cross-sectional data available so that probability distributions and parameters can be assessed.
- **Decision trees** work best when risks can be assessed using past data or population characteristics so that estimates of probabilities of outcomes at each node can be made.
- **Scenario analysis** works best for new and unpredictable risk, even though it offers a rather subjective way of dealing with risk.

Complement or Replacement for Risk-Adjusted Value

- **Decision trees** and **simulations** can be used as either complements to or substitutes for risk-adjusted value.
- **Scenario analysis**, however, can only serve as a complement to risk-adjusted value, as it does not look at the entire spectrum of possible outcomes.

Analysts should always bear the following in mind when using these approaches as *complements* to risk-adjusted value:

- All three approaches use expected, not risk-adjusted, cash flows; therefore, a risk-adjusted discount rate should be used, not the risk-free rate.
- In assessing risk, however, it should not be double counted. If expected cash flows from risky investments are discounted as a risk-adjusted rate, then we should not simply reject them if the variation in possible outcomes is high (as illustrated in Example 1-1).

When using simulations and decision trees as *substitutes* for risk-adjusted valuation, we should keep the following constraints in mind:

- Cash flows should be discounted at a risk-free rate.
- The standard deviation of outcomes obtained from the analysis should be used as the measure of risk in the investment.
- Comparing two assets with the same expected value (obtained with risk-free rates used as discount rates) from a simulation, we should pick the one with the lower variability in simulated values.
- However, in making such a decision we are ignoring the fact that the two assets may contain different levels of non-systematic risk, which can be diversified away.

In Practice

With the surge in data availability and computing power, the use of probabilistic approaches has increased significantly across a wide variety of markets. The following are some examples of simulations being applied in practice:

- In deregulated electricity markets, companies that trade electricity use simulation models to evaluate the impact of demand and supply swings, and of the resulting price volatility. They use the analysis to make important investment decisions (e.g., how much to spend on building new power plants).
- Commodity companies use probabilistic approaches (rather than relying on a single best estimate of future price) to determine how much to bid for new sources for these commodities.
- Businesses use simulations and scenario analysis to model the potential impact on revenues and earnings of the introduction of new technologies.
- Financial companies use simulations to compute value at risk and other risk management tools.

Quant Formulas:

T-Test $= \dfrac{r\sqrt{n-2}}{\sqrt{1-r^2}}$ r = correlation coefficient
$df = n-2$.

reject H_0 if $t >$ positive critical t value
$t <$ negative critical t value

$b_1 = \dfrac{Cov(x, y)}{Var(x)}$. $b_0 = \bar{Y} - b_1\bar{X}$
plug in mean value of x, y.

$t = \dfrac{\hat{b}_1 - b_1}{S_{\hat{b}_1}}$ or

In one X, $t^2 = F$

$SEE = \sqrt{MSE} = \sqrt{\dfrac{SSE}{n-2}}$

$R^2 = 1 - \dfrac{SSE}{SST}$.